A Short History of Canada

DESMOND MORTON

A Short History of Canada

second revised edition

M&S

Copyright © 1994 by Desmond Morton

First published 1983 (Hurtig Publishers)
First revised edition 1987 (Hurtig Publishers)

Canadian Cataloguing in Publication Data

Morton, Desmond, 1937-
A short history of Canada

2nd rev. ed.
Includes index.
ISBN 0-7710-6516-7

1. Canada – History.   I. Title.

FC164.M67 1994   971   C94-931648-2
F1026.M67 1994

The publishers acknowledge the support of the Canada Council
and the Ontario Arts Council for their publishing program.

The support of the Government of Ontario through the Ministry
of Culture, Tourism and Recreation is acknowledged.

Printed and bound in Canada. The paper used in this book is
acid-free.

McClelland & Stewart Inc.
The Canadian Publishers
481 University Avenue
Toronto, Ontario
M5G 2E9

1 2 3 4 5   98 97 96 95 94

To Susan, Jamie, Findlay, and Evan

Contents

Foreword

A nation, said Ernest Renan, is a people that has done great things together in the past. It is not bound by language or by a common culture but by a shared experience. History is what Canadians have in common.

Canadians believe that their history is short, boring, and irrelevant. They are wrong on all counts. The choices Canadians can make today have been shaped by history. The governors of New France launched arguments that federalists and independentists repeat in present-day Quebec. Early fur traders illustrated economic laws that modern-day resource development unconsciously follows. Canadians trying to understand the problems of political leadership deserve a second look at the arts of Sir John A. Macdonald and Mackenzie King.

In each generation, Canadians have had to learn how to live with each other in this big, rich land. It has never been easy. For those who ignore history, it is doubly difficult. This book has been written to make it a little easier for Canadians to know and understand their country.

It would not have been written without the inspiration and firm prodding of Mel Hurtig. That inspiration has been reinforced – unconsciously and perhaps grudgingly – by generations of students at Erindale College, the Mississauga campus of the University of Toronto. Some of them have been new Canadians, committed to an adopted country, yet puzzled by it and reluctant to take its truths for granted.

Because of them, there will never be a final history of Canada.

This is a guidebook to take its readers a certain way. The future is for them to make.

More than most of my books, this one has profited from the patient care and perceptiveness of my editor, Sarah Reid, and of my late wife, Jan. Both deserve whatever claims the book may have to be readable. Where it fails, they could not prevail over stubbornness. Clara Stewart has been more than a typist. She and Kathie Hill have reminded me that readers deserve wit and clarity as well as facts. For this edition, Alex Schultz has been a faithful editor.

Any new edition of a book is better than its predecessor, if only because colleagues and reviewers have generously suggested corrections and improvements. I have benefited particularly from the erudition of Vincent Eriksson of Canmore Lutheran College. Neither he nor the many others bears any responsibility for errors and misinterpretations which persist in the name of what *The Book of Common Prayer* calls "invincible ignorance."

This book is a product of its birthplace, a suburban campus in a new city, as full of energy as it is of self-doubt. It has been completed as Canadians are asking troubling questions about their future together as a country and a compassionate society. Before we shape our future, we should understand our past. This book has grown out of years of telling students, neighbours, and fellow citizens about how Canada has travelled through its most recent centuries and years. Our history should give us confidence.

PART I

DIFFERENT HISTORIES

I

New Nation

At midnight on July 1, 1867, church bells rang out from Lunenberg to Sarnia. In Ottawa, militia artillery fired the first round of a hundred-gun salute. Crowds cheered the explosions and waited as the militiamen laboured in the dark with rammers and sponges. At dawn, four million people awoke as citizens of a new Dominion of Canada. Some of them, in New Brunswick and Nova Scotia, might resent their fate, but a two-day weekend (for July 1 fell on a Monday) was too rare a treat to be shunned. Picnics, lacrosse tournaments, cricket matches, and excursions focused the day's excitement. Farm families united around groaning kitchen tables. On Toronto's waterfront, a huge ox would roast all day so that dripping hunks of meat could be distributed to the poor.

Carefully respecting the ban on Sabbath labour, George Brown arrived at the offices of his *Globe* that midnight, determined to do editorial justice to events he had helped to cause. Throughout the morning hours, his pen filled page after page with history, statistics, and hope for the new Dominion. Only at dawn was Brown finished. Solemnly he pledged that "the teeming millions who shall populate the northern part of this continent, from the Atlantic to the Pacific shall, under a wise and just Government, reap the fruit of well-directed enterprise, honest industry and religious principles." By then, the express trains that normally carried the *Globe* to readers across the old province of Canada West had departed without it. Brown's hopes would go largely unread.

In the summer of 1867, they were no more than hopes. Confederation covered only 370,045 square miles (958 416.5 km^2), a mere tenth of British North America. Three colonies had become four provinces, but the northern edge of the new provinces of Ontario and Quebec ran vaguely along the watershed that drained into the St. Lawrence and the Great Lakes. The population – 3,816,680 by official count – was a tenth as large as that of the bustling, powerful nation to the south. Many Canadians wondered how long they would survive the American boast of a "manifest destiny" to rule the entire continent.

George Brown's Dominion Day mood allowed no dismay. Small as it was, Canada's population was at least as large as America's had been when the Thirteen Colonies won their independence in 1783. Confederation itself was proof that the divisions between a million French Canadians and two and a quarter million Canadians of British origin could be overcome. If there remained differences of race, region, and religion, prosperity would dissolve them. The *Globe*'s readers could share the editor's intoxication with statistics, marvelling at every aspect of the young country's potential, from ship-building to the vast deposits of rock oil near Petrolia.

In his day, Brown had flailed at the corruption and waste of the railway builders but now he celebrated their achievements: 2149 miles (3458 km) of track in Quebec and Ontario alone, backed by canals, roads, bridges. The Grand Trunk, with 1277 miles (2055 km) of rail, was the world's largest system. Almost two of those miles rumbled across the St. Lawrence River at Montreal on the world-famous Victoria Bridge, completing a line that ran unbroken from Sarnia to Portland, Maine. And soon there would be more. Confederation was nothing if not a guarantee that new rail lines would snake their way east to Halifax and perhaps west across the fabled Rocky Mountains to the Pacific.

Prosperity would depend on the *Globe*'s most faithful readers, the farmers. Across the Dominion, there were more Canadians in farming than in any other occupation. If there was an average farmer of the time, he owned from fifty to one hundred acres, cultivated twenty of them, grew seventy-two bushels of wheat, owned eight cattle and a team of horses. In fact, soil and climate created vast differences. Quebec farmers were poorer, on average, than those in Ontario or the agricultural regions of the Maritimes, but they were recovering from several grim years of depression. Surplus offspring had left for New England mill towns and were sending home the hard-earned sums that would allow the family farm to diversify into dairying. Much of Ontario, soil exhausted and crops ravaged by Hessian fly, was now sliding into its own rural depression.

Social scientists and statisticians barely existed in the 1860s to warn people of national trends. Canadians who gathered for barter or gossip at the local inn or general store knew only of a daughter marrying a man from "the Boston states" or of sons gone homesteading in Kansas. Only the census, every ten years, identified trends: Canadians were leaving the land, and many of them were leaving Canada. Meanwhile, people lived their lives for the most part within the limits of family and community. They looked to politicians not for social or economic programs but for bridges, wharves, and post offices, and sometimes for a personal place on the public payroll.

In spite of localism, broad legislative programs existed. Egerton Ryerson had crusaded tirelessly to make the rural communities of Upper Canada establish and tax themselves for their own public schools. Ontario could boast of the results (and grumble at the cost). In Lower Canada, Ryerson's dynamic counterpart, Pierre Chauveau, became the first premier of the new province of Quebec. The struggle for schools was hard; in the lower provinces, it was not yet won. Rural communities saw no need for those "charitable and eleemosynary institutions" the new constitution assigned to the provinces. Rural families made room for their own orphans, elderly, and insane. If the treatment was sometimes harsh and misguided, were the few publicly-run poor houses, orphanages, and asylums any better? Even police forces had no place in a rural Canada. Magistrates had to turn to the militia or recruit special constables if criminals defied the majesty of the law. A frightened rural community could make its own laws, as the Black Donnellys of Lucan, near London, discovered in 1880. When their sense of justice was aroused, rural communities could also defend their own. The Megantic outlaw, Donald Morrison, was hidden from the law for three years in the 1880s when his

Eastern Township neighbours found no crime in his alleged arson and accidental manslaughter.

Farming lay at the heart of Canadian society and economics in 1867. Closely linked were the other resource industries of fishing and logging. Indeed, there was little distinction. However harsh or inhospitable the coastline, every fishing family cultivated a few acres of vegetables and hay. Settlers on the edge of the Canadian Shield forced the thin soil to grow hay and oats for the logging camps where they and their sons spent the winters. Wheat, square timbers, and fish made up most of the $80 million in exports with which the new Dominion hoped to pay her way in the world.

The future, of course, would be different. It lay not so much with the resource frontier as with the cities that controlled the trade and transportation routes. Once it had been rivers and harbours that made cities, now it was railways that confirmed or denied urban ambitions. The Victoria Bridge confirmed that Montreal would continue as the metropolis of Canada, the first city of 100,000 people. Quebec, with 59,699, would slowly wither as her poor rail connections undermined her claim to be the great port of the St. Lawrence timber trade. Toronto, with 56,092 citizens, would grow because of the river of railway tracks across her waterfront – the Grand Trunk, the Great Western, and her own creation, the Northern, reaching to Collingwood, Lake Huron, and the West. Halifax with 29,582 people and Saint John with 28,805 were the fourth and fifth cities of the Dominion and dominated their own provinces. Their huge merchant fleets allowed Brown to boast of Canada as a great new maritime power. But in the Victorian mansions, where the shipowners displayed their wealth, already there were fears that great ports might become backwaters.

If railways decided the fate of cities, they also created new reasons for urban growth. The costly self-sufficiency of small market towns, producing their own tools, furniture, and boots, ended with the railway. Mass markets justified mass production, costly machinery, and armies of persuasive salesmen. Necessities made locally or in the home could now be supplied year-round with a variety and quality few local tradesmen could hope to match. By

1867, manufacturing employed fifteen per cent of Canadian workers and produced twenty per cent of Canadian wealth. The Massey family's reaper and mower won a prize that year at the Paris Exposition. What could better typify the hopes of Confederation than a Yankee-style pride in home-grown inventiveness? What was more Canadian than delight at foreign recognition? More significant for Canadian development was the process that would carry Daniel Massey's little foundry at Bond Head to the town of Bowmanville and finally, by 1878, to the growing metropolis of Toronto.

The merchants and industrialists of the expanding cities were, for the most part, self-made men: once-penniless clerks and artisans who had saved their money, seen their chance, and seized it. Some were Americans; a disproportionate number, perhaps because they were apprenticed so young and in such a hard school, were Scottish immigrants. Few of these hard-bitten achievers (including George Brown) could spare much genuine sympathy for those who had failed in the struggle for wealth. Confederation coincided with an era when skilled workers were losing the struggle for near-equality with their employers and superiority over the unskilled. Ancient crafts, from shoemaking to typography, were being undermined by new technologies. By luck and strong organization, the printers would save themselves; other occupations would disappear or decline in status.

The average worker in Confederation Canada – almost as mythical a being as the average farmer – echoed the rhyme that "a dollar a day is very good pay." That might be true for labourers; a skilled worker expected twice as much or more for a work week of six days and sixty hours. A mixed blessing of industrialism was that women now found paid work, though at barely half a man's wage. Children earned far less. An employee, of course, paid for his own holidays – even Dominion Day and Christmas – and took his own risks with old age, sickness, and injuries on the job. The cyclical certainty of hard times was met from a worker's meagre savings. Those responsible for municipal relief did their best to make sure that any applicant had first considered starvation as a serious alternative.

Urban, industrial workers were a minority. Most Canadians still worked in a wageless, pre-industrial economy, often, like Gaspé fishermen, in debt to their merchant suppliers. Rural-minded Canadians had no sympathy with arguments for shorter hours, higher wages, or labour unions. When workers in Hamilton and Toronto imitated British industrial workers by demanding a nine-hour day, the Halifax *Witness* delivered an editorial sermon most of its readers would instinctively echo:

> In this new country, where every man who strives may advance in social power and rank, to teach men subordination to class movements is to deprive them of those noble opportunities for personal advancement which are the peculiar glory and advantage of this continent.

If many Canadians pretended to ignore class differences, their political, religious, and cultural leaders offered plenty of alternatives. They began with the barriers between the two "founding nations" of French and English. Few, in the first Dominion census, escaped either category: 202,991 Germans were by far the largest exception, but the census-takers found only 125 Jews and 11 "Hindoos." Yet British origins could hide historic and bitter differences. The 846,414 Irish (by far the largest of the "British groups") had brought with them, refreshed by an ocean voyage, all the hatreds of Green and Orange. They played them out in frequent midsummer riots in Montreal, Toronto, Saint John, or wherever the fires could be struck.

More than the differences of language and culture, the architects of the new Dominion had tried to accommodate the bitter quarrels of Catholic and Protestant. Few politicians had escaped the temptation or the risks of mixing religion and politics. It was misleading, of course, to claim that Protestants were united (the census distinguished six varieties of Presbyterian and eight of Methodist). Nor were all Canadians united in Christianity (the census also found 1884 "pagans" and 20 atheists, almost all from Ontario).

For Brown's Toronto, for the twenty thousand people of the sweltering little logging town of Ottawa, for Montreal business-men with renewed visions of a transcontinental empire, Confed-eration was a triumph. For others, half-devoured by the long struggle with the land, the forest, or the sea, it was a matter of deep indifference. For some, like those who draped the entrance to the Halifax *Chronicle* in black bunting, or those who gathered at Montreal's *Institut Canadien* to hatch schemes to bring down that "sell-out," George-Etienne Cartier, Confederation was already an enemy before it was born.

It was Cartier, the man of action, not words, who had urged, cajoled, and manoeuvred his fellow French Canadians into Con-federation. The man who had composed *Avant tout, soyons Cana-diens* ("Before All Else, Let's Be Canadians"), who sang it in his rough, raucous voice whenever the company could endure it, was also the man who insisted that Confederation created a "new nation." It was, Cartier insisted, only within a new political nation of British North America that the cultural nation of French Canada could be safe from American conquest or English assimilation.

The new Canadian nation was not the outcome of a long struggle for liberation or even of the effort, so common in nine-teenth-century Europe, to revive a half-buried language and cul-ture. The Dominion had no common language or agreed-upon symbols. Even the beaver, "a most respectable animal," as Sir Wil-liam Dawson of McGill University acknowledged, was "a type of unvarying instincts and old-world traditions. He does not improve and becomes extinct rather than change his ways." Canadians cer-tainly shared a climate – harsh, interminable winters that might, if one believed the dangerous new doctrines of Charles Darwin, breed out the feeble and the weak-willed. Winters were more pop-ular with the wealthy than with workers who faced routine wage cuts and layoffs when the cold months approached. Canada's image as "Our Lady of the Snows" would repel the investment and immigration which so preoccupied the Fathers of Confederation.

July 1, 1867, was a time of hope and fresh beginnings. In fact, Confederation had not broken with the past. Unlike the American revolutionaries, who deliberately concealed their borrowings from colonial tradition, the Fathers of Confederation built deliberately, pragmatically, and cautiously from their own historical experience. They and their critics carried their memories intact across the narrow divide of the first Dominion Day. The history of Canada as a single transcontinental nation begins from that day.

The histories of Canada had begun long before.

2

First Nations

Written history has its limits. It has little to contribute to the first millennia of Canada's human past. Doubtless this makes a book like this blessedly shorter, but it is aggravating to those whose history, being absent, seems to be scorned. Without writing to give an apparent precision and durability to human memory, all history is what English law used to call "time out of mind," and a period that might seem like eternity may in fact have begun only a dozen years before.

For pre-Contact America, all time is out of mind. The people who created the great Mayan and Aztec civilizations, or the smaller but hardly less sophisticated cultures of the Iroquois, the Algonquin, and the Haida, mastered some remarkable technologies, but systematic writing was not among them. European priests, travellers, and traders, with a feeble grasp of native languages and with concerns other than the preservation of "pagan" myths, have been the chief historical source, but how precise were their interlocutors or their interpreters? To know more of pre-Contact history, we must rely on the evidence of archaeologists, anthropologists, and ethnographers, all of whom draw vast inferences from a few tiny fragments of stone, clay, or bone, from speech and language patterns, or from legends. Increasingly we are urged to record and respect the tales of native elders, but are such stories, often the sole basis of a land claim or an ancient rivalry, any less self-serving than those our European ancestors accepted when they were told that the Virgin Mary gave her special protection to the town of Montreal or that God, in His infinite wisdom, had invited the British to rule His vast American domain?

When Europeans reached North America in the 1500s, there may have been about a third to half a million people living in what later would be called Canada, though the numbers fell rapidly. Native people have a variety of beliefs about their creation. A widespread myth features an Earth Diver who plunges into the primeval ocean to emerge with the mud from which land, forests, animals, and humanity are fashioned. Sometimes a great spirit persuades animals to do the diving. Other native peoples believed in the myth of a Great Transformer, occasionally a form of the Trickster common to many native legends. A sometimes comic figure in native folklore, the Trickster stole fire, light, water, animals, and even humanity to create the known world. Among the Haida and Tsimshian it is the Raven, among the Ojibwa, Nanabozo, among the Blackfoot, Coyote. Among the Micmac, Malecite, and Abenaki the world was created by a super-hero of human character and supernatural powers, though some peoples recognized the opposites of cold and heat, good and evil, summer and winter, and imagined two forces contending to create their universe. Common to all native beliefs was the conviction that their origins were here in North America and that they were in fact, rather than in mere seniority among immigrants, the true First Nations.

Archaeologists would insist that North America's first human inhabitants arrived in a more pedestrian way. Twelve to twenty thousand years ago, they had made their way across the land bridge between Asia and the Americas that survives as the Aleutians. Then they made their way south, adapting gradually to the enormous diversity of climate and topography of a hitherto uninhabited continent. Scientists have reinforced the claim by comparing the DNA of natives and their alleged ancestors in Manchuria and Mongolia. At least one native leader has claimed that migration flowed the other way. What is certain is that no ancient immigration officer was on hand to document either migration.

Scientific evidence suggests two great waves of prehistoric migration: the first twelve to twenty thousand years ago, and the second, after an intervening ice age, much later. The cold forced native ancestors to migrate southward, and then, as it receded, settlement pushed northward again. A later wave of arrivals helps explain why the Athapaskans differ completely in language and even physical appearance from the Algonquins, who inhabit the eastern and central belt of woodlands. The Innu are part of a circum-Polar people who may also be found in Siberia.

Whatever they had in common in their origins, the native peoples whom whites encountered had made an effective adaptation to their environment. Traditionally, native groups were classified by their eleven language families, though a simpler division might be based on differing lifestyles. Across most of Canada, from the Yukon to the Atlantic, were two language groups, Algonquins and Athapaskans, sharing a hunting-gathering existence, with small bands, great mobility, and such technological triumphs as the birch bark canoe and the skills in trapping and in curing animal pelts that gave Canada its first staple industry. To their north were the Innu, amazingly adapted to life in the Arctic desert. To this day, no one else has been better able to survive in a region of dark, bitterly cold winters and short summers, almost wholly dependent on fish and animal life. To the south of the forest-dwelling Algonquins were the Iroquoians, people who had learned to farm the soil and to sustain themselves, winter and summer, in substantial villages. Far away on the western plains were people who had adopted the collective organization needed to hunt the huge herds of prairie bison and to survive long prairie winters. Still farther west were people who had adapted to life in the southern plateau regions of the Rockies. Along the Pacific, in the shadow of the coastal mountains, were people who had adapted to a life of fishing, trading, and limited agriculture, and whose towering totem poles and wooden houses bespoke a complex culture and belief system.

Every one of the First Nations had, through millennia of adaptation, found the culture, beliefs, skills, and technology to survive in their part of Canada, whether it was the light snowshoes of the Algonquins, the hunting organization of the Blackfoot and Crees, or the Arctic clothing, kayaks, and igloos of the Innu. All had unique artistic and decorative skills, sophisticated myths and legends to explain their world to themselves and others, and religious beliefs that sustained the human qualities needed for survival. They made war but in moderation, preserving captured women for intermarriage and children for adoption.

Whatever their form of life, native North Americans saw themselves as part of nature, not as its masters. Though they fought other bands and nations, they had very little sense of territorial ownership. Even agricultural societies migrated when the soil was exhausted and rebuilt their villages on other sites. Native beliefs found kindred spirits in the animals they hunted, and misfortune befell those who offended such spirits by killing cruelly or to excess. Of course their lives were hard, and death from hunger, cold, and injury was no stranger. They knew sickness too, though many of the white men's diseases were unknown to them and, in their lack of immunity, contact brought catastrophic death rates.

Native remains and languages show that they traded long before Europeans arrived, exchanging what they produced in surplus for what they could not supply for themselves. Perhaps their eagerness for new technology was their downfall. A less curious or adaptable people might have ignored the Europeans and their goods and left them to live or, more probably, die on their own. Without the full co-operation and assistance of natives in showing the Europeans their methods of survival, their territory, and their resources, the early explorers and settlers would have perished in even greater numbers and possibly abandoned their quest, much as the Vikings had done five hundred years before.

Instead, with the enthusiasm of natural free-traders, they welcomed the Europeans and their goods into existing trading systems. Any second thoughts came too late.

3

Cartier's Quebec

It was not just the natives whose history began before 1867. For George-Etienne Cartier, or any other *Canadien*, the history of Canada began in 1534, when another Cartier had made his landfall on the Gaspé shore of the Baie des Chaleurs. By erecting a cross and claiming the continent for His Most Christian Majesty, Francis I, Jacques Cartier had posted the French bid for North America.

The bid ignored the claims of Indians or Inuit, established for thousands of years since their ancestors had crossed the Alaska land-bridge from Asia. Even Europeans had staked an earlier claim; Vikings, driven west from Iceland to the coast of Labrador, Newfoundland, and perhaps even New England, had recorded their discoveries in Norse sagas. Basque and Breton fishermen had come regularly, returning under strict oaths of secrecy about the origins of their rich catches. In 1497, when the boastful John Cabot came back to Bristol to report schools of codfish so dense "they sometimes stayed his shippes," he merely broke a trade secret.

Cartier had come for a different form of wealth. He had been enticed by vague Indian claims of a wealthy "Kingdom of the Saguenay" and by the great river that he hoped would lead past the rapids of Lachine to a western ocean. When the gold he brought home on his third voyage proved to be iron pyrites, the St. Mâlo seaman was discredited. Anyway, France was too deep in the wars between Catholic and Huguenot to care about distant lands. Seventy years would pass before the French came again. This time, Samuel de Champlain would make them stay.

No nation could ask for a nobler founder than Champlain. Navigator, soldier, visionary, a Protestant turned Catholic by conviction, a man of Renaissance curiosity and eternal fortitude, Champlain created New France. A few bleak winters spent on the Bay of Fundy persuaded him to try elsewhere. Fate then took him back to Cartier's great river, the "Father of Waters." Where Cape Diamond rears up to narrow the St. Lawrence River, Champlain and a few men built their *habitation* in the autumn of 1608.

Champlain's business, financed by court favourites and Rouen merchants, was the fur trade. In its name, he made alliances with Algonquin Indians; fought their dreaded enemies, the Iroquois; journeyed to the Huron country that is now central Ontario; and sent young Frenchmen to learn Indian languages and lifestyles as the first *coureurs de bois*.

Champlain has been condemned for provoking the Iroquois, but his intervention only speeded up the inevitable. Enemies and climate had driven the Iroquois south of the Great Lakes. Their longhouse culture of cornfields and tribal alliances gave them a strength and a stability no other northern Indians possessed. On the other hand, they lacked rich sources of good furs or the swift canoes to carry them to the new European trading posts. Anyone who has tried skinning a rabbit with a stone knife or boiling water in a clay pot will not wonder why Indians were soon desperate for the steel knives and copper kettles the Europeans traded for their furs. Lacking furs and canoes, the Iroquois used their military power to become the middlemen between the stolid Dutch traders at Albany and the Huron and Algonquin suppliers. If these tribes went to the French, they would be punished or even destroyed by the Iroquois.

For almost a century, war with the Iroquois was a recurrent, tragic fact of life for the struggling French settlement. The war made every settler a soldier and a potential victim of death by torture or brutal captivity. One result was a legend of an embattled people, defended by heroes such as Adam Dollard of the Long Sault and such heroines as Madeleine de Verchères. Only divine inspiration could have spared the few hundred colonists or the frail outpost of Montreal, established in 1642 by Paul de Chomédy,

Sieur de Maisonneuve. In the legend of *Canadien* survival, there was little room for sympathy with the Indians, caught between powerful European rivals and struggling with their own ingenuity and courage to defend their interests.

To Champlain and to others, New France meant more than furs or war. The fur trade was a vital commercial foundation for a greater purpose: the conversion of the Indian people. As part of the price for their furs, the Algonquins and the Hurons had to take back with them black-robed missionaries with their strange incantations and their epidemic infections. It was a heavy penalty for the magnificent European goods. In five years, almost half the Hurons had perished.

If commerce led to conversion, Champlain saw that colonization was vital to both. European settlers would give the Indian converts a demonstration of the Christian life while they laboured to make New France self-sufficient.

The interlocking of commerce, colonization, and conversion was Champlain's plan, sustained against adversity, failures, and the first English conquest by the Kirke brothers in 1629. It was Maisonneuve's plan when he established Montreal in defiance of the Iroquois peril. It was the vision that Jesuit missionaries reported in the *Rélations*, the brilliant propaganda newsletters which attracted funds for their enterprise from the ladies and gentlemen of the French court. The plan sent Jesuits to Huronia in the 1630s. A generation later, the few Huron survivors of European diseases and Iroquois invasions withdrew from a devastated land. Only in 1662, when a newly powerful Louis xiv finally extended his royal government to his remote and embattled subjects, was Champlain's concept altered.

In fact, the three elements of Champlain's scheme had never worked together. Traders preferred to leave their customers as they found them. Missionaries were scandalized by trading morals and methods. Colonists rarely measured up as role models for the few Indian converts. As well, they were too attracted to the freedom of the fur trade, too busy defending themselves from the Iroquois, and often too untrained as farmers to be successful producers. The *habitants*, as they proudly called themselves (in distinction from the proper term of *censitaire* or "tenant") cleared trees and laid out the characteristic strip farms running back from the river banks, but even the Iroquois peril could not persuade them to leave their own land and live in forts and villages. With effort and good weather, the settlers could enjoy a rude plenty. As often, however, the colony was close to starvation. Always the annual trading fleet had to make room for food and livestock as well as for the cloth, hardware, and brandy the fur trade demanded.

Under royal government, the missionary impulse weakened. The autocratic Bishop François Montmorency de Laval established a stern tradition of religious authority in the little colony, but the officials of Louis xiv could be certain of royal backing against any bishop's pretensions. It was far harder for them to resolve a dilemma which persisted throughout the French regime and, in some form, has remained with the leaders of French Canada ever since. Were the people of New France to be *habitants*, cultivating their small colony in the valley of the St. Lawrence, or were they to be *voyageurs*, carrying the fur trade, Catholicism, and French influence throughout the continent?

The instructions of Louis xiv's minister of colonies, Jean-Baptiste Colbert, were clear. His Intendant, or business manager, Jean Talon, must expand the population, improve farming, and develop industries in a compact, self-contained colony. Talon and his successors did their best to obey. Shiploads of women were brought over to provide brides and to balance the sexes in the male-dominated colony. Though immigration slowed to a trickle after 1700, impressive rates of natural increase sent the population of New France soaring from only three thousand at the start of royal government to sixty thousand a century later. As in the English colonies to the south, the legal and administrative structures of the old world were simplified and adapted to the new. Seigneurs served as settlement agents, and any who fancied themselves as feudal lords could swiftly be brought to earth by a rude reminder from the Intendant.

The seigneuries along the St. Lawrence and its tributaries formed one version of New France. On his farm, the *habitant* could fish or hunt. The long strip of land, rolling back from the river to the forest, would be divided among his sons. Rents and taxes were low. An efficient, reasonably cheap court system allowed the *habitant* to indulge a proverbial delight in lawsuits. Officials and clergy might seem all-powerful but they were also paternal. The forest and the fur trade were outlets for the ambitious or the discontented. Since officers' appointments in the colonial garrison were reserved for the sons of influential colonists, there was even access to the lower rungs of the French aristocracy. By the 1750s, visitors from the old world claimed that a new kind of French people was emerging along the banks of the St. Lawrence.

The pressure to expand created another version of New France. As Talon complained, his efforts to create a compact settlement were undone by the unscrupulous but plausible rogue Louis xiv had appointed governor of the colony. Sent to the new world to escape his creditors, Louis de Buade, Count Frontenac, saw only one way to rebuild his fortune and return in splendour to court. Whatever it might cost in renewed war or humiliating treaties, Frontenac had to reach past the Iroquois and revive the fur trade. First he built a fort at Cataraqui (now Kingston) where the St. Lawrence becomes Lake Ontario. Then he sent Robert de la Salle to build another fort at Detroit. Soon agents for the trade, missionaries, and *coureurs de bois* reached out along the Great Lakes, the Ohio and the Mississippi rivers, and north to Hudson Bay to find new Indian bands, new converts, and, above all, new sources of fur.

For governors, soldiers, and ordinary *habitants* there was really no other source of wealth. A journey to the West, with its dangers and back-breaking labour, netted a *voyageur* enough to buy the livestock or land that might turn subsistence farming into a chance to support a wife and family. A successful licence at a trading fort could give a young officer the quick fortune he wanted to support the status of minor nobility in France. Governors and even intendants took their cut of fur-trade revenue, from selling licences to taking a share of the fur price. Nothing else was as profitable. Talon developed shipbuilding and the iron deposits at St. Maurice near Trois-Rivières, but never with commercial success. Only when the French king poured a fortune into fortifying Louisbourg and into wartime garrisons could corruption provide an alternative source of wealth. By then, the fate of the French regime was sealed.

The price of expansion was a far more dangerous rivalry than the Iroquois or the Dutch had represented. The English colonies, sheltered behind the Appalachians, looked as compact and settled as the seigneuries on the St. Lawrence. In fact, they were quarrelsome, divided, and, by the 1750s, ready to explode beyond their borders.

Two dissident *coureurs de bois*, Pierre Radisson and Médard Chouart des Groseillers, bedevilled by Talon's restrictions on the fur trade, had managed to interest English merchants in the opportunities of Hudson Bay. In 1670, the English established the Company of Adventurers Trading into Hudson's Bay. There is now no doubt that the French were more skillful at trading with the Indians than the English. Their goods, from Europe's leading manufacturing nation, were superior to most that the English could supply. The long Indian wars had forced the *Canadiens* to become tough, efficient wilderness soldiers. What the French lacked in the developing struggle for North America was a powerful navy and the will to match the thousands of English emigrants who left annually for the Thirteen Colonies. Embattled in Europe, France was forced to treat her remote colonies as valued but sacrificial pawns.

In a game of historical might-have-been, the compact colony of New France might have escaped conquest by a sort of armed neutrality. That never seemed possible. The frontier wars, with their lightning raids, burnings, and massacres, cried out for vengeance. A legacy of fear and hatred of the Iroquois and their American backers grew up in New France, to be matched with equally horrifying memories in New England and northern New York. Even more significant was the role that the expansionist fur trade came to play in French strategic thinking.

At the French court, New France was only a pawn in a European power game. Louis xiv's decision to occupy New Orleans and the later plan in the 1750s to build a belt of French forts along the Ohio and Mississippi rivers were part of complex schemes to help France's Spanish allies and to distract the British. They owed nothing to the commercial needs of the fur trade for there were few pelts to be gained from the Ohio region. The French-Canadian militiamen who struggled and died in the brutally mismanaged expedition to build Fort Duquesne (at present-day Pittsburgh) were expendable pieces in a board game played far away at Versailles. When first the Virginians, under George Washington, and then the British, under General George Braddock, were sent reeling back from the Ohio valley in humiliation or defeat, the French congratulated themselves. In fact, by provoking the stronger British, the French strategists had sealed the fate of New France.

Blockaded by the Royal Navy, preoccupied by wars with its European neighbours, France could spare only a few thousand regular troops to back its gamble in the new world. Louisbourg, the vast fortress built on Cape Breton Island to protect the approaches to the St. Lawrence, fell in 1758 because France had too few warships to relieve it. The French military commander in New France, the Marquis de Montcalm, detested his superior, the Canadian-born governor, Pierre de Rigaud, Marquis de Vaudreuil. Their bitter rivalry, far more than the gross corruption of the last Intendant, François Bigot, doomed the colony. Though Montcalm's outnumbered regulars won against incredible odds, notably at the battle of Carillon or Ticonderoga in 1758, the general's insistence on mixing Canadian militia with his soldiers was a big factor in their defeat on the Plains of Abraham in the following year. An almost accidental last-minute victory by General James Wolfe and his redcoats was made certain by confused tactics in the French ranks. In the fall of Quebec, the French and the *Canadiens* discovered how little they had in common.

In September 1760, with Quebec in British hands and Montreal surrounded, the surviving French troops burned their standards, boarded ships, and went home. So did most of the merchants and leaders of the colony. The remaining *Canadiens*, abandoned in the hands of their enemies, would retain an enduring suspicion of remote imperial strategies and their bloody consequences.

It had taken a century and a half to create New France but now the French were finished with it. To the French Ministry of Marine, the colony had represented huge costs, small returns, and no advantage that fishing concessions off Newfoundland could not match. Voltaire's blunt dismissal of Canada as "several acres of snow" became the official consensus. The British seemed hardly more interested. His Majesty's new Province of Quebec would be made as hospitable to British settlers as the imposition of English law and an elected assembly reserved for Protestants could make it. Narrow boundaries for the new colony cut off the fur-trading hinterland, but incoming British merchants would presumably find other ways to become rich. The conquered *Canadiens* would undoubtedly accept the blessings of the new regime and become English-speaking, if not necessarily Anglican.

Not for the last time, however, the *Canadiens* defied the inevitable. The first British governor, General James Murray, and his successor, Sir Guy Carleton, detested each other, but their aristocratic souls both rejoiced in the ordered, rural, and seemingly dutiful society that had survived the capitulation of 1760. Under its Catholic clergy and a scattering of remaining seigneurs and merchants it was, claimed Murray, "perhaps the bravest and best race upon the Globe." To both governors, it was intolerable that the handful of shifty merchants and camp followers who had accompanied the British army to Montreal and Quebec should now monopolize power simply because British law excluded Catholics. Murray's good will was immediately apparent. The Catholic bishop of Quebec had died on the eve of the conquest. Without a bishop, no new clergy could be ordained. With Murray's help, a successor was chosen, sent to France to be consecrated (since the Catholic church was illegal in Britain), and returned to Quebec. The British gained a staunch clerical ally.

The British had imagined that a flood of settlement would soon help anglicize Quebec. Few people came. By 1772, Sir Guy Carleton, Murray's successor, had absorbed an obvious point: "barring a catastrophe shocking to think of [Carleton probably meant smallpox], this country must, to the end of time, be peopled by the Canadian race." A more troublesome principle followed: they must be governed by institutions and practices familiar to them. Carleton's arguments persuaded the British government. The Quebec Act of 1774 restored the kind of regime Quebec's clergy and seigneurs desired. The Church regained its legal right to tithes and the seigneurs regained the old civil law. The earlier promise of an elected assembly vanished. If the community of English-speaking merchants at Montreal raged at this betrayal, they were more than compensated. The huge fur-trading hinterland to the west, removed from Quebec in 1763, was now restored. Indians and traders would not be disturbed by settlers.

Carleton could not foresee that his Quebec Act would help drive the Thirteen Colonies to open revolt, but he was certainly confident that the Act would rally both the Indians and gratified *habitants* to the British side. He was disappointed. When Americans invaded Quebec after the Declaration of Independence in 1775, the clergy and seigneurs appealed almost in vain for people to rally to Carleton's aid. The Americans, as they advanced to besiege Quebec City, had little better success in winning over the *Canadiens*. Only when starving Americans began to raid livestock and food supplies, leaving worthless paper from the Continental Congress as payment, did the *habitants* choose sides. By the spring of 1776, the Americans had been driven away.

The American Revolution undermined Carleton's prediction. Quebec would not be forever *Canadien*. Ten thousand Loyalist refugees poured into the province up the old invasion route of the Richelieu River and across the Niagara River. Beyond the seigneury of Longueuil, Loyalists and German veterans of the war were granted land.

The cataclysm of the American Revolution forced the British to reconsider the government of the scattered colonies that remained to them. Once again it was Carleton (now Lord Dorchester) who tried his ingenuity. He would split the old province of Quebec. Beyond Longueuil, Upper Canada would develop as a model British society that *Canadiens* and Americans could admire – and perhaps even ask to join. The eastern portion, Lower Canada, would also have an elected Assembly, an appointed upper house or council, and an executive – replicas of the British Commons, Lords, and Cabinet – but the *Canadiens* would also keep their language, their civil law, and their religious institutions. The Act of 1791 confirmed the arrangements.

And the *Canadiens* seemed to prosper. If a high birthrate is a symptom of a nation's well-being, rarely have a people been happier. The sixty thousand *habitants* of 1760 were a hundred and ten thousand by 1784 and three hundred and thirty thousand by 1812. The Colbert-Talon dream of a compact, prosperous rural society was fulfilled. The methods were primitive – farmers piled their manure on the ice to float downriver at the spring breakup – but wheat production climbed and seigneurial fortunes rose. The long war between Britain and revolutionary and Napoleonic France that began in 1793 awakened few old loyalties among Lower Canadians. Instead, wartime scarcities promoted wheat exports and a growing timber trade from the St. Lawrence. The Church opened colleges to train its clergy. Wealthier *habitants* sent their sons to train for such professions as law and medicine.

The avocation of these newly educated *Canadiens* would be politics. The aging anglophile seigneurs and local notables who had represented the *Canadiens* in the Assembly in its early years soon gave way to younger, more critical men. Politics provided an outlet for new grievances. Despite their dramatic population growth, the *Canadiens* felt threatened. Land that their children would someday need was now being granted to Americans who had not even been Loyalists. Quebec's new Anglican bishop, Jacob Mountain, made no secret of his hope that a state-endowed "Royal Institution," through its schools, would systematically anglicize the French. Through the Assembly, French-Canadian politicians could fight back.

In spite of the *Canadien* predominance, there were signs that Lower Canada was becoming anglicized. By 1812, most of the thirty thousand Montrealers spoke English. So did a majority in Quebec City. Whether the French-speaking merchants were vanishing through intermarriage, deliberate preference for the seigneurial life, or because of brutal competition, the business of Lower Canada was being done in English. Beyond those who purchased seigneuries as a source of income, few merchants cared about the over-population or the shrinking harvests of the rural districts. Their concerns lay with the fur trade or improving the St. Lawrence route to the wheat and potash trade of a thriving Upper Canada. Financing canals to get past the St. Lawrence rapids would cost money. Like most prudent men, the Montreal merchants wanted others to foot the bill.

In Lower Canada, the Assembly soon became the battleground where *Canadiens* could challenge the harsh verdict of the conquest. Their leader, Etienne Bédard, taught the young notaries, doctors, and lawyers that *Canadiens* could win their fight by using the institution the British themselves most admired: Parliament. By 1810, Bédard's determination had led him to prison. However, with war imminent on the American frontier, the British removed his antagonist, Sir James Craig, replacing him with a more sympathetic (and bilingual) governor, Sir George Prévost. In French Canada, Craig's name would remain a symbol of English oppression to the *Canadiens*.

The War of 1812 rarely crossed the Lower Canadian border. When it did, both *Canadiens* and the Assembly could take pride in their patriotic role. Among the officers of the French-Canadian militia was Louis-Joseph Papineau. Eloquent, handsome, seemingly self-confident, Papineau was the logical choice for Speaker of the Assembly in 1815. A professed believer in British institutions, Papineau was also a proud and by no means benevolent seigneur and, thereby, a firm guardian of French Canada's most basic institution. Above all, Papineau was a man of words, concealing a tragic streak of indecision behind billowing rhetoric.

In the wake of the War of 1812, there was much that was seriously wrong in Lower Canada – economic stagnation, crop failures and declining yields, over-population in the seigneuries. Montreal's English-speaking merchants urged reunion of the Canadas and costly improvements of the St. Lawrence route; Papineau and the *Canadien*-dominated Assembly refused. When the merchants pushed their ideas with the appointed council and executive in 1822, Papineau and his allies visited England to defeat the reunion plan. Far from returning triumphant and grateful, Papineau came home disillusioned by Britain and her institutions. Every issue was soon reduced to an uncompromising battle between Papineau and his *patriotes* and those he sweepingly denounced as a "Château Clique" of *bureaucrates*. Leaving more moderate allies in his wake, Papineau set an increasingly radical course, halting all public works, preventing payment of official salaries, and making administration of Lower Canada almost impossible.

Papineau's goals were unclear. In religion he was almost a free thinker; as a seigneur, he was highly conservative. At times, he preached the merits of an American-style republic. Above all, he denounced the control of patronage by the governor's appointed advisers. This issue had strong appeal for the growing *Canadien* elite of educated professionals, condemned to remain as ill-paid village notaries and doctors. Constitutional arguments also aroused English-speaking followers like Wolfred and Robert Nelson, ready to believe that British liberties were at stake. George-Etienne Cartier, studying law and sharing the circle of Montreal's French-speaking elite, was only one of scores of ardent young men who took up the *patriote* cause.

In the Lower Canadian countryside, the mood was different – grimmer. The growing population had become a terrible burden. The narrow strips of land, subdivided for the sons in each generation, could be split no more. Seigneurs, French and English, had become oppressive landlords with no Intendant to restrain them. The land could no longer support its people. Wheat fly and exhausted soil produced shrinking yields. For the first time, a class of landless labourers appeared.

Since the end of the long European war in 1815, a tide of immigration had swept up the St. Lawrence. Most of it had moved on to Upper Canada or the United States; often only the poorest remained. So did the cholera epidemics. The first of them invaded Lower Canada in 1832. Hundreds died miserably from a plague no medical knowledge could cure, and there were those who echoed the *patriote* orators who insisted that the British had deliberately plotted the death of the *Canadiens*. Suspicion and hatred were mutual. The old cordiality of a merchant class that had intermarried, learned French, sometimes even converted to Catholicism, was not inherited. British governors, assailed by hostile *patriote* politicians in the Assembly, also worried about the growth of a rancorous, bitter "English party" in Montreal. The violent attacks by journalists like Adam Thom and the military drill of young men in the Doric Legion only spurred Papineau's followers to fresh extremism in language and tactics.

In 1837, the clash came. Three years before, Papineau had compiled every imaginable Lower Canadian grievance into what he called "Ninety-Two Resolutions" and despatched them to London. The Assembly, he promised, would let the colony stagnate until Britain acted. In 1837, Lord John Russell's Whig government sent its reply, in the form of the "Ten Resolutions." These instructed the governor to reject the Assembly's demand for executive power, ordered him to give hard-pressed officials their back pay, and to govern the colony with or without an elected Assembly.

It was a terrible year to provoke a political conflict. While the colony had stagnated, tensions had risen. Endless rains in the summer and autumn of 1837 had ruined crops. In the United States, President Andrew Jackson's anti-banking crusade had led to a commercial collapse that affected Montreal. Huge, sodden rallies of *habitants* gathered to hear Papineau, echoing his outrage but ignoring his unexpected appeals for prudence and patience. Papineau's indecision was beginning to show, just as the avalanche of anger he had helped to build was beginning to move. Angrier, harder men, like Wolfred Nelson, a wartime surgeon, began drilling men at St. Dénis.

In Montreal, both the *patriotes* and the English drilled. When the governor banned the Doric Legion, it reformed under another title. Suddenly there were clashes; one violent riot threatened Papineau's house and only the arrival of British troops saved it. Fearing arrest, Papineau fled to the countryside. The cautious, peace-seeking Lord Gosford resigned as governor; Sir John Colborne, one of the British army's ablest soldiers, succeeded him.

Given time and a united leadership, the *patriotes* of 1837 might have been a formidable force. At St. Dénis on November 23, Nelson's men drove off two hundred British regulars. Young George-Etienne Cartier shared in that victory, but Papineau had fled St. Dénis, slipping across the border to Vermont. Other *patriotes*, like Louis-Hippolyte La Fontaine, hurried to Quebec City in a vain effort to make peace. An impatient Sir John Colborne gave the rebels no more time to drill or debate. Beaten at St. Dénis, the British troops mounted a swift counter-attack on the rebel centres on the Richelieu River. With the winter freeze-up, Colborne sent his men north of Montreal to crush rebels at St. Eustache. His ill-disciplined irregulars spread across the countryside, leaving the *habitants'* homes blazing behind them. Colborne would be remembered in the historical mythology of French Canada as "*Vieux Brûlot*," the Old Firebrand.

Long after the futility and self-interest of Louis-Joseph Papineau and the *patriotes* had been forgiven, the bitter memory of fire and sword would remain. As in 1760, the *Canadiens* had been defeated. The bitterness of a second conquest engulfed the Lower Canadian leaders, leaving them paralysed and despairing. Others would have to find strength and ingenuity to survive.

4

English Canadians

English-speaking people in Lower and Upper Canada had a different memory of their history – sometimes several different memories. To them, Canada dated from John Cabot's discovery of his "New Founde Lande" in 1497. The French had been the hereditary enemy, conquered in 1759 when James Wolfe led his soldiers up the narrow, ill-guarded Anse au Foulon to occupy the Plains of Abraham.

All memories are selective. Most English Canadians forgot those New Englanders, ransomed from Indian captors, who so fully joined in the life of New France that they refused to go home. Men from Wolfe's army, most of them Scots, stayed, married, and also assimilated, becoming ancestors of such French-speaking Quebec premiers as J. G. Ross and Daniel Johnson. The English also forgot the deft calculation which had helped persuade French diplomats to abandon New France. With no threat from Quebec, the French had reasoned, the American colonists would fight each other. Within fifteen years of the capitulation at Montreal, Britain and her American colonies were indeed at war. Within a decade of the Quebec Act of 1774, the British had absorbed their worst defeat of the century.

The Treaty of 1783, ending the American Revolutionary War, left Britain with the cold, unprofitable remnants of the continent. Perhaps something might be made of them. After all, Montreal still sat astride the only route to the heart of America. The vast interior of the continent had changed hands too often to assume that the Treaty of 1783 was the last word. Preferring profits to politics, most of the American merchants at Montreal had remained loyal. British garrisons and their Indian allies would continue to hold the interior until the claims of dispossessed Loyalists were satisfied. That might be a long time.

For the moment, the top priority was to cope with the columns of refugees pouring into the province of Quebec. Tools, rations, and livestock were as necessary as land. Bewildered officials, wrestling with problems of wilderness logistics, were cursed as hard-hearted or corrupt. In the wake of the war, ten thousand Loyalists were struggling to build homes and farms in the forests along the upper St. Lawrence or below the Niagara escarpment. Iroquois of the Six Nations, forced into exile as British allies, found their own pockets of settlement up the Grand River. Pennsylvania Germans, bound by language and culture as well as loyalty, drove and floated their big Conestoga wagons even further up the valleys of the Grand, the Speed, and the Eramosa rivers.

History is preoccupied with politics, ideas, and movements. In the 1790s, as perhaps in any age, these were luxuries only a few could enjoy. For pioneers in a harsh and unfamiliar land, survival was a preoccupation, to be achieved only through relentless, back-breaking work. The forest was the enemy. Huge first-growth trees resisted the puny axes and saws of the settlers as they struggled to clear fields or even to break through the overhanging gloom to the sun. The forest accentuated loneliness. Pioneers were described as being reduced to an unsmiling grimness by loneliness and labour. Women faced the terror of childbirth without even a neighbour to help. A single careless blow with an axe could cripple a man or leave him to die in the stench and agony of gangrene. The dark side to pioneer life was only partly veiled by the almost frantic revelry of militia reviews, barn-raisings, and "bees," or by the fervour of camp meetings summoned by Methodist circuit riders, the best agents of frontier Christianity.

Yet politics and ideals mattered because they gave shape to the thousands of individual struggles for survival. Newcomers they might be, but the King's "old subjects" from below the border had strong views about the political society they wanted. When they turned from their grinding tasks, they could count on outspoken leaders to state their case. Sir John Johnson, superintendent of

Indian affairs in New York, became a leading Loyalist in the Canadas. It was he who led the campaign to split the colony to help guarantee an elected Assembly for at least Upper Canadians. William Smith, the former Chief Justice of New York and now of Quebec, argued for a federation of all the British North American colonies, a precursor for the eventual idea of Confederation in 1867.

The British response was both generous and conservative. The Constitutional Act of 1791 created the two Canadas sought by Johnson, provided them both with the structure of governor, executive council, and elected assembly, and fostered institutions which, in the hopes of Colonel John Simcoe of Upper Canada, might create "the very image and transcript" of English society. Since taxes had provoked the American Revolution, in the Canadas, government would be financed by reserving a seventh of all land for the Crown. Another seventh would finance an established Protestant clergy. Though proposals for a titled aristocracy in the Canadas were abandoned, insistence that legislative councillors possess up to six thousand acres was intended to foster the keystone of the English constitution, a well-entrenched landed gentry.

If Champlain was the founder of New France, Upper Canada was almost as much the creation of John Simcoe. A successful commander of Loyalist troops, Upper Canada's first Lieutenant Governor could not resist trying to reverse the verdict of the American Revolution. With incredible optimism, Colonel Simcoe imagined that he could make his raw, backwoods colony so attractive that Americans would repent their disloyalty and renew their allegiance. His energy matched his ambition. Survey parties vanished into the forest to lay out the gridiron of concession and side roads that still shape rural Ontario. Soldiers and settlers drove highways of the future through swamp and bush – Yonge Street north from Lake Ontario to Lake Simcoe; Dundas Street west from Yonge Street to Hamilton and to the tiny inland settlement of London. The Kingston Road struggled eastward to the garrison town where Frontenac had once built his fort. At the junction of these roads was the muddy little village of York, set in malarial lakeside swamps, where Simcoe moved his capital. London, his first choice, had been vetoed as too remote. From his little bungalow, Simcoe dictated letters, dispatches, instructions, and promoted a flood of proposals for everything from hat-making to a mining industry.

Simcoe's energy was guided by a dream. To prosper, Upper Canada would need far more than the fourteen thousand people who had reached it by 1791. As a bustling, progressive success story, the province would be a haven for all who, Simcoe boldly predicted, would be weary of the mismanagement and corruption of the American republic. Unmoved by the warnings and protests of Loyalists, Simcoe boldly invited any of His Majesty's late subjects to renew their allegiance in return for excellent free land. Moreover, people came. Allegiance was a small matter on the frontier; land was everything. Upper Canada, particularly its lower peninsula between Lake Erie and Lake Huron, was directly in the path of the American frontier surge. Simcoe's critics sneered at "late Loyalists" but the ox-teams with their overloaded wagons poured into the colony. By 1811, almost ninety thousand people had settled in Upper Canada and distinctions between early and late Loyalists had been worn down by the common pioneering experience.

By then, however, Simcoe had been gone for fifteen years. He was not even knighted for his services. His successors were lesser men, reluctant exiles in a colonial backwater of long winters and steaming, mosquito-ridden summers. Most of Simcoe's vision left with him, but the people still came, for by now even the colony's tiny elite had realized that their huge land grants would be worthless without the pressure of settlement. A fertile tract surrounded by prospering farms would grow in value. In the meantime, one might live respectably on the salary and profits of government office.

If Upper Canada seemed a backwater to British officials, it was the front line in British-American relations. South of the Great Lakes, the British clung to their old trading posts, holding out for compensation for the Loyalists and unconsciously encouraging the Indians to resist the advance of American settlers. In 1791, a small American army was destroyed by the Indians. The British were blamed, even though they had warned the Americans of the danger. Britain's government saw the folly of another war with the United States at a time when the French Revolution was blazing on their own doorstep. In 1794, they conceded the futility of their hopes of receiving Loyalist compensation and withdrew, abandoning their Indian allies to the tide of American settlement. The result was the decisive defeat of the Indians, under their great chief, Tecumseh, at the Battle of Fallen Timbers.

Other factors heightened Anglo-American hostility. In the long war that dragged on in Europe (with brief intervals) from 1793 to 1815, neutrals found little sympathy. Even the Swiss and the Swedes became involved. American ships were seized and boarded by British and French alike. The lure of war profits helped the ships' owners to adjust, but American opinion boiled at each insult to the young flag. Bitterness grew as one moved west, to mingle with outrage at alleged British backing of the Indians. In the 1812 elections, the western States sent angry "warhawks" to Congress, demanding that President James Madison declare war and promising swift and easy conquest of Canada. "I verily believe," boasted one of them, young Henry Clay of Kentucky, "that the militia of Kentucky are alone competent to place Montreal and Upper Canada at your feet." In June 1812, Madison delivered his message: there would be a second War of Independence.

Most people called it the War of 1812 and shrouded it with myths. On paper, Clay was right. Seven and a half million Americans could overwhelm half a million British subjects, a fifth of them "late Loyalists." Major-General Isaac Brock, with fifteen hundred regulars to defend Upper Canada, concluded that he would have no help from his legislature and very little from local magistrates and militia colonels unless he won some rapid victories. Backed by Indian allies such as Tecumseh and his Shawnee warriors, Brock seized the initiative. A handful of regulars and Indians captured the American fort at Michilimackinac, holding the entire Middle West for the rest of the war. While American state militias debated whether to cross the border and aged generals left over from the Revolutionary War trembled for their scalps,

Brock and Tecumseh captured an entire army at Detroit. In the final battle of 1812, at Queenston Heights, Brock died, but his angry redcoats and a revived Upper-Canadian militia hurled American invaders back across the Niagara River.

That one year, 1812, gave Upper Canada most of the national myths it would ever have, from Brock's leadership to the gallantry of the militia (which, for the most part, had waited until the regulars and the Indians determined the outcome of the war). The struggle continued for two more years of hard-fought victories, painful setbacks, and murderous devastation of frontier communities. The Americans would remember the war for a series of ship-to-ship battles, forgetting the fighting that ravaged the Upper Canadian landscape. In fact, the Americans lost the ocean war by 1814 because of the British naval blockade, while their strength, resources, and new regular army steadily grew in the inland campaigns. In 1813, American control of Lake Erie allowed raiding parties to ravage Upper Canada from Sandwich to Norfolk. In 1814, American shipwrights were outbuilding the British dockyard at Kingston. Once the Americans won Lake Ontario, Upper Canada would fall.

Instead, British negotiators had ended the war even before its last – and almost its bloodiest – battle was fought at New Orleans. The war changed no boundaries, brought no reparations, avenged no wrongs. The Canadian hope that somehow the old fur-trading hinterland might be restored turned out to be forlorn. Upper Canadians seeking compensation for burned-out farms and slaughtered livestock would get no reparations from the Americans who had done the deed. They must look to Britain, and the British, exhausted after a generation of war, could not afford to be generous.

From the War of 1812, English Canadians took both proud and bitter memories. In Lower Canada, they felt a pleasing, if temporary sense of solidarity with the French Canadians. The battle at Chateauguay was hardly Waterloo, but a French Canadian, Colonel Charles de Salaberry, had commanded both British regulars and his own *Voltigeurs* in driving off the Americans. Upper Canadians could be proud of Queenston, the murderous battles of

Stoney Creek and Lundy's Lane, and the odd little legend of Laura Secord driving her cow through the American lines to warn Lieutenant James Fitzgibbon of an enemy attack. Even more important were the memories of those who had stood loyal and unafraid in the early days of disloyalty and confusion. Archdeacon John Strachan, the Scottish convert to Anglicanism, with his megalithic convictions of righteousness, had faced American invaders with the same resolution he would show to Methodists and unbelievers. John Beverley Robinson had shown courage on the battlefield and brutal resolution at the Ancaster assizes. Robinson's prosecution had sent eight late-Loyalist traitors to the gallows and had confirmed him, though he was barely out of his teens, as Upper Canada's Attorney General. In Upper Canada, the Loyalist tradition had always been questionable. The War of 1812 gave the colony's elite new credentials of loyalism. If there was a Family Compact in Upper Canada, it was really an unspoken alliance of those who had led and organized the colony in its most threatened years, who had run great risks and who expected the rewards.

As the colony struggled after 1815 to rebuild from wartime wreckage and to adjust to an economy no longer fed by huge British military spending, Upper Canada's leaders cancelled Simcoe's old welcome to Americans. By insisting on war, the American warhawks had helped to cancel a process that might have led to peaceful absorption of the colony by the United States. Upper Canada would now be British, though at a cost. The tide of superbly qualified American frontiersmen would pass south of the Great Lakes, making the shores flourish with farms, cities, and industries, while Upper Canada stagnated. Certainly immigrants came to the colony after 1815, lured by promises of land and opportunity, but they came from a Britain where there were now "too many spoons for the broth." Very few had the skills or the capital to transform wilderness into crude but productive farms. In time, the "late Loyalists," with their mixed allegiance, would be submerged in a tide of English, Irish, and Scottish settlers, but Upper-Canadian landowners would still grumble that abstract principles had hurt their profits.

The post-war colony was full of grumblers. In part, this was because a generation of relentless labour had paid off. Pre-war settlers had won the leisure to observe the Upper-Canadian scene. With a franchise broader than most Britons would enjoy until 1832, there were few barriers to political participation for prosperous farmers or tradesmen. Newspapers were few and costly, and their proprietors depended on government advertising, but they also satisfied an appetite for gossip and controversy. A red-wigged tempestuous newcomer named William Lyon Mackenzie was one of those who filled this need. An honest man with a huge bump of self-righteousness, Mackenzie travelled the backwoods and filled his *Colonial Advocate* with the grievances he uncovered, together with serialized novels, moral tracts, helpful hints, and the reports of curiosities that he loved to collect.

The grievances were many and most grew out of jealousy of the greener fields on the American side of the lakes. Upper Canada seemed a backwater, short of bridges, roads, and other public works vital to a pioneer society. By American standards, officials were grossly overpaid. Land policies which left vacant the tracts of crown and clergy land, adding to the weary trek of farmers to their markets, were inevitably blamed on corruption. In a province that was Methodist if it was anything, how dare Archdeacon Strachan claim to the British government that Upper Canada was Anglican? There was really no mystery: Strachan wanted the clergy reserve revenues for his own denomination. In young Egerton Ryerson, the Methodist dissenters found an eloquent and fearless champion.

The history of Upper Canada has been dominated by one-sided versions of its political struggles. Historians have been captivated by the persuasive venom of Mackenzie's editorials; they have treated the slogans of reformers as though they were factually true. Probably Upper Canada's leaders were as honest and conscientious as the times allowed; their fault was their conviction that they must manage everything in the colony, including successive lieutenant-governors. Like most elites, they saw no distinction between their own best interests and those of the community.

They succumbed to the dangerous error of treating critics, from Robert Gourlay to Robert Baldwin, as mortal enemies.

Whatever monetary cranks like Mackenzie might claim, the colony needed the Bank of Upper Canada, but did the bank need to be switched, by legislative chicanery, from Kingston to York? The elite also backed William Hamilton Merritt's Welland Canal with its own funds, but, when the project ran beyond their means, they had no hesitation in using Upper Canada's credit. It was a shrewd stroke to invite British investors to create the Canada Company as an agency to market the crown and clergy reserves and then, by agreement, to force the company to develop the huge Huron Tract between Guelph and Goderich. Was it wise, though, to impose Strachan's son-in-law as the company's Canadian manager?

Oligarchies are rarely self-critical. Upper Canada's leaders could sometimes seem petty and vindictive in their use of power; they did not defy the law. When sons of York's elite threw Mackenzie's press into the harbour, a court ordered prompt and generous compensation. Mackenzie's own speeches and editorials were evidence to contemporaries that free speech prevailed in Upper Canada. Leading reformers like Dr. William Baldwin and his eloquent son, Robert, often found the excitable editor an embarrassment, but Mackenzie's following of farmers and small-town tradesmen was valuable to their loose coalition. Unlike Papineau's *patriotes* in Lower Canada, who commanded a one-sided majority in the Assembly, the reformers and the Tory oligarchy in Upper Canada each commanded only a knot of loyal supporters. Other members floated with the wishes and needs of their frontier constituents, stern against corruption but eager to bargain for a badly needed bridge. In any case, the Assembly could be ignored by legislative and executive councillors who believed themselves appointed for life.

That conviction was suddenly challenged. In a seeming political cataclysm, Britain's Whigs came to power after more than half a century of Toryism. In the excited political mood, it seemed the Radicals might not be far behind. The turmoil was easily exaggerated. The new men were as wealthy and almost as cautious as the old. The great Reform Bill of 1832 gave Britons the franchise

Canadians had enjoyed since 1791. A succession of Whig aristocrats at the colonial office differed little from their Tory predecessors though they were a little more willing to listen to professed "Reformers" from the colonies and to give credence to claims of "Family Compacts" and "Château Cliques." When John Beverley Robinson grumbled about Mackenzie having received a hearing in London for his absurd charges, he was dismissed as Attorney General for his indiscretion. In 1836, when the Whigs chose a successor to the valiant Sir John Colborne, some Upper Canadians erected banners welcoming their new Lieutenant Governor as "A Proven Reformer."

Sir Francis Bond Head certainly had radical ideas. No previous governor had worried about Upper Canada's depleting resources or about the land and hunting rights of the Indians. Unlike Colborne, who listened to the oligarchy, Bond Head listened to himself. He appointed Reformers like Baldwin to his executive and dismissed them when they insisted on their own policies. Bond Head is remembered as a figure of fun who conducted official audiences with his short legs stuck rigidly out in front of him. He was the would-be dictator who took the field in the 1836 Assembly elections, raised the loyalty cry, and drove most of the Reformers, including Mackenzie, from their seats.

Most sensible Reformers licked their wounds and bided their time. Assembly elections in Upper Canada swung regularly from Tory to Reform as settlers voted alternately for public works or political fireworks. Certainly there were differences in 1836. The post-1815 flood of British settlers had begun to have political significance. Some signs were ugly. Reformers complained that Tory bullies had attacked their voters at London – though that did not prevent a Reform victory. Orangemen, the Protestant extremists who had been banned in Ireland, surfaced in the eastern districts of Upper Canada to back Bond Head's loyalty call. They were dangerous allies.

For William Lyon Mackenzie, defeat was intolerable. In 1834, he had enjoyed a brief taste of power as the first mayor of a newly incorporated city of Toronto – the old York. A long visit to the United States convinced him that only republican institutions would give Upper Canada the cheap, honest government its yeoman-farmers needed. To Mackenzie, defeat in 1836 was not an electoral mishap but an act of tyranny enforced by a British governor and a corrupt oligarchy. From the analysis came the only possible remedy: revolution.

As in Lower Canada, the times encouraged revolutionary language among angry, American-born farmers in the townships north and west of Toronto. An economic depression had descended on Upper Canada, aggravated by Bond Head's insistence that banks and business houses must keep their doors open and pay off panic-stricken creditors even at the cost of needless ruin. It was no secret in Toronto that both Canadas faced rebellion, but Bond Head sent every soldier he could find to reinforce the British garrison in Lower Canada.

When Mackenzie shared his plans for proclaiming an Upper Canadian republic, most Reformers were aghast. Robert Baldwin drew away. Others decided that Mackenzie's threat, however foolish, might frighten the governor into concessions. Dr. John Rolph, the veteran Reform politician Mackenzie had designated as president of his provisional government, talked discreetly to both sides. In the rural townships, simpler men believed in "Little Mac," read his hurriedly printed manifesto and heeded his call: "Up then brave Canadians. Get ready your rifles and make short work of it."

The work would be short. On December 4, 1837, unaware that Papineau's rebellion had already collapsed, a few hundred men began to gather at Montgomery's Tavern on Yonge Street, a few miles north of Toronto. It was a demoralizing prospect, with rain and wind, and Mackenzie himself in a state of rage and indecision. In Toronto, it was no better. Old Colonel Fitzgibbon, Laura Secord's confidant of 1813, pleaded desperately with Bond Head to abandon his complacency. News of the rebel gathering turned complacency into panic. Then, thanks to Fitzgibbon and a tough young Tory from Hamilton, Allan MacNab, the governor's allies rallied. At dawn on December 7, untrained militia marched up Yonge Street behind bagpipes and bands to meet the frightened, ill-armed rebels. In a few minutes, the battle was over.

Mackenzie fled, sheltered by men and women who risked everything for his safety until he reached the United States. Militia and Indians patrolled every road, checked every barn, and sent sad little groups of prisoners to face jail, trials, and transportation to Britain's penal colonies. There can rarely have been a rebellion that found fewer supporters at the time or more admirers afterwards.

The Rebellion of 1837 failed because it never had a chance of success. Mackenzie had sought to reverse not only the election of 1836 but the rejection of the United States in 1812. Many of his followers would pay a bitter price for his leadership. The absurd little battle north of Toronto was followed by repression far beyond anything seen in Lower Canada in 1837-38. Two of Mackenzie's lieutenants died on the gallows; ninety-two people were sent to penal colonies. In the aftermath, hundreds of prosperous but resentful settlers left for the United States. Yet, as Mackenzie's biographer, William Kilbourn, has argued, perhaps the Rebellion cleared the air. Some of the violence and unreasoning invective went out of Upper Canadian politics. A fresh start was possible, and most of the old players would be gone.

5

United Canadas

The 1837 rebellions were the first formative experience for Cartier, John A. Macdonald, and many of the politicians who launched Confederation thirty years later. Even in the lower provinces, Confederation with the Canadas revived old fears of the violence and disloyalty of 1837. In fact, the rebellions ended an era. They could be bathed in a romantic aura because the old antagonisms died so quickly. Within a decade, Papineau and Mackenzie returned to communities where their luckless followers had been hanged. They were sputtering political relics. Old friends and enemies were too busy making money and finding political compromises to care.

In 1837 Britain was still euphoric at the accession of the young Queen Victoria. The Canadian rebellions had come as a shocking embarrassment. A shaky Whig regime might silence at least some critics by despatching "Radical Jack," Lord Durham, to solve the Canadian problem. As Governor-in-Chief and Lord High Commissioner, Durham's power extended to all of British North America. Unfortunately, it did not reach as far as Bermuda, though it was there that he sent his eight leading *patriote* prisoners, liberating the rest. It was wise clemency but Durham's English enemies crowed that he had exceeded his jurisdiction. After a bare four months, an ailing, exasperated Durham quit. Two years later he had died, after years of chronic ill-health.

Those four summer months of 1838 made his reputation. A man of firm liberal convictions did not need long to reverse the judgements of his military predecessors. The commercial dreams of Montreal merchants and Robert Baldwin's political frustrations made sense to Durham; the claims of French Canadians or the Upper-Canadian oligarchy did not. Durham did not have to talk to people to reach conclusions obvious to any intelligent European liberal. "There can hardly be conceived a nationality more destitute of all that can invigorate and elevate a people," Durham reported of the *Canadiens*. They had no history, no literature, and, accordingly, no future. He spent ten days in Upper Canada, one of them with Robert Baldwin, others devoted to convivial attempts to improve relations with Americans at Niagara Falls. The journey sufficed to convince the governor general that there indeed was a "Family Compact" to be dispossessed.

Both judgements were highly dubious but they lay at the heart of Durham's analysis. So did two solider facts. The Montrealers were right: Canada was an economic unit and the split beyond Longueuil had done great economic harm. Baldwin was right too: colonial self-government was a farce if the governor's officials and advisers could ignore the elected Assembly. The best constitutional experts had insisted that sovereignty could never be split. This, Durham insisted, was nonsense. There were powers vital to a colonial role – foreign affairs, for example, or even crown lands – which Britain must continue to exercise through its governors. There were many more powers which the colonists could be left to manage.

The Canadas must be reunited, Durham insisted, both for economic reasons and to assist the inevitable assimilation of the French. In a single Assembly, their numbers would give them a small majority, but the tide of immigration promised that it would not be for long. In subjects of colonial interest, the executive council must depend on the Assembly for support. No more than in Britain should a colonial administration continue without the confidence of the elected chamber. The Canadas also needed municipal governments so that the Assembly would no longer ring with controversies better settled at the local parish pump.

In time, Durham's report would be much admired. When it first appeared, it was cordially abused. Then, as often happens, large parts were implemented, and small, but significant, features were not. The Act of Union of 1840 created the United Provinces of Canada. The large debt of Upper Canada was merged with the modest debt of Lower Canada. English would be the language of government and legislature, but even the temporary risk of an Assembly dominated by ex-*patriotes* was avoided. Each of the old colonies would have forty seats. Nor was Durham's notion of "responsible government" to be entertained. Governors general would choose their advisers and manage the Assembly as best they could.

The British might be forgiven their caution. Throughout 1838, rebel exiles and their warm-hearted American hosts had plotted feverishly. Secret societies called Hunters or *Chasseurs* proliferated. The border became an armed camp; the internal conflict of 1837 became, for many Canadians, a patriotic struggle against American invasion. Hours after Durham's departure, a new *patriote* thrust crossed the border south of Montreal. Within a week, Colborne's men had crushed the invaders but leniency in Lower Canada was given no second chance. Twelve *patriotes* were executed and fifty-eight Lower Canadians were sent to the Australian penal colonies.

In Upper Canada, the drawn-out border conflict and the savage repression discredited Mackenzie and his Tory enemies alike. When Lord Sydenham, the veteran politician chosen to manage the awkward new Union, summoned his first Assembly at Kingston in 1841, Robert Baldwin's moderate Reformers won an easy ascendancy. In Lower Canada, the mood was utterly different. Their rebellion crushed, their leading *Canadiens* gave way to despair. Yet life went on and the new game would have to be played. Durham's verdict might be appealed. Already the young François-Xavier Garneau had set out to defy Durham's judgement that French Canadians had no history by writing it in massive detail. Etienne Parent, editor of *Le Canadien*, argued, like Bédard before him, that the British constitution could still be the best safeguard for French-Canadian survival. Forget Durham's errors, Parent urged, go to the Assembly and fight for his idea of responsible government.

The suggestion would be adopted, without much acknowledge-
ment, by the ablest colonial politician of the 1840s. Louis-
Hippolyte Lafontaine was a plump Montreal lawyer with a fancied
likeness to Napoleon and a comparably authoritarian personality.
He had split from Papineau in 1837, suffered a brief and beneficial
martyrdom in prison, and now was prepared to teach the *Canadiens* how to survive in the new regime. The principles, most of
them announced to the voters of Terrebonne in 1841, were clear
enough; winning support took a little longer. French Canadians
must forget the divisions which had separated the anti-clerical
Papineau from the Church or middle-class leaders from *habitants*.
Clergy and people must form a tight alliance, of faith and nationality. Next, they must be pragmatic and progressive in order to build
an alliance with the Upper Canadian Reformers. Together, they
must dominate the new Assembly and in time they would win the
constitutional struggle.

The essence of Canadian political history in the 1840s is the
slow completion of Lafontaine's strategy. Lafontaine's alliance
with the Reformers was sealed when, defeated in Terrebonne, he
accepted Baldwin's invitation to campaign for an Assembly seat in
Mackenzie's old territory north of Toronto. Later, Lafontaine
would return the favour for Baldwin. Together, their supporters
almost dominated the Assembly. A succession of governors did
what they could. Sir Charles Metcalfe, Sydenham's successor, was
in constant pain from a fatal cancer, but he did better than most.
He waged the 1844 election campaign virtually as his own party
leader, using arguments against patronage and its corruption
which a Whiggish breed of Canadian constitutional historians
later preferred to ignore. At stake in responsible government, he
insisted, was the determination of Baldwin and Lafontaine to dis-
tribute offices and public works as spoils to their followers.
Metcalfe was perfectly right. High-sounding arguments about
British parliamentary institutions and vice-regal tyranny camou-
flaged the fact that colonial politicians wanted to reward followers
and punish opponents in a very American fashion. Lafontaine
argued that it was wiser to sprinkle appointments, commissions,

and salaries among the frustrated professionals of Lower Canada, than to let them plot new *patriote* uprisings.

Britain did more for the Canadas than send a new constitution and a succession of able but unhealthy governors to enforce it. Durham had also underlined the desperate need for public works on the St. Lawrence rapids, so long delayed by Lower Canada's political impasse. In the 1820s, Britain had spent far more than she wanted to on fortresses and the Rideau Canal in the event of a repetition of the War of 1812. Now, more grudgingly, she guaranteed huge loans. The colonial economy, lagging as usual behind an American recovery, spurted forward.

Hardship in the 1830s had helped drive emigrants from Britain; the prosperity of the 1840s was what now attracted them to Canada. The appeal had to be strong. Big, leaky timber ships from Quebec crammed their "'tween-decks" with steerage passengers, doubling the owner's revenue at whatever cost in human misery. Despite the quarantine station at Grosse Ile, the cholera came up the river. So did the old country quarrels of Orange and Green, of Connaught-men and Cork. Canadians complained that better-fitted and more prosperous immigrants most often had plans to continue to the United States. But still, people came, filling the new counties of Canada West (Upper Canada), sending the population climbing at twice the rate of that in Canada East (Lower Canada). For the first time, too, many immigrants came without the means or prospect of acquiring land. The Irish, driven out by poverty, overcrowding, and then by the terrible potato famine of the 1840s, formed the first waves of that huge, anonymous, forgotten army of labourers who dug the canals and would build the railways, the mines, and the cities of a developing Canada.

Prosperity and then famine in the 1840s had a revolutionary impact on British colonial policy. Long before, in narrow intellectual circles, the radical ideas of Adam Smith, Thomas Malthus, and Jeremy Bentham had gently undermined old convictions about the necessity of maintaining a self-sufficient empire. Surely, as the greatest manufacturer and trader in the world, Britain should be the greatest foe of all constraints against free trade? Buying timber or wheat in the cheapest market rather than from Canada or New Brunswick would not only benefit Britain, it would remove a hidden tax from the poor.

The Canadas were a good illustration of why the new free-trade ideas made sense. Huge spending on defence and the continuing cost of a garrison only aggravated the Americans and brought no return to Britain. The Rebellions of 1837 surely proved that British colonial policies had failed. Prosperity in the early 1840s showed that protection was not needed. The Irish famines were aggravated by tariff barriers to cheap food. The complex system that had protected the markets of English landowners and colonial farmers alike crumbled.

Nothing happens overnight. Even in the 1820s, Canadian timber and wheat had had to compete harder in the British market, yet it was hard for colonials to see that arrangements they took for granted could ever fundamentally change. Whig or Tory, British politics seemed so immovable. Prosperity is also an anaesthetic, and in the 1840s everything was booming. In 1841, twelve thousand tons of shipping cleared the port of Quebec; in 1846, the total reached forty thousand tons. In Montreal that year, died Joseph Masson, the wealthiest merchant in Canada and a reminder that *Canadiens* too could prosper in trade. Even the church put its money into canal companies, steamships, banks, and the first little portage railways. A visitor to Toronto in 1842 marvelled: "All is in a whirl and a fizz and one must be in fashion; everything and everybody seems to go by steam." There was money for education too. As Chief Superintendent of Schools for Upper Canada, Egerton Ryerson had moved on from Methodist concerns to launch a public system of "non-discriminational schools." For the rest of his life, he would bully, prod, and inspire the cause of public schools. Strachan's dream of an Anglican monopoly of higher education crumbled as Presbyterians and Methodists used prosperous times to launch their own colleges. In Montreal, Bishop Ignace Bourget brought back the Jesuits and helped to revive a dream as old as Champlain, the conversion of an entire continent. French

Canadians as far away as Oregon and as near as Toronto became bishops. Bourget too was an educator.

Disasters are rarely predicted and seldom come singly. Montreal had lavished hope and capital on its new canal system as the great route to the Atlantic, not only from Canada West but from the central United States. The Irish canallers had dredged a way across the Niagara peninsula, built locks to pass the Lachine and Soulanges rapids, and cleared a way from Montreal to Detroit. No sooner had they finished than the Americans dropped their duties and enticed traffic down the Erie Canal from Buffalo to the Hudson River. Wheat exports through Montreal dropped in the year 1848 from 3.9 million to 2.2 million bushels. As the Irish famine of the 1840s dumped shiploads of penniless, starving people in Canadian ports, the triumph of free trade in Britain wiped out Canada's only real export market. If that were not enough, Americans seized the Oregon territory on the remote Pacific coast and demanded that the boundary be set at 54.40', vowing war if they did not get their way. British territory would be shut off from the ocean.

Considering all this, it seemed almost irrelevant that the latest governor general, Lord Elgin, was allowed to concede the principle of responsible government to a Lafontaine-Baldwin ministry after its election success in 1848, or that he would open the ensuing legislative session with a speech in both English and French. By now, the Canadian Parliament had moved from Kingston to a new building in Montreal – a suitable gesture to the commercial (and largely English-speaking) metropolis of the United Provinces. In the circumstances, though, with Montreal's merchants facing utter ruin and thousands of people unemployed at the busiest season, Lafontaine and Baldwin showed a surprising lack of tact. The first test of their new power, designed to bury forever the bitterness of 1837, was a Rebellion Losses Bill for Lower Canada. *Patriotes* and innocents alike would be recompensed for the depredations of *Vieux Brûlot*, Sir John Colborne, and his Montreal militiamen.

English Montrealers were furious. The bill was a political insult to cap their economic woes. On April 25, 1849, they stoned and threatened Lord Elgin as he returned from giving the law his assent. A mob pillaged and burned the new parliament buildings. Some business leaders went further. If Britain had abandoned them, why not seek annexation with the United States? Among the names on the angry manifesto were Alexander Tilloch Galt, William Molson, John Redpath, and a future prime minister, John Abbott. Louis-Joseph Papineau's name was there too. So were those of ardent new admirers who now called themselves *rouges*, from their ribbons and banners of revolutionary red.

Even as the English crowds raged through Montreal, the annexationists had their answer. In 1849 there were huge finds of gold in California, fuelling an economic boom that would last, with breaks, to the early 1870s. Despite its deepening conflict over states' rights and slavery, the United States surged with prosperity. When merchants stopped complaining long enough to check their ledgers, they found that their British orders had not dried up after all and Americans were becoming buyers of Canadian wheat and timber as well as fish from the lower colonies. In 1854, Lord Elgin went to Washington to resolve disputes about trade and fisheries. He returned with a ten-year Reciprocity Treaty which virtually wiped out the boundary as a factor in the trade of natural products. The U.S. Congress ratified the arrangement that August. American critics complained that Elgin's proposals "floated through on champagne." Southern slaveholders voted for the treaty only after Elgin promised that it would keep the colonies British. They wanted no more "free-soil" states.

Baldwin and Lafontaine retired, their work complete. Canada had its framework of government, education, and municipalities. George-Etienne Cartier would soon complete a modernized civil code for Canada East which would see the gentle extinction of seigneurialism. In ten years, the *Canadiens* had taken a constitution designed to destroy them and made it work for them. Indeed, they now rather liked the Act of Union. If it had been fair in 1840 to give each province equal representation, it would surely be fair for a long time, even if Canada East now had only 1,111,566 people to the West's 1,396,091.

The old issues were gone and so were old alliances. As always, there were those who were fed up with compromise. Youthful *rouges* from the old *patriote* strongholds of the Richelieu valley stirred with nationalist passion and a nervous anti-clericalism. It seemed impossible that they could ever make common cause with the austere Protestant farmers in the "great western peninsula" of Canada West, with their anger at privilege, corruption, and government spending. "Clear Grits," they called themselves, "pure sand and not a particle of dirt." In the 1850s, though, the big, craggy-faced Scot named George Brown who had created the Toronto *Globe* and who never questioned his own wisdom, would take the Grits in hand. They would be purged of Americanism and disciplined. Above all, Brown reminded them, Protestant English Canadians must show as much solidarity as the French or their own religion and rights might be forfeit.

Those who held power had outgrown such preoccupations. Lafontaine's men, re-mustered by Cartier, now called themselves *bleus*, to contrast with *rouges*. They were, appropriately, cool realists from a province that had learned pragmatism. There were Baldwinites, too, like the cunning Francis Hincks, but more and more weight lay with the Tories, with heirs of the Family Compact and Metcalfe's 1844 campaign. Yet, whether it was the gawky young lawyer from Kingston, John A. Macdonald, or old Sir Allan MacNab, once Bond Head's adviser and champion in 1837, these also were pragmatists. "Railways are my politics now," MacNab blandly confessed. The title of their party, the Liberal-Conservatives, surely welcomed anyone who wanted a share in power.

MacNab was typical. The railway boom had crossed the Atlantic. Cities, towns, and nimble speculators pestered the legislature for charters, planned routes, and interviewed contractors. Francis Hincks went to London to negotiate a line to Halifax with representatives from the lower provinces. Angry Maritimers felt cheated when the Canadians pulled out. Torontonians had even better reason to cry foul when the same Francis Hincks was caught out, with the mayor of their city, in an ingenious stock swindle with their beloved Northern Railway. Hincks dropped out of sight, but railway promotion was irresistibly corrupting.

In 1850, Canada had about 55 miles (88.5 km) of track. Four years later, Sir Allan MacNab's Great Western Railway covered 254 miles (408.6 km) from Niagara to Windsor. Hincks' London visit had not been wasted. The great British contracting firm of Peto, Brassey, Jackson & Betts persuaded itself that there would be profit from a vast trunk railway through Canada from Portland, Maine, to the American Middle West. No one seems to have warned them about rivers, politicians, labour costs, or the effect of Canadian winters on track, locomotives, and rolling stock. By 1861, the line was complete to Sarnia but the company's largely-British shareholders had to recognize that the Grand Trunk was not only effectively bankrupt, but that the system would never pay a penny unless even more money was poured into it. To illustrate their imperial vision, Grand Trunk interests bought control of the Hudson's Bay Company and fantasized about the profits to be made from a real trunk railway across the continent. Meanwhile the company had to find a scheme to keep conductors from "deadheading" passengers for free trips, the cheapest way to get their tracks standardized to the North American gauge, and how to relate British railway technology to Canada's winters.

Booms end and love affairs cool. By the late 1850s, both fates befell railways in Canada. Politicians who had shared in the "great barbecue" were suddenly suspect. In the pattern of double-barrelled ministries which Lafontaine and Baldwin had established as a makeshift for their un-United Province, George-Etienne Cartier and John A. Macdonald had emerged as leaders. In the prevailing morality, Cartier saw no sin in being both attorney-general and the Grand Trunk's well-paid lawyer. Indignation at railway corruption could unite George Brown and the party he preferred to call "Reformers" with Antoine-Aimé Dorion's *rouges*. An Assembly with a large number of "shaky fellows," "loose fish," and "waiters-on-providence" (as Macdonald scornfully called independents) meant that no unpopular government was safe for long.

Trivial, emotional issues are always the trickiest. After Montreal's violent behaviour in 1849, the province's capital alternated (on a costly three-year cycle) between Quebec and Toronto. A firm choice of a capital had to be made. Tactfully, the choice was left to Queen Victoria, guided by pleasant little watercolours done by officers of the Royal Engineers. Photography might have been safer. The queen chose Bytown, an ugly lumber town on the Ottawa River. Not even monarchists accepted the choice and the Cartier-Macdonald government fell; Brown and Dorion had a chance to govern. Two days later, when the Assembly members had recovered their composure, the Reformers and *rouges* were defeated. This "double shuffle" returned Macdonald and Cartier to power and left Brown fuming on the sidelines.

By now the Upper Canadian Reformers had an issue the *rouges* did not share: representation by population. Supporters made it a slogan, "Rep by Pop," and the issue lent itself to simple emotions. Late in 1852, after Upper Canadians had drifted home from the long legislative session at Quebec City, the French members voted to impose Catholic public schools on an overwhelmingly Protestant Canada West. Brown and his followers were outraged at such sectarian meddling; they held firmly to the doctrine that separated church and state. With Brown's inspiration, still more grievances were developed against the Lower Canadians. By the 1850s, Canada West's share of the population had become a large and growing majority. The equality of representation imposed by the Act of Union in 1840 had become anathema.

By the 1860s, "Rep by Pop" had taken hold as a popular cause in Canada West, and support for Macdonald's Liberal-Conservatives diminished at each election. The slogan pitted English against French and, since religious prejudices outweighed race, Protestant against Catholic. Orange riots in the towns of Canada West were matched by Catholic violence when apostate priests, Gavazzi and Chiniquy, insisted on evangelizing in Montreal and Quebec for Protestantism. With no efficient police forces to control mobs and the British garrison cut by the need to send troops to the Crimea and India, the province reluctantly organized a five-thousand-man "volunteer militia." The forebear of Canada's armed forces found its primary role as a riot police.

The thought of sectional conflict might have been farther from people's minds if the example of violence had not been so near at hand. Canadians formed the largest group of immigrants to the United States; hundreds of thousands of *Canadiens* who had trekked to the New England cotton mills, easing the poverty and over-population of Canada East, kept their relatives aware of American events. Meanwhile, the American slavery issue was brought to Canada West by hundreds of black fugitives, helped into British territory by the men and women of the "Underground Railroad." Blacks in Canada experienced plenty of racial discrimination, but their presence was a reminder of the "irrepressible conflict" tearing the United States apart. When it came in April 1861, the American Civil War divided Canadians as well. Both sides also recognized that the American crisis could easily develop into a threat to Canada as well.

To most Canadians, defence and foreign policy were British responsibilities. Even Canada's tiny volunteer militia was left to languish after a few early years of enthusiasm. Suddenly, war was imminent. President Lincoln's secretary of state, W. H. Seward, publicly declared that war with Britain might rally the divided states. Others argued that the conquest of Canada could compensate for the departed Confederacy. When an American warship removed Confederate delegates from a British mail steamer, Britain had a solid justification for a declaration of war. In an instant, the British forgot their colonial indifference. At no thought of the cost, thousands of regular troops were despatched to Canada to forestall an American invasion.

The troops were still there in 1862 when the legislature rejected a modest defence program largely as a pretext to defeat the corrupt, tired Cartier-Macdonald government. The success fell to John Sandfield Macdonald, a Catholic reformer who disliked Brown. Macdonald believed with his partner, Louis Sicotte, a disaffected *bleu*, that "double majorities" of French and English members worked perfectly well. In Britain, the twist in colonial politics produced outrage. The patriotic mood of 1861 that accepted war for Canada if necessary curdled into fury at the foolish and ungrateful colonials. Moreover, as the huge military potential of the United States was mobilized for the Civil War, British strategists came to the cold realization that they could never repeat the victories of the War of 1812. A report in 1864 by a trusted staff officer confirmed the conclusion: without efforts no British government could afford, the Canadas were indefensible.

That was a secret no colonist could be allowed to know, but it lent harsh urgency to the British determination that something be done about the North American colonies. It was a determination shared by a number of influential private investors in the Grand Trunk Railway. In Canada, too, there was a growing sense that a more profound constitutional change was necessary. Sandfield Macdonald and his closest allies, Luther Holton and the *rouge* A. A. Dorion, had no real policy beyond cost-cutting and hope. Plans for an Intercolonial Railway – a year-round connection to the lower provinces and the ocean – were on hold. So was expansion westward to the Red River colony and the Northwest. In 1863, the American Civil War reached its climax. After Gettysburg, the North could be certain of victory, and who knew what dangers that might bring to Canada?

By 1864, everything seemed necessary and nothing seemed possible. The two Canada's were trapped in their own histories and by their own geographies. On March 21, its support flaking away, Macdonald's government resigned. There had been deadlock: now there was nothing.

6

Lower Provinces

Beyond the mouth of the St. Lawrence lay four proudly self-reliant British colonies. John Cabot's crew was almost certainly not the first to see Newfoundland when the *Matthew* sailed into the future harbour of St. John's in 1497. The history of these colonies would have been the oldest in North America if Basque, Portuguese, French, and English fishermen had left records of their voyages and discoveries.

Since they had no cheap source of salt, some fishermen, notably the west-country English, needed to go ashore. The cod must be landed and dried on long racks, or "flakes." To do more, to develop whole colonies of fishermen on this distant shore, would give them a six-week head start before the rival fleets could arrive from England. Men might be left to guard and repair the flakes, but a few early attempts at settlement convinced the English that Newfoundland, with its harsh climate and thin soil, could never support serious agriculture. People came anyway, ignoring laws and periodic attempts at deportation, somehow surviving the hardships. Mass starvation remained a hazard of Newfoundland life as late as the 1820s.

In later years, on the rare occasions when Maritimers thought about what they insisted on calling "Upper Canada," they frequently deplored the incessant squabbles of French and English, Catholic and Protestant. Yet their own region had the same troublesome diversity and the same propensity to quarrel with neighbours and subjugate them if they could. Indeed, this existed within each colony. There was a distinction few people in either region fully appreciated. The Canadians were forced together in their lives and their quarrels by the long, indivisible avenue of the St. Lawrence and the Great Lakes. Each of the lower colonies developed as a ring of shoreline settlements. People depended on themselves and their chosen neighbours. If they sought space, they could look out to sea. In all but Prince Edward Island, much of the interior was a rocky, inhospitable wilderness. Very few river valleys – the St. John, the Miramichi, the St. Croix – beckoned farmers and timber merchants inland. Between the shore and the forest, the more favoured regions offered a chance to farm. Towns and cities developed at harbours. There was timber for ships and housing and export, but for generations, the only real wealth of the region came from the sea.

Most Acadians were heirs of the few French who had remained in the area when Champlain had chosen to move up to the St. Lawrence. Tossed, for a few turbulent years, between French adventurers and New England pirates, the Acadians were then left to themselves for a century. They learned to dike the rich bottom land of the Minas Basin against the Fundy tides. In 1713, when the Treaty of Utrecht transferred Acadia to the British, perhaps sixteen hundred Acadians were included. It seemed to make no difference to them.

Unhappily for the Acadians, war outpaced fishing and subsistence farming as an industry for the region. The French settlers and the friendly Micmac and Abenaki Indians had provided a passive flank defence for New France. After 1720, they were supplemented at the far corner of Ile Royale by the huge new French fortress of Louisbourg. For all its strength, a British naval squadron and New England militia took the fortress in 1745, only to see it returned to the French by English diplomats. As the French hurried to repair the damage, the British countered by developing the huge natural harbour of Halifax. With its forts, its dockyard, and its garrison mentality, Halifax became a city that subsisted on government and thrived on war. Having ignored the Acadians, both sides now demanded their loyalty. Old loyalties favoured the French, but neither Quebec nor Louisbourg sent protection. Instead, backed by the harsh rules of war, British troops rounded up thousands of Acadians in 1755 and sent them south to be scattered among the Thirteen Colonies. In 1758, with Louisbourg taken again, more Acadians were expelled.

The dispersal was neither complete nor permanent. Many Acadians fled into the woods; others returned when the war was over to find their farms sold to American speculators. The returning Acadians went on to Ile St. Jean and Ile Royale – renamed respectively by their English conquerors Prince Edward Island and Cape Breton Island. Others went to the Saint John River valley and later to the Madawaska. The French government, which prudently limited its North American commitments to fishing rights on Newfoundland's French shore, sent Acadians to help populate the tiny islands of St. Pierre and Miquelon, all that remained of Champlain's great venture.

Like the Acadians, the American settlers who took their place and who spread themselves along the southern and western shores of Nova Scotia largely ignored the self-important little government of merchants and officials at Halifax. They sent home grim corrections to the glowing propaganda which had enticed them to "Nova Scarcity," but, while New Englanders' minds turned to revolution, Nova Scotia's Yankees turned their few leisure thoughts and moments to the "New Light" movement, a passionate religious revival. With a British fleet and garrison at Halifax, the few sparks of revolt in the 1770s were swiftly extinguished, and the missionaries of the "New Awakening," alarming though they seemed to Halifax Anglicans, sought revolutions in morals, not governments. Merchants in Halifax and other ports made too much money from the war to feel rebellious.

The Revolution came to Nova Scotia anyway. Loyalists arrived in shiploads from Boston in 1776, and then tens of thousands more came after the British had abandoned New York in 1783. It was a flood of bitter, defeated exiles, who had suffered much and lost everything for the Crown. The thirty thousand who came to Nova Scotia were not like the toughened farmers who went to Upper Canada. At Shelburne, where a large townsite with special districts for servants and for blacks had been laid out to welcome them, thousands of once-wealthy Loyalists landed. Promptly, they set to work planning a city hall, street names, and where to house the little fire engine presented by King George III. Unfortunately, no labourers appeared to build their houses. Not even the toughest frontiersmen could have tilled the rocks and swamps beyond the town. A little poorer and wiser, most Loyalists moved on.

At Halifax, Governor John Parr and his council lost patience with "New York office-grabbers." The answer, as in the Canadas but for different reasons, was separation. In 1784, New Brunswick and, for good measure, Cape Breton, became separate colonies. The leading Loyalists were delighted. In New Brunswick, they would build a society that would become "the most gentleman-like on earth." Whole regiments, under their officers, would settle on grants up the Saint John River, with colonels and captains receiving much larger grants to support their social status. Fredericton, safe from American attack up the river, would be a little gem of a capital. In a verdant paradise, Tory values would thrive.

Reality was different. The first fleet reached Saint John on May 18, 1783, to find bare rocks, swamps, and an endless vista of burned-over forest. As the ships departed, one woman felt such a terrible loneliness that ". . . although I had not shed a tear through all the war, I sat down in the damp moss with my baby and cried aloud." A second fleet, with thirty-five hundred people, arrived at the end of 1785 with no time to do more than pitch tents or erect crude huts before winter descended. Brave men simply lay down on the frozen earth and died.

Many Loyalists left. Others accepted the ruin of their dreams and made the best of it. When the huge trees of the Saint John valley were cleared, the soil was good enough for farming, and the timber slowly formed the basis of a major industry. Saint John grew slowly as a commercial centre, gradually justifying the premature charter that made it the first city of British North America. Behind the genteel Loyalist myth was a hard-grubbing, impoverished existence, mocking the memories of cultivated life in New York or Boston. More than a few Loyalists took their chances and slipped back to the United States, making links that others would later join.

New Brunswick was a victim of emigré illusions. Cape Breton was the little colony almost everyone but its Highland settlers forgot. Both were spared the casual disaster inflicted on Prince Edward Island. In a display of greed blatant even for the time, English speculators fastened on the island as soon as it was transferred from France in 1763. Sixty-seven "proprietors" drew lots for sixty-seven equal townships of twenty thousand acres on which they promised to pay quit-rents, develop the fishery, and establish a hundred Protestant settlers within the decade. Only one of them, Samuel Holland, kept his promise. Two others made a feeble attempt. The rest simply waited for squatters to occupy the land and then sent agents to collect the rent. As a result, what was potentially the richest Maritime colony never grew up. By dint of keeping the ear of the British government in London, the proprietors could milk the settlers and do nothing in return. Settlers had no incentive to improve the land or even their homes. They were even reluctant to build schools or churches. Every political issue seemed to focus on the distant "grantees" and on the officials who always seemed to enforce the proprietors' rights and condone their broken promises.

Loyalist leaders in the Atlantic colonies had concocted a grandiose economic role for their new home. The rich business of supplying food to Britain's slave islands in the Caribbean would be barred to the rebel Americans and switched to the loyal provinces. As rebel Americans looked on, rich cargoes of food and timber would travel south in Nova Scotia and New Brunswick ships. West Indies rum and sugar would move east across the Atlantic. It was absurd. It was only because of the squatter-farmers of Prince Edward Island that the Maritimes could feed themselves much less the West Indies. In any case, Britain was determined to make friends, not enemies, of the King's late subjects, the Americans.

The salvation of the Atlantic regions came with war. The struggle with Revolutionary France that began in 1793 and ended with the final defeat of Napoleon in 1815 transformed the economy of each of the lower provinces. The naval weakness of Revolutionary France guaranteed near-immunity to the ships and ports of the colonies, but wartime fleets and garrisons meant customers who paid in gold. French victories in Europe, and French alliances which closed off vital supplies sent British agents searching for replacements. When Baltic ports would no longer supply the Royal Navy's timber and spars, the forests of North America had available, if inferior, substitutes. Merchants shifted their operations to Saint John and the mouth of the Miramichi. In Newfoundland, the peacetime arguments against allowing local settlement and fishing collapsed. In 1809, the huge, unexplored mass of Labrador had been passed back to Newfoundland as though in recognition that the island colony now mattered. By war's end, St. John's had become capital of the island's fishing industry, and in 1817 the first resident governor arrived.

The war was a spur to shipbuilding in every major port of the region. Even minor harbours set up stocks to build schooners for the rich wartime cargoes. There was another more risky but vastly more profitable trade in "privateering," a form of licensed piracy on enemy merchant ships. For young Samuel Cunard and other Halifax merchants, privateering became the foundation of huge shipping fortunes.

As for the War of 1812, it was the bonanza on top of good fortune. While Upper Canada fought for its existence, New Brunswickers lived in peace with their American neighbours. The furious speeches about seamen's rights and taming British pride had only been Yankee bluster. Humiliation, felt the New Englanders, was a small price to pay for the huge profits they could draw from wartime trade. By declaring war, President Madison had destroyed the most lucrative mercantile era the northeastern states could remember. They might cheer the victories of the few American frigates but they would not fight the war. British colonists had no such inhibitions. Battalions from Newfoundland and New Brunswick fought in the defence of Upper Canada. Privateers found new and richer prey. In the final months of the war, British troops brushed aside feeble resistance to occupy much of Maine. Intercepted American customs revenue helped endow Halifax's Dalhousie University.

Whatever many a Maritimer might secretly wish, war could not last forever! Peace brought an economic collapse. In Halifax and Saint John, firms went bankrupt by the hundred. The shacks and shanties of St. John's vanished in a huge fire in 1816, and by the following winter ships brought pathetic appeals for food to fend off imminent starvation. Methodist missionaries newly arrived in Newfoundland tactlessly chose the moment to blame Catholics for the terrible predicament of the area. Religious riots enlivened the misery.

Yet the prosperous years had left their mark. Halifax's Province House stood as the finest public building in British North America and an Education Act in 1811 had pioneered secondary education in Nova Scotia. The cheap labour of French and American prisoners had built streets and fine houses. Even Prince Edward Island had found the first few leaders to resist the grantees. The nervous Scottish philanthropist Lord Selkirk had given the island an influential voice in London as well as a few hundred Highland settlers. Shipping and timber might be sluggish in the first post-war years but protection would last for thirty more peacetime years. Then, as in the Canadas, American markets would be sought.

In the language of development, the war years had given the lower provinces as good a chance for economic take-off as they would ever have. Memories of a golden age of Maritime prosperity would be shared by only a few. The lives of Maritime farmers, seamen, loggers, and fishermen could be brutally hard and financially precarious. Shipping records show a terrible toll of lives in vessels that were helpless in a winter storm on a lee shore, where lighthouses were rare and life-saving non-existent. Romantic images of lumber camps and the spring log drives overlook the reality of bad food, dangerous work, and a record of disease, crippling injury, and early death. In the colonial assemblies, employers were in control, whether they spoke as Tories or Reformers. The first unions in British North America had appeared among Halifax and Saint John longshoremen during the War of 1812. Afterwards, the appearance at regular intervals of laws banning them suggest that at least feeble workers' organizations persisted.

By the 1850s, workers in Saint John had enough self-confidence to announce their wage-rates in newspaper advertisements, and civic officials welcomed union floats and marchers in the city's periodic processions. The reason was simple. The flood of immigration largely bypassed the Atlantic colonies, adding only a healthy quota of Irish to the region's population. Workers were scarce enough to command a price, and merchants and mill-owners were prosperous enough to pay it.

Workers with bargaining power because of skills or local scarcity were the exception. Coastal fishermen, particularly in Newfoundland, had no such advantages. Most of them were soon hopelessly in debt to fish merchants who supplied their needs and kept them dependent. The transfer of the merchants to Newfoundland brought few benefits beyond providing St. John's with a small middle class and the beginnings of a cultural and social life the people of the bays and outports would rarely glimpse. A pattern of debt and deference developed in Newfoundland with even more serious social consequences than the antagonism of proprietors and tenants in Prince Edward Island.

All of the colonies had assemblies, even Cape Breton until it returned to Nova Scotia in 1820. Everywhere, cosy local oligarchies monopolized power, resembling Upper Canada's Family Compact in all but its energy and creativity. Political opposition was much slower to develop, perhaps because of the tradition of expecting little from government. Farmers, the obvious critics of urban elites, remained few and scattered. Assemblies were like unambitious town councils, willing to share out modest public works and then adjourn. Would-be reformers seemed easy to isolate as "troublemakers." In Newfoundland, a short-lived experiment in parties degenerated into such a bitter Catholic-Protestant conflict that in the 1840s, by common consent, the Assembly was suspended for six years. When it revived, the old divisions remained, but Catholics proclaimed themselves Liberals and Reformers while the Protestant communities along the north coast would call themselves Conservatives. In New Brunswick there were no real parties at all until the 1850s when the issue of prohibiting liquor finally split the colony. Prohibitionists, or "smashers," rallied behind a young Saint John druggist named

Samuel Leonard Tilley. His opponents, the "rummies," preferred to consider themselves Conservatives.

Nova Scotians could be disdainful of such crude and primitive politics. Largest and wealthiest of the colonies, Nova Scotia's economy diversified from fishing, farming, and shipbuilding to mining and a little manufacturing. The province had slowly out-grown its self-perpetuating merchant elite and perhaps even its parade of stuffy soldier-governors. Thomas McCulloch's Pictou Academy gave early notice that brains and ability could be found outside Halifax. In 1835, a young Haligonian journalist, Joseph Howe, made himself a hero of the hinterland, first by denouncing the Halifax oligarchy and then by winning acquittal when he was tried for libel.

Like Mackenzie in Upper Canada, Howe was the angry spokes-man for Nova Scotia reform, but he was no rebel. His pride combined with an almost mystical faith in Britain and her consti-tution. He denounced the 1837 risings not only for delaying Nova Scotia's constitutional progress but for their disloyalty. He would carry vestiges of this mistrust of the Canadas for a very long time. Through the 1840s, Nova Scotia Reformers articulated and then urged Lord Durham's idea of responsible government. In 1846, new instructions to the governor, Sir John Harvey, made the change. It was done, boasted Howe, "without the shedding of a drop of blood, . . . the breaking of a pane of glass." On February 2, 1848, James Uniacke, Howe, and the Reformers took power. Cau-tiously, and in their own time, the other lower provinces followed suit. In New Brunswick, local politicians themselves delayed party government until 1856. Even then, they were moved more by embarrassment at being last than by real party differences.

Constitutional change came slowly because societies in the lower provinces were smaller, less deeply divided by great issues. Ambitious men like Howe combined immense pride and devotion to their communities with an acute yearning for new worlds to conquer. "Boys, brag of your country," he told Nova Scotians. "When I'm abroad, I brag of everything that Nova Scotia is, has or can produce; and when they beat me at everything else, I turn around on them and say: 'How high does your tide rise?'" Yet Howe *wanted* to be abroad, and he pestered the British shamelessly for appointments. He dreamed boldly. Howe promoted railways and promised listeners that in their lifetime they would hear train whistles in the distant Rocky Mountains. Like growing numbers of Canadians, some Maritimers had a vision that reached as far as British North America. Others, and Howe was among these too, dreamed of an imperial federation in which Nova Scotia might someday be an equal partner with England and Scotland.

Behind the dreams came nagging practical worries. Free trade had frightened the Maritimes as badly as the Canadas, and the ten-year Reciprocity Agreement with the United States, signed in 1854, was vital for the region's fish and timber trade. If the American market should vanish, could the Upper Canadians ever provide a substitute? There was an urgent need for a connecting railway through British territory. It was easy to blame Hincks and the Canadians for the earlier failure, but the real problem remained the route through New Brunswick. Military considerations insisted that it follow the line of meagre little Acadian settlements along the north shore; New Brunswick politicians insisted that it come down the Maine border, along the Saint John River valley, to Fredericton and Saint John, where most of their voters lived.

By the 1860s, the maritime colonies faced tough choices. It was not conservatism but a sense of dangerous, uncontrollable choices that hung over the Confederation debate in the Maritimes.

7

The Great Northwest

People emigrating to Canada have had an awkward tendency to assume that nothing much worthwhile has happened before their arrival. Champlain presumed that Indians would be honoured to transform themselves into good Catholics and subjects of his king. The Loyalists, in both Nova Scotia and Quebec, insisted that these colonies should be readjusted to meet their desires. The British immigrants who poured into Canada after 1815 felt obliged to correct the obvious "Americanism" of Upper Canadians. Later waves of immigration have felt equal freedom to make over the country in their own image and to denounce opposition as intolerant and old-fashioned.

The Canadian Northwest has been a particular victim of such assumptions. The amiable Canadian assumption that the West is somehow "new" and the North is newer still, ignores the fact that these regions have probably known human habitation longer than any others on the continent. The two hundred thousand Indians who met the Europeans in the 1600s were heirs to millennia of experience which probably began in the far Northwest. Fragmentary archaeological evidence suggests that they may have encountered even earlier human inhabitants. The ways of the Indian (and the amazing Inuit north of the sub-Arctic tree line) were very old indeed.

The long native heritage was at least as valuable to the early European invaders as any technology they brought from Europe. The light birchbark canoes of the Algonquins covered distances at a speed that astonished the first explorers, and their snowshoes made travel possible in the winter. The concoction of buffalo meat, fat, hair, and berries the Indians called pemmican might seem nauseous to Europeans but it was the only food nourishing and light enough to carry travellers across the Great Plains. From the tough, adaptable Naskapi of Labrador to the sophisticated Indian culture of the Pacific coast, native people were the best guides to adapting to the new continent. Only their lack of formal records and writing barred them, by pure convention, from having a "history."

In the sixth of Canada covered by the United Provinces and the Atlantic colonies, the 23,035 Indians who remained by 1861 had been bullied and enticed into the life pattern devised by Sir William Johnson, the first British superintendent of Indians. It was Johnson who devised the treaties of surrender and the reserves which shaped the Indian policies of both Canada and the United States for two centuries. As a means of easing consciences and removing Indians, treaties and reserves were a success; as a basis for equality between Europeans and native people or as fair compensation, Johnson's system would prove a failure. Unfortunately, no one then or later offered acceptable alternatives.

Beyond the limits of the settled colonies, there was no Indian policy at all and no need for it. In five-sixths of British North America, whites and native people lived in what, theoretically, was a simple market relationship of willing seller and willing buyer. Europeans had manufactured goods; Indians had furs. Simplicity was deceptive. Both sides brought bitter national, commercial, and private rivalries to the transactions. As the Iroquois had shown, there was nothing primitive in the Indians' understanding of competition, middle men, or the benefits of playing one tribe of white men against another. From the European side, too, there was nothing simple about a trade that depended on the vagaries of fashion, conducted a thousand or more miles from the nearest seaport among complex and therefore unpredictable people.

Whatever criticisms might be made of the beaver's habits and intellect, there was an excellent reason for adopting the hardworking rodent as a Canadian symbol. Instinct and common sense would have pulled traders and explorers southward in America; the beaver pulled them north. The best pelts came from the colder regions. Diplomacy, not furs, pushed the French into their southward venture into the Ohio valley in the 1740s. So far as commerce, not aggrandizement, was their goal, traders had every reason to stay north of the Great Lakes and well above the invisible line that a later age would identify as the forty-ninth parallel. If the British wanted to share the continent with an expansive United States the beaver's natural preferences kept Canadians away from the American juggernaut.

That was why the trading rivalry that mattered most in North America was not between the French and the Dutch and English merchants who operated from Albany. A pair of disaffected French traders, Pierre Radisson and the Sieur de Groseillers, showed the English where real profits could be made, and the "Governor and Company of Adventurers of England Trading into Hudson's Bay" acted. There was literally almost nothing on the European maps to explain what Charles II meant by "Rupert's Land" in the 1670 Hudson's Bay Company charter. When the clerks wrote about waters draining into Hudson and James bays they were describing the vastest empire any private company ever controlled.

The English posts, perched nervously at the mouths of the Moose, the Albany, the Churchill, and the other rivers draining into the bay, transformed the fur trade. English trade goods were by no means superior to most that the French could offer, and the methods were cautious to the point of timidity. The Indians had to make their own toilsome way across the barren "starving country," but the Company's ships could come direct from England, cutting off a thousand miles of portages and trans-shipments, and getting closer to the best furs than any French trader could.

The French were forced to fight back. In brilliant campaigns, three of them led by the Canadian-born sailor Pierre le Moyne d'Iberville, the Hudson's Bay Company posts were steadily captured and destroyed. By 1713 only one remained. Then, for reasons of European diplomacy, they were restored. In the years of quasi-peace, the French tried other tactics, planting their own posts up-river from the English, proclaiming alliances and allowing licences to men such as La Vérendrye and his sons, who would probe as far as Lake Winnipeg in search of new business. The tactics worked, though the Indians were shrewd enough to share part of their trade with the English. The Crees, new middlemen in the northern trade, understood even better than the Iroquois the virtues of competition.

After 1760, France was gone, but her complex, aggressive trading system of forts, depots, and highly organized canoe brigades was simply inherited by the Scottish and New England merchants who followed the British armies into Montreal. The *bourgeois* or boss might now speak another language, but the *voyageurs* still gathered in the spring to make their marks on the careful, notarized contracts and then to set off in their heavily laden *canots de maître*. They were small, tough men who could paddle twenty hours a day, measuring distances by the time it took to smoke a pipe of tobacco. At Grand Portage they met the smaller canoes of the wintering partners, as far away again from the distant posts. As they transferred their loads and dickered over the trade goods that custom allowed each *voyageur*, the "pork-eaters" from Montreal wondered whether the freedom and adventures of their western counterparts outweighed the hardships and long winters. The men of the upper country, the *pays d'en haut*, were different. Many took Indian wives, vital intermediaries in the trade, cementing in fact and in custom the trading alliances of white and native. In time, these would be mothers of a new mixed-blood people. Their sons and daughters would grow up divided between Indian ways and the Scots-Presbyterian or *Canadien*-Catholic heritage of a trader or *voyageur* father. The French-speaking would be Métis; the English-speaking "country born" or half-breeds.

Nothing in 1760 had ended the rivalry of the Hudson's Bay Company and the "pedlars from Quebec." Indeed, the "pedlars" themselves were in ruinous and sometimes murderous competition. Outsiders rarely understood how costly and risky the trade was. It took four or five years of packing, storage, and transportation before goods ordered in England could actually be paid for. Traders carried an impossible load of debt and even a small disaster could mean ruin. Business logic dictated the only possible solution, a cartel. A first small experiment in 1770 led by 1787 to the fully grown North West Company. Systematically its few rivals were included or wiped out. The last was the short-lived XY Company, formed by traders driven from the southwest by the Americans.

It was the "Nor'westers," the wintering partners and their servants, who learned from the Indians how to live in the West and to find their way along its rivers and lakes. The rough American Peter Pond reached Lake Athabaska in 1778. Alexander Mackenzie, seeking a way over the mountain barrier, first followed the river that would bear his name in 1789. He called it "River of Disappointment" after it had led him to the ice-floes of the Arctic Ocean, but he persisted. With better navigational instruments and after terrible dangers, he could mark his name on a rock near the Dean Channel on July 22, 1793; the first white man to travel overland to the Pacific Ocean. Others followed; between them, Simon Fraser and David Thompson confirmed the shape of the great rivers and mountain ranges of the Pacific slope. Their purpose, almost always, was business.

The North West Company waged a desperate, Montreal-based struggle to fend off Americans like John Jacob Astor from the south and the Hudson's Bay Company from the north. The HBC responded, questioning its old policy of waiting for trade. "The sleep by the frozen sea," as scornful critics termed the Company's policy, had to end. The benefits of cheapness (and of leaving the Indians undisturbed) no longer weighed in the ledger. In 1774, Samuel Hearne, having explored on his own as far as the Coppermine River and the Arctic Ocean, went inland to build an HBC post at Cumberland House. Other posts soon followed. Rival posts competed with all the cunning and occasional violence their traders could devise.

By 1811, the Hudson's Bay Company had a new strategy. For years, those few veterans of the trade who loved the country or who would not abandon their Indian wives had settled in the relatively sheltered valley of the Red River. Their half-breed and Métis offspring had settled there too, the former turning to farming, the latter to the more adventurous but indispensable life of the buffalo hunt. The annual slaughter of the huge animals that seemed to supply every need of prairie life provided the Nor'westers with their pemmican. As part of their rivalry with the hated HBC, Nor'westers assured the Métis that, through their mothers' blood, they were the true and only inheritors of the land. Young people, growing up proud in the lore of two cultures, took pleasure in seeing themselves as a "New Nation" with the semi-military structure of the buffalo hunt as their first cultural institution. Leaders like Cuthbert Grant gave the Métis a sense of power. In law, of course, that old charter of 1670 was clear – the Red River valley was part of Rupert's Land. The philanthropic Lord Selkirk, having settled destitute Scottish Highlanders in Prince Edward Island and Upper Canada, now purchased a big block of Hudson's Bay Company stock and proposed to settle still more of his people on its highly recommended Red River land.

In 1811, the Company gave Selkirk 106,000 acres at the forks of the Red and the Assiniboine rivers for his colony. To every imaginable pioneering misery, from frost and floods to grasshoppers, Selkirk's settlers could add an extra calamity: the utter hostility of the Nor'westers and their Métis allies. Nor'westers saw no mystery in the Hudson's Bay Company's motive in planting a colony across their main route to the West and on top of their most basic food supply. Led by Cuthbert Grant and encouraged by the "New Nation" argument that the land was theirs, the Métis harassed the unhappy Highlanders and trampled their crops. At Seven Oaks in 1816, Grant and his Métis shot down twenty-one men from the colony and mutilated some of the corpses. The remaining settlers were driven out, finding refuge at the far end of Lake Winnipeg.

Selkirk took rapid vengeance. Collecting Swiss mercenaries, disbanded after the War of 1812, he headed west. At Fort William, now the Nor'westers' trans-shipment base, he seized prisoners and trading goods and sent his men on to restore the colony. The nervous settlers returned to the Red River, and both Métis and Scots seem to have come to a surprisingly smooth reconciliation. The whole dispute entered the courts which, unfortunately for Selkirk, were held in the distinctly pro-Nor'wester atmosphere of the Canadas. By the time he had finished with judges, lawyers, and charges of false imprisonment, both the philanthropist's fortune and his health had withered away.

Even the battle with Selkirk was too much for the North West Company. Dissident partners plotted joining with the rival company. Sir Alexander Mackenzie, the explorer, had urged such a merger years before. The logic of monopoly was, as usual, inescapable. In 1821, the Hudson's Bay Company absorbed its competitor, cut the long link with Montreal, and secured a twenty-one-year licence for its monopoly from the British government. The Nor'westers, with their reputations for audacity, endurance, and the wild drinking of their Beaver Club, joined their old rival or applied their capital to other commercial dreams in Montreal. Some of them sank into obscure poverty.

In the West, a short, stout Scot named George Simpson emerged as "the little emperor" of the Hudson's Bay domain. By 1839, he had cut out most of the competing posts, reduced costs, and firmly suppressed any costly schemes for settlement or administration. He also established his headquarters in Montreal, though his strict supervision hardly slackened. In 1841, teams of paddlers took him from Fort Churchill on Hudson Bay to Astoria at the mouth of Columbia in only eighty-four days.

Astoria was part of the Pacific domain Simon Fraser and David Thompson had won from John Jacob Astor for the Nor'westers. Politically, its status was controversial. Britain and Spain had drifted close to war in 1790 over the ownership of Nootka Sound, but the firmness of Captain George Vancouver had made the Spanish accept a diplomatic withdrawal. The War of 1812 had proved a great setback for Americans like Astor, but the tide of history was on their side. In 1818, Britain and the United States had agreed to joint occupation of the distant Pacific coast, and in 1839, the Hudson's Bay Company settled a potential threat from the Russians in Alaska by trading them food supplies for a post.

Sensible Company officials knew that they held the coast on borrowed time. American missionaries had entered the Oregon territory, traders had followed, and troops to protect them were not far behind. So were settlers, pouring through the mountain passes into the rich valleys. Company officials hurried to harvest furs. In 1846, Oregon was gone, passed to the United States, and the whole coast would have followed as American politicians and editors cried for "Fifty-four-forty or fight." But a new fort had been opened at the tip of Vancouver Island, and British diplomats held firm behind a weak hand. They insisted that the international boundary along the Great Plains, the forty-ninth parallel, be extended over the mountains and pushed through the Straits of Juan de Fuca. (Even then, no one knew that San Juan Island straddled the line, and another war scare would occur in 1860 before the Americans won that prize.)

All things considered, British North Americans were lucky in their boundary settlement. As usual, they were utterly unprepared for war, and this time the Americans really were in a fighting mood; they went off and fought the unfortunate Mexicans instead. As for the Hudson's Bay Company, it had suffered a serious blow. The Company's prestige depended on an aura of permanency, summed up by the rude version of the letters on its flag – "Here Before Christ." Canadians and imperial-minded Britons awoke at last to the realization that a trading company was a very feeble steward for choice territory. The new free-trade ideology was utterly out of sympathy with government-licensed monopolies. Still, actually doing something would be troublesome too, and the Company got a second chance. In return for promising serious colonization within five years, it was given Vancouver Island to manage as a crown colony.

Even if the Company could have changed its ways, in 1849 every conceivable colonist set off for the gold fields of California. A few retired officials, two tiny parties from the Red River, and some accidental tourists were all that the Company could muster by 1851 when a hardened veteran of the Company service, James Douglas, became governor. People seemed to have forgotten about the colony until suddenly, in 1858, British Columbia had its own gold rush. Thousands of miners, prospectors, and hangers-on poured up the Fraser valley and on to new discoveries in the Cariboo. It was the moment for a tough old autocrat, and Douglas rose to the occasion in the full knowledge that he faced another Oregon. A separate mainland colony was proclaimed. A smart detachment of Royal Engineers arrived, not as a garrison but as road-builders and as discreet backing for an extraordinary one-man embodiment of a ruthless brand of British justice, Matthew Baillie Begbie. It would take months before the colonial secretary in London could consider a sentence, Judge Begbie informed one convicted murderer, "but you will not be interested in what he decided, for you are to be hanged Monday morning."

By 1866, both the gold and the rush were gone, leaving two tiny colonies, two capitals (at Victoria and New Westminster), and one large debt – for roads were not built cheaply through the mountains. With much grumbling, the colonies were reunited, the Company relinquished its power (in 1867), and in 1868 the capital was restored to Victoria. The nearby British naval base at Esquimalt provided some reassurance and a source of gunboats for frequent expeditions to overawe coastal Indians.

The Company had prided itself on maintaining good relations with Indians – mainly just by leaving them alone. Now growing numbers of missionaries found a humanitarian audience in Britain for their sometimes scurrilous allegations of Company neglect or sharp practice. A tiny British garrison in Red River, sent ostensibly for the Oregon crisis, was needed to maintain dwindling Company authority. Neither the troops nor the military pensioners who replaced them were much use as police.

In 1849, Guillaume Sayer appeared at the Red River court to be found guilty of breaking the Hudson's Bay Company's monopoly. Since he brought several hundred fellow Métis with him, the judge prudently decided that no punishment was in order. The high-wheeled Red River carts would be free to screech and squeal their way south to St. Paul as they pleased. The Métis had become formidable. In 1851, as their women and children sheltered behind the carts and loaded their rifles, the buffalo hunters slaughtered attacking Sioux at the battle of Grand Côteau.

The Company itself also collected its supplies from St. Paul. Steamboat and railway connections were now better than the old route from the Bay. Old links with Canada revived. So did Canadian interest. The Company had deliberately given the impression that the prairies were a sub-Arctic wasteland and the harsh experience of the Selkirk settlers had confirmed the image. French-Canadian missionaries to the Métis, mindful of the Jesuit *Rélations* and the blessings of martyrdom, exaggerated their sufferings. The Grit farmers of Upper Canada were unimpressed. Like their American cousins, they looked on the frontier as a heritage for their sons, and they had not the slightest respect for the Hudson's Bay Company. When, in 1857, the British Parliament appointed a Select Committee to review the Company's licence renewal, George Brown and his Reformers made sure that Canada was present in strength.

Precise information on the area was still scarce. In 1857-58, two expeditions, one British and the other Canadian, set out to report on prospects for western settlement. John Palliser for the British concluded that the wooded parklands of the Red, Assiniboine, and North Saskatchewan river valleys were suitable for agriculture, but the treeless prairie to the south was too arid ever to be farmed. Henry Youle Hind, a professor of chemistry at the University of Toronto, delighted his Canadian sponsors by reporting rapturously on prospects for the entire region. Strong supporting evidence came opportunely from Lorin Blodgett, an American, who showed that lines of identical temperatures ran northwest and southwest, not along latitudes. Farming *was* possible. Suddenly, a new shape for British North America became an exciting prospect.

PART II

A MARI USQUE AD MARE

I

Confederation

In an almost continent-wide coincidence, by the 1860s all British North Americans had been obliged to take thought for their future. A decade of railway-building had shown that it was possible to break the barriers of distance and climate but at a cost that no single colony could afford. The railway boom had also brought foreign investors to the region. Their perspective was broader, if no less self-interested, than that of local people and their politicians. However parochial they might be, all British North Americans could understand the threat of the United States.

In 1847 the Americans had absorbed Texas and California with quite unnerving speed. In the 1850s the Fraser and Cariboo gold rushes might well have been pretext enough to gain British Columbia. South of the little Red River colony, Minnesota was now a state and its politicians made no secret of their annexationist intentions. By 1861 Americans were preoccupied with their Civil War but, as the Montreal-Irish orator D'Arcy McGee warned, war was an appetite that grew with feeding. Even after four years of fighting and half a million dead, the United States' military strength seemed to keep on growing. If Washington wanted a pretext to turn northward, one would not be hard to find.

A few young Canadians, captivated by the South's romantic image, had helped Confederates use Canadian bases to plot their attacks. Some of the Southerners launched a murderous raid on St. Albans, Vermont, escaped to Canada, and went free. The furious Americans promptly closed their borders, enforced the use of passports, and announced that the cherished Reciprocity Agreement would end in 1866. It was one more reason for the British colonies to look to each other, if only as substitute markets.

Some form of union was no new idea. A British staff officer had suggested it as early as 1783. William Smith, the Loyalist Chief Justice of Quebec, had devised a scheme for a central legislature in 1785. Among the ideas that had cascaded through William Lyon Mackenzie's mind was a colonial union. Lord Durham had promoted the notion when he had summoned lieutenant-governors and their councils to meet him in 1838. James W. Johnson, Howe's opponent in Nova Scotia, had been so impressed with Durham's idea that he had pushed the proposition during the 1850s. So had British governors like Lord Elgin and his able successor, Sir Edward Head. It was hardly astonishing. The colonies were all British – Canada East no less than the others – and they all lived in the shadow of the largest, if not necessarily the happiest, federal union in the world.

If the military and economic threat from the United States was the firmest prod in making the British colonies consider closer union, the breakdown of American federalism was also a useful warning. The real issue in the Civil War, as contemporaries understood matters, was not slavery but states' rights. The South's "peculiar institution" had led to secession in 1861 but it was the claim of state sovereignty that had allowed the Confederacy to raise armies and had paralysed the will of the rest of the nation. Federalism might seem a logical answer to the problems of the United Provinces or even of British North America as a whole, but the experience of the best available example was not reassuring.

Still, the experiment had to be considered. In 1859, when the Reformers of Canada West had met in convention, impatient in their demands for representation by population, George Brown had led them to consider some form of federalism as a possible compromise. The year before, the one-time annexationist and voice of Montreal business, Alexander Tilloch Galt, switched from the Reformers to Macdonald and Cartier on condition that they take up the notion of a British North American federation.

Cartier and Macdonald did as little as was necessary to retain a valuable new partner; neither man was much taken with constitutional novelties.

By the spring of 1864, the idea was no longer a novelty but an opportunity. If Macdonald could not stem the tide of votes to Reform and "Rep by Pop," his career would end. Cartier could now foresee a political battle his *Canadiens* could not win. Two years of feeble government under John Sandfield Macdonald had proved to all but the stubborn Reform leader that a double majority drawn from each of the United Provinces would not work. Sandfield Macdonald's bitter rival, George Brown, saw both the need and an opportunity. By 1864, there had been two elections and four governments during three very dangerous years. Outsiders knew that Brown and the Tory leader, John A. Macdonald, were mortal enemies. The bibulous opportunist and the self-righteous autocrat hated each other. They might also use each other.

On June 14 a short-lived Macdonald-Cartier government was defeated. In the confusion George Brown rose to announce his willingness to enter a coalition pledged to find a way out of the constitutional impasse. An ecstatic but tiny French Canadian *bleu* clambered up the massive Brown and embraced him while the House cheered. By June 30, under the titular leadership of Sir Etienne-Pascal Taché, a veteran of the War of 1812, the Great Coalition was announced. Its constitutional policies were easily drawn from a legislature committee, chaired by Brown through much of the 1864 session. What was needed was a place to present them. News that leaders of three of the Atlantic colonies would meet at Charlottetown on September 1 suggested the opportunity. At once the Canadians asked for and received an invitation.

Maritime union, the original Charlottetown topic, was at least as old an idea as British North American federalism. It was just as obvious and just as impossible. It was a favourite of British lieutenant-governors like John Manners Sutton and Arthur Gordon in New Brunswick. How better might they advance the region (and their own careers)? Nova Scotians fancied the idea if only because they would obviously dominate the union, but it took all of Gordon's persuasion to make New Brunswick's Premier Tilley even a lukewarm supporter. As for Prince Edward Island, it was thought best to hold the Maritime Union Conference in Charlottetown to make sure that the Island's leaders showed up. Indeed, it may have been only the unexpected inquiry from the Canadians that ensured that the Conference happened at all.

In the circumstances, the Charlottetown Conference was an unexpected triumph for the Canadians. Since the Maritimers had nothing much to discuss, they cheerfully agreed to hear their visitors. Well-briefed and rehearsed, Macdonald, Cartier, Brown, and Galt each spoke brilliantly in their field of expertise. Lavish entertainment ashore and on the Canadians' ship, the *Queen Victoria*, made the first week of September pass like a dream. Next the Canadians and their hosts moved on to Halifax and then to Saint John with more speeches, banquets, and toasts and an agreement that all would meet at Quebec on October 10.

The Quebec meeting was longer, tougher, and much more specific. It almost began with tragedy when the *Queen Victoria*, sent to collect delegates, wives, and marriageable daughters, nearly foundered in a storm. At Quebec, Newfoundland was represented as well. So was Britain. Colonel W. F. D. Jervois, who believed Canada to be indefensible, obediently went to Quebec to tell delegates that a modest military effort could keep British North America safe. Details of discussion at the closed meetings are sparse and one-sided, taken largely from minutes kept by Hewitt Bernard, Macdonald's secretary, and from the letters sent home by George Brown to his young wife. Once again, the Canadians were the best-prepared, and almost all the seventy-two resolutions adopted between October 10 and 28 were their work.

The speed and good humour of the meetings concealed real differences. Macdonald made no secret of his preference for a single legislative union. Federalism, he insisted, had been discredited by the American experience. To a large degree, he had his way. Confederation, as it emerged from Quebec, gave the central government infinitely greater powers than Washington possessed. In the division of responsibilities, the future Section 91 not only gave the central power a healthy list of tasks to ensure "peace, order and good government" but left any "residual" or unspecified powers to the centre as well. Provincial responsibilities were so modest as to be almost municipal in scope – education, local roads and improvements, and "charitable and eleemosynary institutions." Moreover, provinces would be limited to the meagre revenue from direct taxes and their laws would be suspended or even disallowed by the central authority.

Yet Macdonald did not win. It was his partner and closest ally, George-Etienne Cartier, who insisted on a federal system. On behalf of his French-Canadian colleagues, Cartier argued that the provincial powers, which would be their only bulwark against an even larger Anglo-Saxon majority, would be very real indeed. "Property and civil rights," for example, was the phrase from the old Quebec Act that had guaranteed the *Canadien*'s identity; it must now be a provincial concern. Cartier's chief ally was a short, bespectacled Ontario reformer named Oliver Mowat. In the light of events, an astonishing amount of discussion was focused on the proposed upper house of the new federal Parliament, and even that debate concentrated on the provincial shares, not the decisive fact that all senators would be federal appointees.

At the end of October 1864 the Confederation agreement was set. Many delegates headed on to Montreal, Toronto, and the West to see the vast potential of provinces most of them had never visited and to share the heady excitement of banquet oratory. Both the coalition and the British, contented midwives for the process, could congratulate themselves on an easy victory.

In Canada, the coalition government approached the provincial Parliament with some confidence. Meeting for the last time at Quebec, with their speeches recorded and published, members tackled the Confederation issues with energy and occasional flashes of vision. Some criticisms were predictable. The intercolonial railway demanded by Nova Scotia would be too costly; financial terms for the lower provinces were too generous. French Canadians obviously had much to lose. Cartier and his deputy

Hector Langevin did their utmost to keep nervous *bleus* in line, boasting of the powers left for the new province of Quebec and insisting that *Canadiens* would now be masters in their own jurisdiction. A. A. Dorion and the *rouges* condemned the new arrangement as fatal to French Canada, and a number of younger *bleus* like Honoré Mercier abandoned their allegiance. Minorities would have minorities of their own. The elderly Christopher Dunkin, speaking for the English of Canada East, predicted that too many interests – regional, racial, religious, and political – would persist in the new Confederation to allow any new national community to develop. His warnings would be remembered.

Macdonald, Cartier, Brown, and especially the fiery D'Arcy McGee, cajoled, persuaded, and occasionally lifted their supporters' emotions above mundane criticisms. As they spoke, the great Civil War was winding to its end and the threat of the blue-clad Union armies hung over the debate. If the Americans came, talk of local rights, and especially of French-Canadian survival, would be academic. Everyone knew it. The vote was decisive. Members from Canada West voted 54-8 for Confederation; from Canada East the margin was 37-25, though the French-speaking majority was only four. The next business, a $2-million loan for fortifications, passed swiftly, and the leading ministers left at once for London to pursue both matters with the British.

Confederation had passed, though more painfully than its architects in Canada had expected. In the lower provinces, it was another story. The euphoria of September 1864 had vanished by November when the delegates came home. It was obvious almost at once that neither island colony would join. Prince Edward Island delegates had opposed "Rep by Pop" at Quebec and had lost. Was that a foretaste of Confederation? Times were good; the little island would manage on its own. It could even afford its own railway without going on bended knee to Canadians. Newfoundland too would turn its back. St. John's, where political and business power met, was closer to London than to the newly designated capital of Ottawa. Its merchant elite had no plans to share power. Hard times had justified sending delegates to Quebec, but now fish prices were climbing again, prosperity began to breed confidence, and the Water Street merchants of St. John's spread the word: Confederation meant conscription and Canadian taxes. In the 1869 election, the pro-Confederates lost.

In Nova Scotia, James Johnson and Charles Tupper had brought the Conservatives to power back in 1864, so at least time was on their side. Opinion was not. Joe Howe had left politics in 1863. Perhaps he had squandered some of his influence by his anti-Catholic bigotry but his power was immense. At times Howe had backed a North American union but his real dream remained an imperial federation with Britain. Early in 1865, Howe acted. The pro-Confederation editor of the Halifax *Chronicle* was fired. Soon, the paper's columns carried "The Botheration Letters," brilliant invective against Confederation and its sponsors. The author was anonymous but every Nova Scotian knew the voice of their most outspoken politician – Joe Howe. Tupper, premier since 1864, could feel his support slipping.

Across the Bay of Fundy, matters were even worse. Tilley did not have time. His Liberals had held office for a decade, accumulating splits and enemies. An election was due and Governor Gordon insisted that it be held before the legislature could endorse the Quebec Resolutions. The anti-Confederates were ready. Tilley, they said, had sold New Brunswickers for eighty cents a head – the $200,000 the Quebec proposals would pay the colony for its customs revenues. By the end of March 1865 Tilley was out and his old enemy, Albert J. Smith, was in.

Without the two island colonies, Confederation could go forward; without New Brunswick to link Nova Scotia to central Canada, it was dead. Somehow, the idea must be resuscitated. The British would do their utmost to help. A pro-Confederate governor arrived in Nova Scotia and in New Brunswick Arthur Gordon got new orders to help Tilley if he could. The Canadians in London got a guarantee for their fortification loan and a vague but seemingly valuable pledge that if they would take their own defence seriously, "the Imperial Government fully acknowledged the reciprocal obligation of defending every portion of the Empire with all the resources at its command." That was an answer to Maritimers who insisted that Confederation would tie them to a defenceless interior.

Unknowingly, the Americans helped as well. The termination of Reciprocity, with its accompanying fishing agreements, in 1866 hurt the lower provinces as much as Canada. Albert Smith had boasted that he could get a better deal from Washington than from any Confederate politician. He returned empty-handed and humiliated. His support began to crumble.

The huge American armies had disbanded with astonishing speed after the Civil War, but they left a bitter residue. In the cities of the North, the Fenian Brotherhood, pledged to liberate Ireland from English rule, had recruited widely among the Union's Irish soldiers. By recruiting hardened veterans with ready access to arms and American sympathy, the Fenians planned to form an army to conquer Canada and hold her hostage for Ireland's freedom. It was a wild scheme, growing ever wilder in the reports sent by informers and secret agents to British and Canadian authorities. Thousands marched, applauded fiery speeches, and went home; there were hundreds, patriots and unemployed, who might act. In response, British troops and Canadian militia trained, planned, and occupied frontier posts. Border towns buzzed with rumours and false alarms.

Suddenly, the rumours came true. At Fort Erie on May 31, 1866, sixteen hundred Fenians scrambled ashore. By June 3, they had all fled or been captured, but not before they had defeated two small forces of Canadian militia. At Pigeon Hill, just over the Vermont border, another eighteen hundred Fenians camped for a day before American authorities seized their leaders and supplies. The most fatuous but also the most significant incursion had ended a month before when Fenians clustered on the Maine border had tried to raid Campobello Island. For New Brunswick, it was traumatic. Not even in the comic-opera Aroostook War in the 1840s, when the contested boundary with Maine had finally been settled, had the colony felt so threatened. Now a few hundred confused, ill-led Fenians suddenly made a union with Canada appear sensible. Smith's support collapsed and the lieutenant-governor discreetly used his power to require a new election. Funds from Montreal reinforced the cause of Confederation. This time Tilley was triumphant.

Both Tilley and Charles Tupper avoided asking their legislatures to endorse the Quebec Resolutions. Instead, they sought a mandate to negotiate still better terms in Britain. The hint was hardly needed. The Canadians had manoeuvring room and the British were now almost beside themselves with eagerness. The reasons were unflattering. British investors feared for their money in the hands of any of the individual colonies. Some of them had vast plans at stake, from expanding the Grand Trunk to creating a transcontinental railway line. Politically, the doctrines of free trade and imperial separation had reached their height. "I cannot shut my eyes to the fact that they want to get rid of us," an unhappy Galt reported from London in 1865. "They have a servile fear of the United States and would rather give us up than defend us, or incur the risk of war with that country."

When delegates from Canada, Nova Scotia, and New Brunswick met in London at the Westminster Palace Hotel, the mood of the Quebec Conference had revived. Tilley and Tupper got better financial terms and the educational rights of religious (though not linguistic) minorities were improved. The Intercolonial Railway, merely discussed before, became a legal obligation. In their own draft, the Canadians, monarchists to the core, had proposed that their creation be termed "the Kingdom of Canada." The British warned that American sensibilities might be aroused. The devoutly Christian Leonard Tilley offered both an alternative and a national motto by thumbing his bible to Psalms 72:8: "He shall have dominion also from sea to sea, and from the river unto the ends of the earth."

Without particular ceremony or sense of occasion, the British Parliament passed the act as Canadians had designed it, correcting a word or phrase here or there as legislative draftsmen advised but giving the colonials, for the first time, a constitution that was as home-made as it could be. One lapse went unnoticed: nowhere did the British North America Act, 1867, explain how the colonists would share in its future amendment.

Lawyers and historians would amuse themselves for more than a century with debate about what the Fathers of Confederation had really meant by all their torrents of words between 1864 and 1867. Were the Quebec Resolutions a treaty, inviolable by the participating provinces? Macdonald and Cartier certainly said so to fend off would-be amenders in their Canadian Parliament but they cheerfully altered terms when they got to London in 1866 and they would change them later. Was the Act a compact, either among the three original colonies, or among the two founding nations of French and English, or even, most far-fetched, among all current and future provinces? Such a notion would become fashionable in the 1880s, supported by the diligent collection of random quotations. As an historical interpretation of what happened in the 1860s, the compact theory is absurd. Before and long after Confederation, sensible Canadians have understood that peace, order, and good government in their country have depended on the reasonable long-run harmony of French and English. That notion was not embodied in the British North America Act; it was left for ensuing generations to rediscover or neglect at their peril.

2

Nation-Building

Confederation had been a means to many ends. By 1867, one purpose mattered more than the others: the bid to establish a transcontinental nation. Sir John A. Macdonald, newly knighted and summoned as the Dominion's first prime minister, would never forget that goal.

First he must form a government. The big gothic-style buildings at Ottawa and the timid bureaucrats of the United Provinces would form a suitable foundation. Few officials would leave the lower provinces. As for the new governments of Ontario and Quebec, they would start from scratch. Forming a cabinet was harder. In the Canadas, ministers had represented interests as well as departments. That would continue but it was now so much more complex. Quebec, for example, must have four ministers: one for the English Protestants and the others to balance the rivalry of Montreal and Quebec City. There was no room there for the brilliant D'Arcy McGee: he would have to wait. Nine months later, still a mere MP, McGee lay dead in the Ottawa slush, the victim of a Fenian bullet.

By November 1867 Macdonald was ready to face elections. The outcome reflected the Confederation debate. In Nova Scotia, only Tupper survived the anti-Confederate tide. New Brunswick split narrowly for Tilley. Quebec went solidly for Cartier's *bleus*. In Ontario, where George Brown had worked since 1865 for a Reform sweep, the *Globe* publisher lost his own seat. Sir John A. Macdonald was exultant. In Ontario, Macdonald shrewdly invited Sandfield Macdonald to head a "patent combination," a coalition of Tories and old Reformers. Again Brown was worsted. In Ottawa, the Dominion's first Parliament would pit 108 government supporters against a mixed bag of 72 *rouges*, Reformers, and Maritime anti-Confederates.

Safe in power, Macdonald had much to do. Joseph Howe's campaign to repeal Confederation was making no headway in Britain but Nova Scotia's bitterness was not allowed to fester. By 1869, Howe had accepted as "better terms" a richer subsidy than the original eighty cents a head and, despite the resulting cries of treason, had joined Macdonald's cabinet. Newfoundland would not come for eighty years yet; her 1869 election saw to that. (In 1895, Canada had another chance – but balked at the cost of $5 million in financial help. A generation of Newfoundlanders concluded that Canadians were a mean-minded folk.) Prince Edward Island was different. The fatal lure of railways had left the tiny colony $3 million in debt. Frightened island politicians turned to Ottawa and got terms they could not refuse: complete transfer of the provincial debt and hard cash to buy out the notorious "proprietors." By 1873, the island was a province.

A far more nerve-wracking issue to Macdonald was holding the West. At last the Americans were moving. In 1867, they bought Alaska from the Russians for $7.2 million and they sent a consul to the Red River. Canada saw that it was time for her legal haggling with the Hudson's Bay Company to end. In 1868, Cartier and William McDougall went to London and simply purchased Rupert's Land for $1.5 million and a guarantee that a twentieth of the land in the fertile belt would remain with the old Company. Formal transfer would come soon, "at a date to be determined." Meanwhile, Canada would send survey crews and a road-building gang to link the Red River settlement with Lake Superior.

It was really too good to be true. McDougall, the long-time campaigner for the Northwest as an outlet for farmers' sons, would become governor. An appointed council and a small police force would keep the peace and shut out American troublemakers. Warnings from Catholic missionaries and aged Hudson's Bay officials were discounted. Cartier, the perennial optimist, knew that all would be well. McDougall reported that he had dependable informants among Canadians at the Red River.

Both men were wrong. The Canadians, with their knowing-newcomer arrogance, were detested. Company authority, shrinking since 1849, vanished under the strain of the unpopular land transfer. English-speaking settlers might accept their fate; the Métis would not. Their disciplined hunting organization made them a force. Their old belief that as the "New Nation" they had inherited the land gave them a unifying cause. They were backed by Catholic priests, fearful of an influx of Protestant farmers. Still, Métis resistance might have been mere grumbling without young Louis Riel. The ambitious son of a respected father, Riel had gone to Montreal for a classical education. He had found no vocation for the Church or the law and had drifted home qualified for no career but politics. The man and the moment met. The combination derailed Macdonald's transcontinental plans. A national council of the Métis became the real authority in the Red River.

McDougall actually helped the Métis. As the would-be governor approached, the Métis formed a committee, mustered their forces, and seized Fort Garry, the Hudson's Bay Company's main base. No sooner had McDougall crossed the border than Métis guards expelled him. On December 1, the frustrated official again stepped a few feet over the boundary line, proclaimed Canadian sovereignty, fluttered a Union Jack in the icy wind, and retreated to his hotel room to command all loyal Canadians at the Red River to support his authority. The few Canadians who did so promptly found themselves in the freezing cells of Fort Garry. Louis Riel finally had an argument for proclaiming his provisional government: no other power existed in the colony.

In Ottawa, Macdonald was aghast. By his folly, McDougall had revealed Canadian impotence to Americans and Métis alike. If annexationists wanted a pretext to interfere, they would have a whole long winter before Canada could do anything. A steady stream of visitors and intermediaries, from old Joe Howe to Donald A. Smith, Hudson's Bay Company commissioner in Montreal, set out for the Red River. Riel met most of them with threats and legitimate suspicion. Smith proved by far the ablest. With patience and shrewdness, he manoeuvred Riel and the varied factions in the colony into stating their demands, choosing delegates, and despatching them to Ottawa. Riel's ambitions, after all, were not bizarre: he wanted Red River to be a province like the others. If the French could become Canadians, so could the Métis.

Unfortunately for Donald Smith, Riel and many other people, the patriotic Canadians in the Red River knew nothing of Macdonald's patient strategy. Their loyalty and their injured pride demanded more heroic action against the man McDougall had designated as a rebel. In February 1870 a new and even more bungled assault was mounted; once again the perpetrators were swiftly captured by Métis horsemen. This time, the mood was different. Riel's authority was slipping. Dissuaded by Smith and the community from executing C. A. Boulton, one of the Canadian leaders, he seized on smaller fry. Tom Scott, a big, raw-boned Ontarian, had already been savagely beaten for insulting his guards. On March 4, 1870, after a Métis court martial, he was taken out and shot. "We must make Canada respect us," Riel told Smith in melancholy justification.

It was worse than a crime; it was a blunder. Scott was an awkward martyr. Since he had earlier led a strike over unpaid wages and was certainly an Orangeman, most historians have generally agreed with Riel that Scott must have been a man of bad character. No one should be shot on such evidence. Contemporary opinion declared his death a murder. Reports from the Red River stoked the fires of Ontario Protestantism. Brown, the *Globe*, and the Grits had an issue the smallest mind could understand: Macdonald was bargaining with a murderous rebel. Quebec, at first dismayed by the killing, rapidly decided, after the Ontario furore, that Riel must be forgiven. Riel's friends in Montreal were long-suffering but loyal. They now regarded the Métis as guardians of a part of the French-Canadian patrimony most Québécois would rather admire from a distance.

Macdonald kept his eye on his purpose. Red River delegates were escorted past Ontario law officers, their desires were met, and they returned triumphant with virtually all any of them had sought. The colony would become the eleven-thousand-square-mile province of Manitoba. The duality of French and English, Catholic and Protestant, as it had existed in 1870, was secure forever. There would even be an upper and a lower house for the provincial legislature and, best of all, Ottawa would pay the bill. Only one desire was unsatisfied: an amnesty. It had been promised and expected, but that was before Scott died.

To confirm the transfer from what officially had been British sovereignty to Canadian rule, a joint Anglo-Canadian military expedition would show the flag to Americans, Indians, and the disaffected. With a mixture of land hunger, curiosity, and vengeful patriotism, young Ontarians flocked to join; young *Canadiens* did not. The Red River expedition of 1870 turned out to be a logistic triumph, navigating the old *voyageur* route from Port Arthur to Fort Garry without losing a man. It was also a political misfortune, introducing the young Dominion to the West as a punitive authority. A small garrison remained in Manitoba until 1877. As for Riel, he prudently fled before the approaching troops. A stabler and more robust personality might well, like Mackenzie and Papineau, have resumed a conventional political career, most probably in the Conservative ranks. Certainly Riel remained a hero to his Métis people, but by killing Scott he had robbed himself of immediate recognition as the founder of Manitoba.

The Red River was only one part of the West. In contrast, drawing British Columbia into Confederation proved deceptively simple. When gold ran out the miners departed, leaving behind a largely British and Canadian elite of officials, ranchers, and professionals, and a very large debt. The colony's leaders would have preferred the status quo; some merchants eagerly agitated for annexation with the United States. The editor of the Victoria *Colonist* (a Nova Scotian named William Smith who had renamed himself Amor de Cosmos) insisted that the Canadians be approached. A new British governor agreed, and, in the summer of 1870, two delegates made their laborious way to Ottawa via San Francisco. Macdonald was away, spending a restful summer in Charlottetown, but Cartier was on the job eager to make a coup. British Columbia needed money: for purposes of subsidy, Ottawa would pretend that it had sixty thousand people instead of twenty-eight thousand. (No one had even counted the colony's Indians – a loosely estimated eighty-two thousand!) The delegates hoped for a wagon road across the Rockies; Cartier had not forgotten the old Grand Trunk dream – British Columbia would have a full transcontinental railway within a decade of joining Confederation. It was an offer British Columbia could not possibly reject. By July 20, 1871, it was a province.

Between British Columbia and the Red River lay what an officially sponsored traveller, Captain William Butler, called "The Great Lone Land," peopled by Indians, a few Métis, and even fewer white trappers, traders, and missionaries. Herds of buffalo, sole livelihood for the inhabitants, headed relentlessly towards extinction. Repeating rifles and an American slaughter policy, designed to starve the warlike Sioux Indians, devastated the herds. Canada could not afford Indian wars. Her officials set out to negotiate a system of Indian treaties and surrenders with reserves, payments, medals, and a "medicine chest" as incentives for each band to clear the land for settlers. Ottawa could not stop there. The savage slaughter of an Indian party in the Cypress Hills and the establishment of American whiskey-traders at Fort Whoop-up in Canadian territory were warnings of early trouble. The mounted police force that had been planned for the Red River was revived. Policemen traditionally wore blue, but scarlet tunics would leave no doubt that a different sovereignty prevailed above the forty-ninth parallel. The North West Mounted Police was Macdonald's fondest creation. Canadians would later pretend that they were uniquely devoted to law and order. In fact, the peace and good order of the remote territories were practical necessities if American cavalry or vigilantes were to have no excuse for invading Canadian soil.

That soil would now also have to support a railway. Cartier's pledge was almost as worrying to his colleagues as MacDougall's folly had been in 1869. A three-thousand-mile railway from Montreal to the Pacific was a huge undertaking, especially at a time when Ottawa was pouring money into the Intercolonial Railway. The Pacific line would have to be a private venture, financed, if possible, by huge western land grants. Fortunately, two rival syndicates were bidding for the contract. Senator David Macpherson in Toronto was Macdonald's old friend, but he was a front for the Grand Trunk and no vote-conscious government would dare help that greedy and unloved company. In Montreal, the ruthless shipping magnate, Sir Hugh Allan, formed a rival group secretly backed by American railroad interests. Allan had money and he used it, buying up newspapers, young lawyers, even priests, to pressure Cartier and the entire Tory government.

With his national achievements and prosperity, Macdonald should have been impregnable. He was not. The Riel affair had turned both Ontario and Quebec against him. At the end of 1871, Ontario Liberals had used Riel and the Red River to batter Sandfield Macdonald into defeat. In Quebec, conservative Catholics concluded that the Church should resume the kind of political leadership it had exerted after the conquest. The pragmatic and corruptible *bleus* must be disciplined; the anti-clerical *rouges* must be destroyed. In New Brunswick, a new provincial government had belatedly introduced a single tax-supported non-demoninational school system, deliberately rejecting the Ontario model of dual public and Catholic schools. French and Catholic protests had led nowhere. In Ottawa, the Conservatives refused to disallow the New Brunswick act, insisting that central governments should not interfere in provincial jurisdictions. It was an argument as important to Quebec as to any province but furious Catholics and *Canadiens* were not appeased. In 1871, Quebec's ultramontane bishops approved a "Catholic Program" and commanded faithful voters to support candidates who endorsed it. It was a weapon primarily against *rouges* but it was also designed to split the *bleus* and to shatter the convenient alliance that Lafontaine had forged in the 1840s. The Macdonald government was in trouble.

In politics, problems never come singly. By 1871, the British had claimed their price for Confederation: liberation from North American entanglements. Eager to save money and worried by the new power of Germany in Europe, William Gladstone's Liberal government wanted Britain's colonial garrisons brought home. The troops stayed just long enough to join the Red River expedition and to fend off the last Fenian attacks in 1870, but by the fall of 1871, red-coated regulars remained only at Halifax. A few hundred Canadian gunners, hurriedly recruited to guard abandoned forts, were no substitute for the $6 million a year the British garrisons had represented for the Canadian economy.

Since, as Colonel Jervois had concluded in 1864, Canada was indefensible, the British decision made military sense. It made equal diplomatic sense, for Canada's sake, to clean the slate of Anglo-American grievances. The list was long, ranging from Britain's responsibility for Confederate commerce-raiders to American negligence in the Fenian raids. Long before the plenipotentiaries met in Washington in 1871, with Sir John A. Macdonald a reluctant participant, the scenario could be predicted. Americans would bluster and threaten; the British would retreat. Canadian claims against the United States would be traded against American claims on Britain. So it happened. Canadian expectations, from fishing rights to hard cash, scattered in the wind when the Treaty of Washington was signed. Exasperated by his supercilious fellow British delegates, Macdonald had to accept their argument that lasting peace with the Americans was an inestimable benefit. The problem was that voters would not estimate it either.

Winning reelection in 1872 had become a desperate struggle, to be waged by every trick in the book. To the despair of its chief engineer, Sandford Fleming, the Intercolonial was used as a vast funnel to pour contracts and patronage into the Maritimes. In Ontario, where George Brown had had his striking printers arrested, labour votes might be garnered by a law legalizing unions. Employers were reassured by an even tougher law against most strike activities. It was not enough. Everywhere, government candidates faced trouble. "Confederation is only yet in the gristle," a worried Macdonald wrote to a friend, "and it will require five years more before it hardens into bone." It was the kind of argument that usually precedes questionable expedients. Already Cartier had turned for cash to Sir Hugh Allan, and, as the campaign intensified, Macdonald followed. "I must have another ten thousand," he wired the magnate's solicitor in August 1872. "Will be the last time of asking. Do not fail me."

Macdonald won – narrowly – with 104 seats to 96, but there were too many "loose fish" on both sides to be certain. In Montreal, Cartier had lost his seat. In Ontario, farmers were furious that Macdonald had not rescued Reciprocity at Washington. Without Manitoba and a solid British Columbia, now eager for the railway, there would have been no victory. Sir Hugh would have his reward. For a million acres of land no official had ever seen and a list of other conditions, the government handed Allan a railway charter – on condition that his American partners be cut out. The old rogue agreed. The partners did not. Had they not fed most of the money to Allan for the election? The opposition would soon have the proof. A secret raid on the office of Allan's solicitor delivered a bag of evidence, including Macdonald's desperate message. Either $350,000 or $162,000 had been poured into the campaign. In any case, when even the prime minister earned only $8000 a year, the sum was enormous. The conclusion was obvious. "The Government got the money," explained Edward Blake, Ontario's Liberal premier, "and Sir Hugh Allan the Charter."

Brown, Blake, the dour Alexander Mackenzie, and other Ontario Liberals had always insisted that Macdonald was crooked as well as tricky. At last they had proof. Committees, a Royal Commission, and procedural delays could not stop the "loose fish" from swimming to safety. Among them, no defection counted more than that of Donald Smith, the successful negotiator of Red River. On November 3, fuelled by discreet glasses of gin, Macdonald offered a superb defence, but fatigue and alcohol sent him to bed for two days. By the time he revived on November 5, his government had collapsed. Members simply switched sides.

Macdonald's career was finished as certainly as anything in politics can be certain. His party might well follow him into obscurity. The Liberals could inherit his achievements – if they could form a government. The obvious leaders – Blake, Brown – would not serve. It was left to honest, grim Alexander Mackenzie, the immigrant stonemason who had made good in Sarnia, to become Canada's second prime minister and to create some unity out of the factions that had sat in opposition. On one thing they and the country could agree: wickedness must be condemned. The elections, spaced over weeks and with open voting, so that safe Liberal seats showed the trend, gave Mackenzie 138 of the 206 seats. The Conservatives held a mere 67, almost half of these in Quebec.

From Manitoba came a solitary independent, willing to risk signing his name and taking his oath before fleeing for safety. The signature was that of Louis Riel.

In opposition, Liberals had assailed every nation-building policy, from better terms for Nova Scotia to the great railway. It had been easy for Macdonald to convince supporters, including Lord Dufferin, the latest governor general, that Confederation was unsafe in Liberal hands. Yet Mackenzie had backed the project and he backed it still. The change of government brought rational, overdue reforms. Electoral corruption would surely be harder if voters used a secret ballot and if general elections occurred on the same day, not at the government's convenience. The Supreme Court, promised in the British North America Act, was created as a sop to nationalists – and promptly undermined by allowing appeals to continue to the Judicial Committee of the Privy Council in London. At Kingston, Mackenzie opened a tiny Royal Military College of Canada to train not simply officers but the engineers that a young country needed.

Yet governments inherit far more than they create. By 1876, the Intercolonial was complete to Halifax but Mackenzie's ruthless efforts to prune away corruption and waste never could correct the wandering tracks or the politically appointed employees. The ICR was a cautionary tale for enemies of public enterprise. When Mackenzie cancelled the Allan contract and announced that the promised Pacific railway would be built in slow stages and by the government, British Columbians claimed betrayal and promised secession. Mackenzie's critics promised another dose of corruption. What they got was painful progress from the Lakehead to the thriving little town of Winnipeg.

Progress was slow for an unexpected reason: Canada was suddenly deep in an economic depression.

The post-Confederation years had been a hot Indian summer of prosperity, continuing two decades of almost unbroken growth. Regions and industries might occasionally suffer a little but recovery came soon. Even the loss of Reciprocity in 1866 had seemed relatively painless. Good times had made Confederation easier to promote. Assuming debts, building railways, and improving transfer payments from Ottawa seemed a good idea when revenues grew even faster than spending, from $14 million in 1867 to $25 million in 1874. The first signs of trouble were visible in 1873, with banks failing in distant Vienna and trade and credit suddenly contracting. By 1874, the danger signs were so obvious that businessmen and politicians changed the subject. By 1875, the economic slump was unmistakable.

As usual, many individuals and whole communities escaped with no more than worries; some prospered so mightily that some economic historians would later deny that a depression had occurred. Contemporaries knew better. Revenues, based on import duties, fell drastically. Innocent of theories of counter-cyclical financing, Mackenzie's government set a public example of cost-cutting and, with deep regret (for free trade was Liberal gospel in Canada as well as Britain), raised tariff rates to seventeen and a half per cent. George Brown went to Washington on Mackenzie's behalf, negotiated and actually won a new reciprocity treaty only to see it trampled to death in a protectionist United States Senate. No wonder there was no money for British Columbia's railway. In a grudging compromise, extorted by British mediators, Ottawa agreed to spend $2 million a year and complete the line by 1890.

The economic crisis, with its thousands of hungry unemployed, spread to every part of Canada. By grim coincidence, the timber and shipping industries which had built the prosperity of both the Maritimes and the St. Lawrence faced new problems. The age of "wooden ships and iron men" was passing. Iron, and soon steel, hulls displaced the great ships which had drifted down the ways in Saint John, Quebec, and a dozen other Canadian ports. Nova Scotia's coal mines and a primitive iron industry could not hope to compete with British yards. Prudent merchants could shift their capital to new investments; seamen and shipyard workers simply had to move away. At Quebec and Montreal, *Canadien* shipbuilders waged violent battles for the jobs of Irish longshoremen. In Saint John, long, hopeless strikes brought the city's proud labour unions to the edge of extinction. In 1877, a disastrous fire left thirteen thousand homeless. It was a common enough catastrophe but it was almost more than the beleaguered New Brunswick city could endure.

Labour violence shifted easily to the old issues of sect and race. In 1875, Toronto police fought bloody battles to protect Catholic marchers from Protestant mobs. In Montreal, Orange processions organized to protest the local killing of members were simply banned. After the Liberal victory in 1874, Catholic Programmists no longer divided their fire between *rouges* and *bleus*. Bishop Bourget and his supporters now waged virtual holy war on the Liberals, provincial and federal, Catholic or secular. Clergy, thundering from their pulpits, had no trouble reminding the faithful that Heaven was blue and Hell was not. In 1877, the young Wilfrid Laurier was beaten in a savage by-election in his native Drummond-Arthabaska. Weeks later, he won a seat in Quebec-East. Quebec City's Archbishop Taschereau had an old hatred for Bourget and the Jesuits and a discreet affection for conservative young Liberals. Nothing was ever quite as monolithic as it seemed in French Canada.

Wilfrid Laurier and the Liberals would have a future. The frail, handsome lawyer insisted that he was the heir of Englishmen like Gladstone and Bright, not of European anti-Catholic liberals. Yet, for Liberals as a whole, that Gladstonian free-trade heritage brought political paralysis. The depression did not lift, as conventional wisdom insisted it should. Sir Richard Cartwright, the big, bewhiskered, blustering man who served as the Liberals' minister of finance, was an ex-Tory with a convert's fanaticism. Free trade was his gospel and he would not change it, whatever arguments might be offered by powerful deputations of businessmen and manufacturers. If Americans sent tariffs soaring, they were wrong and free trade was right. A wealth of conventional wisdom sustained him. So did his prime minister.

Sir John A. Macdonald thought differently. He had somehow survived his own despair, a near-defeat in Kingston, and inevitable party disaffection. Perhaps it was simply his durable, unquenchable charm. "When fortune empties her chamberpot on your head," he told a friend in 1875, "smile, and say 'we are going to have a summer shower.'" The shower had ended. Memories of the

Pacific scandal were buried now by awareness of a depression, misery, hopelessness, and a government seemingly unwilling to do anything to help. Tariffs were not a heresy to Macdonald – nothing was if it won votes. Prominent manufacturers, fed up with American dumping of goods over the seventeen-and-a-half-per cent tariff barrier, had a point. They also promised more financial support than Hugh Allan had ever mustered. A summer of political picnics across Ontario in 1876 and another in 1877 taught Macdonald what people wanted and how to put his case.

Once again, Macdonald assured them, he would be the nation-builder, urging not "protection" but a "National Policy," a "judicious readjustment of the Tariff," to "benefit the agricultural, the mining, the manufacturing and other interests of the Dominion."

On September 17, 1878, for the first time in their history Canadians voted on the same day. Mackenzie was utterly confident. There might be local setbacks but huge meetings had cheered him and the rightness of his policies. Macdonald's sly scheme to tax ninety-five per cent of Canadians for the benefit of five per cent would surely destroy the Conservative party.

Instead, it destroyed Mackenzie. The 1874 election was more than reversed, with 142 Conservatives to only 64 Liberals. The popular vote, when the last figures trickled in, of 52.5% for the Tories to 46.3% for Liberal candidates. It seemed that voters preferred Macdonald drunk to Mackenzie sober; warm humanity to dry integrity.

At sixty-three, Sir John A. Macdonald could resume his work.

3

National Policy

In only ten years, the Dominion had met most of the goals of Confederation. Seven provinces and the huge North West Territories ran from one ocean to the other. In 1880, when the British transferred to Canada their claims to the Arctic, Canadians heard of a third ocean few had considered in 1867. In Ottawa, the French-English stalemate was over. Even under the Liberals, Macdonald's policy of strong central government had largely prevailed. In the bad times of the 1870s, most people blamed politicians, not Confederation.

Now Macdonald was free to implement his "National Policy" and to retire triumphant. To most Canadians, it was now "NP"; as comforting and vague as any good political slogan. Sir Leonard Tilley would manage the details of the new tariff, and the corridors outside his office thronged with business deputations. More powerful capitalists met discreetly with Macdonald in a comfortable Toronto hotel room the suspicious *Globe* promptly christened "the Red Chamber." The NP forged a new alliance of business and government and so long as Liberals raged at protection capitalists would cling to the Tories as though their economic lives depended on it.

On March 14, 1879, Tilley finally announced the new tariffs. Amid the inevitable grumbling one thing was clear: from textiles to farm machinery, Canadian manufacturers could depend on a safe national market. Making that market grow was the next priority. The recipe was simple. By filling the empty Northwest with people, a flood of natural products could pour eastward to pay for a returning flow of manufactured goods. The Pacific railway must be hurried forward not simply to reassure British Columbians but to serve the government's prime economic strategy. Mackenzie's policy was too slow to suit anyone.

The most promising private developer was a Montreal-based syndicate that had bought out a bankrupt railway running from St. Paul, Minnesota, north to Winnipeg. At its head was the respectable George Stephen of the Bank of Montreal, but there were also fuzzy links with J. Hill, promoter of the Northern Pacific Railroad. Stephen's major partner was the man who had deserted Macdonald in 1873, the ubiquitous Donald A. Smith. Macdonald hardly hesitated; grudges were not his style. For $25 million in cash, twenty-five million acres along the line, a twenty-year monopoly and permanent exemption from local taxes on its property, Stephen's syndicate would build the line.

Again the Liberals thundered at the prodigality of the terms and the lack of guarantees. Their outrage aligned Macdonald and business more closely. The new railway would create a huge corporation whose fortunes would be bound to the Conservative party. But there were enemies too. In London, officials of the Grand Trunk warned investors against the new Canadian Pacific Railway Company. Experts warned that it would be impossible to fulfill the CPR plan of building along the northern shore of Lake Superior. The experts were wrong. The impossible simply took a little longer and cost a lot more. A formidable American engineer, William Van Horne, managed the construction and galvanized the huge labour gangs. To cut off the Northern Pacific from future Canadian business, the company abandoned Sandford Fleming's original northerly route to the Yellowhead Pass and headed straight west across the prairie, through the Palliser Triangle. Again experts snorted that the CPR would never sell the arid land. They knew nothing of a more frightening risk. As Van Horne's crews raced westwards across the flat prairie, and Andrew Onderdonk's Chinese labourers struggled eastwards through the coastal mountains, surveyors had yet to discover a pass through the difficult Selkirk Range. Only in August 1882 did reports come that a way had finally been found.

In the mood of that year, Canadians might have forgiven such colossal risk-taking. A little prosperity had returned with the new decade and the adventure of nation-building was again in style. The Liberals, now led by the high-principled but ponderous Edward Blake, offered crushing condemnation of each Macdonald policy. His "voluble virtue" could not bury the suspicion that, back in office, Liberals would either do the same as the Tories or nothing at all. Meanwhile, the government could claim credit for each new factory and job. There were many.

An unconscious victim of the National Policy was Canada's merchant fleet, the fourth largest in the world in 1867. Ottawa worried about railways, manufacturers, and farmers; shipping policy was limited to a penurious attempt to make coastal navigation a little safer. Not even the Maritime region's powerful political spokesmen, Charles Tupper, John Thompson, and William Fielding, crusaded for the kind of laws which Britain had used to foster her own merchant marine. In the 1870s and 1880s Canadian shipping grew impressively in vessel size and efficiency; "Down-East" skippers and crew won a high reputation. It made no difference. Falling shipping rates persuaded owners to put their money elsewhere. A great industry was dying and few Canadians even mourned its passing.

In the Maritimes, new fortunes were being made. Manufacturers regularly complained that they got no protection from "Upper Canada"; in fact, they prospered. Along the line of the Intercolonial, factories sprouted in towns like Moncton and Amherst. Coal from Pictou and Cape Breton promised to fuel the new Canadian industrial revolution. Certainly growth was fastest where markets were already largest – in southern Quebec and Ontario. Railways confirmed the favourites – Montreal, Toronto, Hamilton – but they also fostered smaller cities where cheap labour could be drawn from over-sized farm families. The flow of *Canadiens* to New England mills could be diverted to Scugog, Valleyfield, and other new textile towns.

In time, Canadians would learn to condemn the new factories and the squalid houses and streets that grew up around them.

Governments had cast-iron economic principles as well as political friendships to deter them from meddling with long hours, unsafe machinery, and harsh factory discipline. Factory safety laws, adopted by Ontario and Quebec by 1887, were ill-enforced and were mainly concerned with discouraging the employment of women and children. The few trade unions organized skilled workers in construction jobs, the railways, and a few old crafts like printing. The Knights of Labor, a radical and idealistic working-class movement that swept into Canada from the United States in the 1880s, won short-lived political influence for workers in Ontario and Quebec and left a residue of radical ideas and leaders, but it was almost dead by the end of the decade.

Middle-class humanitarians did as much as workers to ease some of the worst consequences of urban and industrial growth in the wake of the National Policy. Defending the sanctity of the family from drunkenness, prostitution, and bad sanitation gave the wives and daughters of the middle class their first excuse to demand a political voice. Dr. Emily Stowe, Canada's first woman doctor, mustered a variety of reforming forces in the 1880s when she helped launch a campaign for women's suffrage. Some clergy cautiously added their weight to reform causes but the intractable problems of urban life in themselves forced city councils to create more efficient police forces, recruit health inspectors, and develop water and sewage systems. Private investors also learned that monopoly franchises to provide street cars, electricity, and telephone service could be highly profitable. A little easy-going corruption among the city fathers helped confirm the deals. In 1886, reform mayors in both Montreal and Toronto waged angry, short-lived crusades against assorted municipal evils from prostitution to pit privies. The horror of contemporary American cities such as Chicago or Philadelphia spurred on their righteous followers.

In the early 1880s, most Canadians were too pleased with themselves to be critical. Benjamin Disraeli had taught British Conservatives that imperialism could win working-class votes. Canadians too were "British" and shared vicariously in the thrill of distant wars. They were flattered when Queen Victoria spared her fourth daughter, Princess Louise, to accompany her husband the Marquis of Lorne to what Disraeli affably described as "one of our great vice-royalties." But their pleasure was spiced with a determination to prove a sturdy indifference to snobbish affectation. As head of the clan Campbell, Lorne was shocked to find Canadian Campbells reluctant to doff their caps to their feudal chief.

In 1881, the Marquis of Lorne, as Canada's new governor general, launched the Royal Society of Canada to honour the Dominion's scientific and literary achievements. The *Globe* dismissed it as "a mutual admiration society for nincompoops." The *Canadiens*, more comfortable with intellectual distinction, rejoiced without reserve when their poet, Louis Fréchette, won the French Academy's Prix Montyon in 1880. In the same year, as part of homecoming festivities to entice *Canadiens* home from New England, Calixte Lavallée composed *O Canada*, a future national anthem.

By 1882, when Macdonald sought re-election, he could count on an easy victory. He took no chances, rigging the boundaries of Ontario constituencies just in case farmers really did deplore the tariff, and supporting Home Rule for Ireland to consolidate his Irish-Catholic support. The British were not amused. Nor did they welcome the creation of a powerful High Commission in London as a quasi-embassy for the Dominion. The British did not vote in Canadian elections, however, and those who did gave Macdonald 139 seats to Blake's 71. It was hard to quarrel with prosperity.

That prosperity depended on the West. In 1881, a record number of immigrants poured into Canada, and many of them headed for Manitoba. By 1883, the postage-stamp province had filled its best farmland, largely with the sons of Ontario. Winnipeg had grown from a few shacks to a town of ten thousand people – ugly, flat, but dotted with churches and schools and vacant lots that sold for an incredible $750 a running foot. Lord Lorne, travelling west in 1881, dutifully inspected the Mounted Police, two thousand loyal Blackfoot warriors, and the Rockies. His entourage of British newspapermen was properly impressed by the prospects for farming and ranching.

Suddenly, in the summer of 1883, the bubble burst. Land prices tumbled. Fortunes invested in land along the expected northerly CPR line vanished when the railway took the southern route. Almost everyone blamed Ottawa. Farmers, furious at the failure of their speculations, met to share grievances over freight rates and elevator monopolies and created the first of many prairie protest movements. Métis, who had sold the land grants received as part of the 1870 agreement and had moved west to the valley of the South Saskatchewan, again met the surveyors and saw in them the vanguard of white settlement. The buffalo hunt was gone; the railway and river steamboats threatened their livelihood as teamsters. Métis settlers wanted title to river-front lots they had staked out. Ottawa hesitated. How could the Métis be discouraged from selling their land again as so many had in Manitoba? The suggestion from Catholic missionaries – giving Métis reserves like Indians – was not helpful.

Indian reserves were not a very encouraging model. Perhaps there was no better solution for native people, once the buffalo were gone, than to form reserves and teach Indians to be farmers. More realistic answers are still hard to find. What is certain was that no one anticipated the patience or resources necessary to turn nomadic hunters into peasants. The government expected the job to be done in a generation. In 1879, when the buffalo finally vanished, Ottawa authorized government rations for starving, destitute Indian bands. Food was used as a lever to force the last roving bands to choose reserves and to pay attention to white farm instructors. After 1883, shrinking federal revenue and official impatience coalesced. To compel Indians to tend their herds and their fields, rations were cut. Ottawa stubbornly discounted police warnings that the Indian reserves were seething with resentment.

Ottawa was not wholly unreasonable, though it was certainly remote. Macdonald, who kept personal control of Indian policy, recognized that transition would be painful whether it was quick or slow, and that it was wiser to strengthen the police than to allow Indians to fantasize about alternatives to their agricultural future. Moreover, the government had more immediate worries as an economic slump returned. By the end of 1883, the CPR was floundering toward bankruptcy. The immigrant flow had stopped. Land sales had not provided revenue. The Grand Trunk's warnings to British and European investors had finally begun to work. In London, Sir Alexander Galt, Canada's new High Commissioner, could not get the British either to invest in the CPR or to assist emigration.

Macdonald himself was ready to retire, but so were too many of his trusted contemporaries. Tupper, urged by his wife to seek the bright lights of London, followed Galt as High Commissioner. Tilley, worn out, withdrew to Fredericton as lieutenant-governor. Macdonald's preferred successor, D'Alton McCarthy, a young Irish-born Protestant, needed his Toronto law practice to pay his debts. John Thompson, a solid, sensible Nova Scotian who had served briefly as provincial premier, came reluctantly to Ottawa in 1885. An age of religious bigotry saw in him a fatal flaw. Protestant-born, he had converted to Catholicism at his marriage, to become, in the vicious language of the day, a "pervert." From Quebec, there had come no successor to Cartier, dead from Bright's disease in 1873. Sir Hector Langevin, the portly, dignified guardian of the alliance with the clergy was, Macdonald curtly admitted, "lath painted to look like steel." Langevin was also enmeshed in the tangled corruption of his Department of Public Works. His rival was Joseph Chapleau, bold, arrogant, and opportunistic. Chapleau spoke for the old pragmatic *bleu* tradition. He despised the *Castors* or Catholic ultramontanes who mustered so many forces in his fiefdom of Montreal. Neither man could unite Quebec; either would destroy the other if he could.

After so much easy success, Macdonald found himself adrift on a sea of troubles. The grievances of Indians, Métis, or settlers were lost in the waves. In 1883, with the unfinished CPR foundering, Macdonald faced a bitter struggle with his own caucus to approve a loan. French-Canadian members, resentful that CPR spending had not helped their province enough, refused to vote until Macdonald pledged funds for the ailing, corruptly managed North Shore Railway from Montreal to Quebec City. New Brunswickers bargained their support for a "short line" that would take the CPR from Montreal through Maine to Saint John. In a single year Canada's national debt rose by fifty per cent. By the winter of 1884-85, the CPR loan was spent, gaps remained north of Lake Superior and in the Rockies, and unpaid employees struck. The paycar sat at Montreal, empty.

Like a kind of *deus ex machina*, on March 16, 1885, came dramatic news. Police and Métis had clashed at Duck Lake, not far from Prince Albert. Twelve police and volunteers lay dead in the snow. The rest had fled. The Dominion faced its first great crisis. The peace and order which were Macdonald's prime goals for protecting and settling the West lay shattered.

The explanations were already in Ottawa, in sheaves of settler and Métis petitions and long, worried reports from police and officials. One of the petitions was the work of Louis Riel, summoned back from self-imposed exile in Montana by a Métis deputation financed by Prince Albert's white settlers. To them, Riel was the man of 1870 who had forced a distant Ottawa to do his bidding. Fifteen years, some of them in the terrible Beauport lunatic asylum outside Quebec, had transformed Riel from a young excitable politician to a moody religious visionary, bitter at his own poverty and failure. At times he now seemed content to draft petitions for land claims and more elected members in the territorial assembly at Regina and in Ottawa, underlining his own professed financial claims on the government. "My name is Riel and I want material," he told a local politician. In other moods, he created *l'Union Métisse de St-Joseph*, dreamed of a Métis empire of the South Saskatchewan and proposed that Bishop Bourget of Montreal should become the pope of the New World. Missionaries and Métis grew alarmed at sacrilege. Indians, summoned to join the new movement, listened and kept their own counsel. In Regina, Lieutenant-Governor Edgar Dewdney sent police reinforcements to the district and planned to go north later in the spring to negotiate face-to-face.

Riel did not wait. On March 18 he seized power, arresting clergy, local officials, and any who disagreed with him. Next day, he proclaimed his new provisional government, an odd theocracy he called the Exovedate. It became his preoccupation during the weeks he expected to wait while the distant government sent negotiators, as it had in 1870. At Duck Lake, he had hoped to capture the police as hostages. The bloodshed appalled him, and he allowed the battered force to escape. At the Cut Knife and Frog Lake reserves, young Cree warriors took the police defeat as a signal for war. Two whites died near Battleford and nine more at Frog Lake, two of them Catholic missionaries. Across the Northwest, panic-stricken white settlers crowded into police forts and wired Ottawa for troops and weapons.

Though caught by surprise, the government had no intention of negotiating. Instead, it improvised brilliantly. The CPR's promise that it would somehow get troops and equipment over its unfinished track was argument enough for a further loan. Within a month, an army of five thousand regulars, militia, and local volunteers had spread across the Northwest. The militia commander, Major General Fred Middleton, was old and a little pompous, but he was also able, clear-headed, and an expert in the kind of mobile warfare the 1885 campaign demanded. Within two months of Riel's proclamation of the Exovedate, Middleton's untrained, ill-armed militiamen had captured Batoche, Riel's stronghold. A few days later, Riel himself surrendered. Though Indians had fought more successfully than Riel's divided followers, their resistance collapsed with the fall of Batoche.

The 1885 Rebellion is a thicket of self-serving mythology. The CPR could pretend that it had saved the Northwest from Riel. In fact Riel saved the CPR from ruin. Canadian troops could have as easily passed through the United States: many did. The Americans were eager to help stop a dangerous threat north of their border. If any corporation made a difference, it was the Hudson's Bay Company. Without its supplies and transport, Middleton could hardly have stirred beyond the CPR track. Middleton's reputation suffered at the hands of subordinates who wanted all the credit. He set out sooner and marched faster than the experts thought prudent, split his forces only at Ottawa's insistence, and did his utmost to protect his raw troops from surprise or heavy casualties.

In both purposes, he succeeded. Middleton's greatest ally was Louis Riel. Having launched his Métis and Indian followers in open revolt, Riel retreated into mystical fantasy, inhibiting every intelligent effort at self-defence. The tragedy of 1885 was not the fate of Riel but that of the people he had led. A Half-Breed Claims Commission, established before the outbreak, settled Métis land claims, but Riel's failure ended any real pressure to reassess Indian policy or the destiny of the New Nation. The rebellion of 1885 was disastrous to Indians and Métis alike.

Riel's egoism remained unquenched. At Regina, where he was allowed to use the police commissioner's office, he wrote to Macdonald to ask for a state trial in Ottawa. Once acquitted, he would like to be premier of Manitoba. Macdonald had other plans. Those who had plotted the outbreak would be punished as a warning to anyone else who might fish in troubled waters. Investigation found no widespread conspiracy, only Riel. He was tried for high treason. Lawyers despatched by the Quebec *rouges* sought to prove that Riel was insane. A Protestant jury might agree, but when Riel spoke on his own behalf he was rational and persuasive, if long-winded. Only one verdict was possible but a jury of Westerners understood Riel's grievances well enough to add their own plea for mercy. The judge condemned him to hang.

A later generation, using a later definition of "treason," sometimes insists that Riel never betrayed anyone. This is undoubtedly true. However, the language of law and that of popular parlance sometimes differs. Since no one had denied that he "levied war upon Her Majesty," it is worth remembering that it was for this kind of treason that he was condemned. Egomania, folly, and religious eccentricity also had nothing to do with the law.

Riel's sentence split Canadian opinion. If there was strong feeling in Ontario, it developed after French Canada had belatedly adopted Riel as a cause. Liberals, for partisan reasons, blamed Macdonald, not the Métis, for the outbreak. *Canadiens* were as shocked by the rebellion as anyone and even more horrified by the murder of missionaries, but they shifted ground as they had in 1870 and closed ranks before the Orange onslaught. Riel became the pathetic madman, alone in his Regina cell. French Canadians had refused to join the flood of western settlement, but the Métis remained their proxies and their grievances were real enough. J. Israel Tarte, a veteran *bleu* organizer, warned: "At the moment when the corpse of Riel falls through the trap and twists in convulsions of agony, at that moment an abyss will be dug that will separate Quebec from English-speaking Canada. . . ." The decision rested with Macdonald, and it had been made long before controversy broke out. Few politicians had more contempt for public opinion – "mere newspapers" he called it – or for the Orange Lodge. Macdonald was a patient man and if Quebec colleagues insisted on allowing appeals or on more medical examinations of Riel's sanity, he would wait. His three Quebec colleagues finally gave their consent. "Old Tomorrow" had learned that political fires sooner or later die down. On November 16, 1885, Riel was hanged.

Macdonald was right. The fires would die, but not soon. On November 22, huge crowds packed Montreal's Champ de Mars. "If I had been on the banks of the Saskatchewan," shouted Wilfrid Laurier, "I too would have shouldered my musket." Even more heard Honoré Mercier, the former *bleu*, now Quebec Liberal leader and emerging as the leader of the *Parti Nationale*, a strange new alliance of *Castors* and *rouges*. "Riel, our brother, is dead," cried Mercier, "victim of his devotion to the cause of the Métis, of whom he was the leader, victim of fanaticism and treason – of the fanaticism of Sir John and some of his friends, of the treason of three of our people who sold their brother to keep their portfolios." In Ottawa, Conservative strategists manoeuvred to control the damage. On a key vote, condemning the government, sixteen French Canadians abandoned the government, but twenty-three English-speaking Liberals deserted Edward Blake's party.

In much of Canada, the scars of the Riel Rebellion soon vanished. In the West, settlers were too busy struggling with homesteads and a serious drought cycle to care very much. The notion of a Protestant Ontario ravening for Riel's blood is an ugly myth perpetuated by lazy historians. Violent editorials from the Orange *Sentinel* or the radical Toronto *News* might be set against a Liberal press which condemned Macdonald as much as Riel for the tragedy. Blake's defence of Riel in 1886 and his insistence on Laurier as his successor in 1887 were two of the decisive steps in determining the future dominance of the Liberal party, but they came from a party whose electorate was still firmly in Ontario.

It was Quebec that was transformed by the Riel affair. Anger forced politics to catch up with reality. To all appearances, Quebec had gained all that Cartier had promised from Confederation. The reward was an almost uninterrupted *bleu* dominance in provincial politics and even the luxury of internal controversy among the factions of *bleus*, *rouges*, and *Castor* ultramontanes. Economically, Quebec appeared to be a major beneficiary of the National Policy, with dozens of new factories. Montreal, confirmed as terminus for both of Canada's major railways, was more than ever a commercial and financial metropolis.

Yet, apart from lawyers, politicians, and a few exceptional businessmen, few *Canadiens* shared the new wealth or opportunities. The factories drew people from rural parishes into cities and towns often dominated by English-speaking Protestant elites. Slums and low-paid jobs were the French-Canadian share. Macdonald's federalism guaranteed Quebec its own cultural and religious institutions, but provinces had little money of their own to spend on projects that might not be a national priority, such as railways north and south of Quebec City or the dreams of colonization urged by the persuasive Curé Antoine Labelle. If children of the *habitants* were not to be lost to New England or the Montreal slums, huge sums were needed to settle them in the "New Quebec" of Lac St-Jean and the Saguenay or on the hilly fields of the Eastern Townships. Churches, schools, and employment must be available from the outset if settlers would accept the brutally hard work of the frontier. It all required money that *bleu* regimes at Quebec City would not or could not collect.

These were mostly dull problems, grinding below the surface. Riel's execution was an explosion. Mercier, eager for power and at odds since 1865 with the Cartier view of Confederation, seized on the feelings of isolation and impotence of French Canadians when their clear, collective desire to save the Métis leader had been ignored. Earlier, when Macdonald had deposed a Liberal-appointed

lieutenant-governor at the insistence of Quebec City *bleus*, Judge
Thomas Loranger had offered as part of an indignant protest a new
view of Confederation as a "compact" or contract between the
two founding nations of French and English. Provinces, not
Ottawa, were the sovereign powers in Confederation. Growing
numbers of Quebeckers absorbed Loranger's legal fiction as
though it were historical truth. If it were, Quebec had been
betrayed by the English and, for that matter, by their own representatives in the government. An embattled people, Honoré Mercier now insisted, could not afford the luxury of political divisions.
It must also abandon false dreams of sharing the great Canadian
patrimony. Surely Riel had tried and now he was dead. From
ultramontanes to *rouges*, French Canadians must unite. Only corrupt *bleu* opportunists would refuse.

The arguments, honed and perfected by Mercier and his lieutenants, recalled the old tradition of the compact colony of New
France, the ruralism of the post-conquest clergy, the cultural separatism of Papineau. They challenged a rival tradition, reinforced
by pragmatism and represented by the memory of Lafontaine and
Cartier and by the very real practical power of the *bleus* in Macdonald's government. There was no monolith but there was movement. On October 14, 1886, after a provincial election in which
Mercier had ridden the corpse of Riel across Quebec, his *Parti
National* won a convincing victory. The Conservative stronghold
was cracked. With Ontario's help, it might crumble.

That help seemed likely. Since 1873, Oliver Mowat as Liberal
premier of Ontario had cemented his provincial power as Blake
never could have. The little bespectacled lawyer rejoiced in the
title of "the Christian Statesman," and he delegated the sordid
side of politics to trusty but remote agents. It was Mowat who
discovered and satisfied an Ontario appetite for moralizing and an
equal taste for tiny but incessant reforms. The provincial legislature was constantly busy. The Ontario premier had also
discovered a new way to fight the old Upper Canadian battles with
Lower Canada. As a Father of Confederation, Mowat had been rare
among the Reformers in urging true federalism and greater provincial powers. He had lost in 1867, but as an insider in the

British North America Act negotiations Mowat had a shrewd idea
of how to attack. The Judicial Committee of the Privy Council in
London, the appeal court for a world-wide empire, revelled in its
assumed expertise in everything from Roman-Dutch law to Tamil
marriage customs. Of the politics and history of Canadian federalism, British judges knew nothing; of classical federalism they
knew all they wanted to know. An able lawyer could do the rest.

Mowat's first major triumph had established Ontario's western
boundary at considerable cost to Manitoba. No one had really
cared very much about the line until rumours were heard of gold
at Rat Portage (now Kenora). Macdonald backed Manitoba's premier John Norquay against Mowat and the Grits. The courts ruled
otherwise, and Premier Mowat had the added bonus of showing
that the Tories had refused to defend Ontario interests. The
rumours of gold soon faded and the remote region lapsed into
neglect. Mowat moved on to fresh issues. A long-drawn but victorious struggle for control over the licensing of taverns elevated the
provincial responsibility for "property and civil rights" over the
newly limited federal role in "peace, order, and good government." It also transferred a rich opportunity for patronage from
federal Tory to provincial Liberal hands. Tavern-keepers would
now be "Grits." Liquor, the best known solvent for a vote, would
be dispensed by Liberals.

Thanks to Mowat, it was Ontario, not Quebec, that began the
steady erosion of the strong central government Sir John A. Macdonald had hoped to entrench in 1867. When Mercier's *Parti
National* took power in 1887 Mowat found an ally. He soon had
others. In Nova Scotia, the anti-Confederate cause, under a Liberal
label, had slowly mellowed as the old slogans lost their potency
and people readjusted. A Conservative provincial government was
perversely defeated on the same day in 1882 that Nova Scotians
gave most of their federal seats to Macdonald's Tories. As boom
turned to bust and the time for re-election approached, Premier
W. S. Fielding and his Liberals returned to their old anti-Ottawa
program. At the end of the 1886 session, J. W. Longley, Fielding's
attorney general, moved to repeal Nova Scotia's membership in
Confederation. After speeches of passionate provincial patriotism,

the motion passed, fifteen to seven with numerous abstentions. Armed with such proof of their devotion to Nova Scotia, the Liberals won twenty-eight of the thirty-eight seats. For the first and almost the only time, a provincial legislature had voted against Confederation.

The trend to provincialism was catching. In 1887, Honoré Mercier summoned his fellow premiers to Quebec City. Mowat, Fielding, Blair of New Brunswick, all Liberals, and a lonely Tory, John Norquay of Manitoba, appeared. Norquay's grievances were notorious. Once completed in November 1885, the CPR had set out to recoup its investment with all deliberate speed. Freight rates were as high as any profitable monopoly would set them. Being a monopoly was a cherished part of the CPR's contract, secured by Act of Parliament. A procession of Norquay's laws permitting rival railways were solemnly disallowed by his fellow Tories in Ottawa. Norquay, Manitoba's first Métis premier, must have known that his political career would be in danger when he consorted in Quebec with the Liberal enemy. A year later it would end.

In any case, the 1887 premiers' meeting accomplished nothing. It was a symbol. The unity of Confederation, so easily taken for granted in 1878, was splitting only a decade later. The second round of nation-building was in trouble. So was Canada.

4

Political Revolution

By now the elements of Macdonald's National Policy were in place. On November 7, 1885, a white-bearded Donald Smith pounded home the last iron spike of the CPR. Passengers could soon travel the three thousand miles from Montreal to Burrard Inlet in a week. On the way, they could see the world's largest nickel deposit, accidentally discovered at Sudbury by CPR survey crews. Settlers, coming west on the CPR's colonist cars, would find land offices ready to help them locate and prove up their quarter-section grants in the vast checkerboard pattern the surveyors had laid on the prairie. At Indian Head, a government experimental farm would soon begin to wrestle with the problems of prairie agriculture. In the East, Macdonald's 1882 victory had convinced even timid investors that protective tariffs would last. New factories opened and old ones expanded, despite the return of hard times.

In Parliament, newspaper editorials, and countless country stores, the merits of the "NP" had been endlessly debated. Riel's execution, symbolically as important as the CPR in showing that the West was open for peaceful white settlement, had helped hand Quebec to Honoré Mercier. By the end of 1887, the CPR's monopoly clause had undermined Norquay and the Conservatives in Manitoba. In British Columbia, the choice of Vancouver as CPR terminus had infuriated both Victoria and New Westminster. When Onderdonk's Chinese labour stayed on as cheap labour for the province's mines and forest industry, white workers got a solid economic basis for their racial prejudices. The result was a durable, radical labour movement, toe-to-toe with powerful employers.

Eastern workers might owe their jobs to the NP's tariffs but they had little else in common with their increasingly wealthy and powerful bosses. Worried commentators warned that Canada would soon see the labour violence of the United States or the class warfare of Europe. A royal commission on the relations of capital and labour, designed to glorify the achievements of the National Policy, collected endless testimony of employer tyranny and greed. "To obtain a very large percentage of work with the smallest possible outlay of wages," a commissioner concluded, "appears to be the one fixed and dominant idea." Such scolding did not lead the Commission to suggest any significant reforms.

Farmers were even more resentful than workers. No policy could have protected them from a cycle of drought, poor yields, and low world prices, but the NP included nothing specific to please them. Western settlers complained that CPR freight rates and policies reflected all the evils of monopoly. Farmers everywhere condemned a tariff that forced them to pay more for their balers, binders, and hay rakes and, for that matter, for the boots, ribbons, and corsets their wives wanted for their Sunday best. In the 1870s, joining organizations like the Grange had helped make some farmers class-conscious but unpolitical. Now the Grange was supplanted by the militant Patrons of Industry, an American-based organization which soon had thousands of members across Ontario and the West denouncing tariffs, monopolies, and the corruption of traditional politics.

Caught between Mercier and Mowat, with his policies under attack and the country plainly in trouble, Macdonald should have lost the 1887 election. Edward Blake wore out himself and his audiences with thoroughly documented evidence of blunders, failures, and maladministration. In Quebec, the ghost of Riel stalked every *bleu*. It was all in vain. Macdonald emerged with 126 seats to 89 and even a tiny majority in French Canada. Sick and humiliated, Blake quit.

Every problem remained and some of them grew worse as Canada followed the world deeper into the depression. Macdonald had won because Blake had been too honest to offer any panaceas. For all his denunciations, the Liberal leader could see no fundamental alternative to the NP – except, of course, his own incorruptible management.

Others insisted that Canadians had alternatives to both the NP and to the shapeless, corrupt compromises of Macdonald's pluralist politics. Since 1884, when Torontonians had formed a branch of the British-born Imperial Federation League, their rising star had been the handsome, gifted young Tory politician named D'Alton McCarthy. His arguments had a powerful appeal for those English-speaking Canadians who believed that their country would be a simpler, happier place if the battle on the Plains of Abraham had represented a final solution. The Riel affair, with Quebec's apparent insistence that the Métis leader go free because he was French, struck McCarthy's followers as a case in point. McCarthy's cold, logical mind rejected the florid excesses of Orange bigotry; it bored through to even more dangerous doctrines. Nations, he insisted, grew from common experiences and language. Canada must be British or French, Protestant or Catholic. The decision must be made firmly and soon. His audiences uproariously agreed.

McCarthy's version of British-Canadian nationalism was a perfect foil for Mercier. In his own way, McCarthy echoed all of Mercier's criticisms of the *bleus.* As premier, Mercier was scrupulously fair to his English Protestant minority, but he displayed himself as the flamboyant champion of a French, Catholic Quebec as no *bleu* premier would ever have dared. He defied anti-clerical opinion by making Curé Labelle Deputy Minister for Colonization. He visited Paris and Rome and returned bedecked with French and papal decorations. He launched railways and public works Quebec could not afford but which it badly wanted. Above all, Mercier settled the tiresome old Jesuit estates issue in a way deliberately designed to tease the Equal Righters and to win more French and Catholic votes.

So far, the Jesuit estates issue had only divided Catholics. Confiscated in 1800 when the last Jesuit in Lower Canada had died, the rich estates had helped finance both Catholic and Protestant schools. When the Jesuits had returned to Canada in 1843, they asked for their land back. Rival Catholic orders had jealously guarded their share of revenue from the land and the quarrel had poisoned Church relations for decades. Mercier's trip to Rome gave him a solution: Protestants were happy with $60,000 in compensation, another $400,000 would be shared among Catholic groups. The pope would serve as final arbiter of the distribution of public funds. The Jesuits would regain their land.

Mercier knew perfectly well that any reference to the pope and Jesuits would draw out Protestant militants and they rose to the bait. Across Ontario and in English-speaking Quebec, protest meetings denounced papal meddling, appealed for "equal rights for all," and demanded that Ottawa disallow the Jesuit Estates Act. Horrified at the bigotry and even more by the political folly of followers like McCarthy who had joined the campaign, Macdonald refused. By a margin of 188 to 13, Parliament agreed with the prime minister. Across the country, newly created Equal Rights Associations hailed the dissenters as the "Noble Thirteen." In the rag-tag of Liberals and Tories, D'Alton McCarthy shone as a leader. Had McCarthy not preferred principle over ambition he might have succeeded Sir John A. Macdonald. In Canadian politics that made him a dangerous man.

In Manitoba, Norquay had been beaten by a lacklustre Liberal named Thomas Greenway. Within two years, Greenway's government was mired in failure and minor scandal. In the summer of 1889, McCarthy visited the West, drawing throngs to the parks and picnic grounds of raw prairie towns. In two decades, immigration had transformed the Red River colony into a little Ontario. Crowds cheered themselves hoarse at McCarthy's assault on separate schools and French. Westerners, he claimed, had the power "to make this a British country in fact as in name." Greenway Liberals, bereft of policy, heard the cheers and took the hint. In 1890, a new law gave the little province its first "national school" system, non-denominational, English-speaking, and publicly financed. Greenway's party won a new and bigger majority. The guarantees that missionaries and Métis had won in the Manitoba Act of 1870 had apparently vanished under majority assault. Now it was up to Ottawa to provide remedies.

Between them, Mercier and McCarthy severely damaged the *bleu*-Tory alliance that had effectively held power since 1854. In Manitoba, McCarthy's views had been seized on by Liberals. For the party's untried new federal leader, that was acutely embarrassing. In retiring, Blake had insisted that Wilfrid Laurier must be his successor. The young Quebec politician hesitated. He had neither the health nor the private wealth for the job. Even worse, in the mood of the times, could a French-speaking Catholic ever be accepted by the Grit strongholds of Ontario? Party elders agreed with the reservations but Laurier would do in the interim while a real decision was deferred. The interim leader lasted thirty-two years.

Party strategists agreed on one point: Blake had lost in 1887 because he failed to provide the "heroic remedy" Canadians wanted. One was now available. Erastus Wiman, a New York millionaire and Canadian expatriate, and Samuel Ritchie, the American who had developed Sudbury's nickel, urged a "Continental Union" of Canada and the United States with a common customs wall against the world. If full annexation followed, so be it. Massive Canadian emigration to the United States and the failure of the National Policy already marked Confederation as a failure. "CU," as the scheme was abbreviated, delighted inveterate free-traders like Sir Richard Cartwright. Ned Farrer, the lively journalist who now edited the *Globe*, took up the idea. So did Goldwin Smith, the former Oxford professor who had moved to Toronto, married a rich widow, and appointed himself Canada's resident intellectual. Annexation, Smith believed, was only a logical first step to an entire English-speaking union. Americans would accomplish what timid Canadians had failed to do: the full assimilation and reform of the French-Canadian Catholics.

For Laurier, annexation was repugnant; even a customs union was too heroic. A more moderate version – unrestricted reciprocity – was ideal. Tariff barriers between the two countries would vanish but each would set its own tariffs against the world. The economic details never bothered Laurier; it was politics that mattered. Unrestricted reciprocity satisfied party veterans like Cartwright. It gave the Liberals a compact slogan to match "NP." Above all, it captivated Ontario farmers, distracting them from Laurier's race and religion and his accented, if eloquent, English. Even loyal Canadians still pined for the old Reciprocity Agreement. The flood of emigrants depopulating Ontario as well as Quebec farms confirmed what visitors reported: the United States was booming while Canada stagnated. Friedrich Engels, Karl Marx's partner, finally had a good word for capitalism when he visited Canada in 1888. After three days of seeing decaying towns and ruined farmsteads, he realized "how necessary the feverish speculative spirit of the Americans is for the rapid development of a new country. . . ." Canadians who agreed could make their choice between CU and unrestricted reciprocity.

Either policy threatened an end to an independent Canada. Did anyone care? By the end of the 1880s, many agreed with Laurier himself: "We have come to a period in the history of this young country when premature dissolution seems to be at hand." In Winnipeg, the *Free Press* warned Newfoundland, bankrupt and considering Confederation, to give the Dominion a wide berth. "There are few provinces, if any, in it today that would not rejoice to be out of it." J. W. Longley, the Liberal who had tried in 1887 to repeal Nova Scotia's membership in Confederation, now travelled the United States as Wiman's agent promoting Continental Union.

Yet envy of the Americans mingled with fear and resentment. In 1890, Canadians had plenty of reason to see the harsh as well as the prosperous side of their neighbours. On both coasts, fisheries agreements had proved costly and painful. In the Bering Sea, American warships seized Canadian sealing vessels in the name of conservation while American sealers went undisturbed. James Blaine, the new Secretary of State, had made his name with Irish voters as an enemy of Britain and Canada. In Congress, the new McKinley tariff promised to end Canada's important grain trade across the border. In his speaking tours in 1890, Macdonald found that farmers could talk of little else.

The Old Chieftain's first notion was to outflank Laurier. He would seek a modest new reciprocity agreement and unveil it for the inevitable 1891 election. But Blaine refused to see an official delegation from a mere British colony. He then told a curious congressman that he knew of no Canadian negotiations, and the scheme blew up.

Macdonald was forced into another strategy – bolder, more dangerous, and yet far closer to his heart. The talk of dissolution and annexation and continental union disgusted him. In 1887, he had fought a winter campaign with draughty meeting halls, icy sleigh-rides, and long hours in unheated railway cars; he did not want another, but time was not on his side. On February 2, 1891, Macdonald called the election. Experts foresaw defeat. Yet, as long as he lived, the old Conservative alliance would survive. Business would fill the party coffers to protect the NP, and William Van Horne could promise that every CPR employee was "a circumcised Tory." And one issue might again pull weary voters back to the Conservatives: loyalty. Louis Kribs, a German-Canadian journalist, coined the slogan: "The Old Man, the Old Flag, the Old Policy."

Across Canada, even in Quebec, Macdonald could summon personal loyalty. There was more. "A British subject I was born, a British subject I will die," he told his audiences. "With my utmost effort, with my latest breath, will I oppose the 'veiled treason' which attempts with sordid means and mercenary proffers to lure our people from their allegiance." Posters, more elaborate than in any earlier elections, depicted Laurier and Cartwright negotiating with Americans behind the Old Chieftain's back. Two weeks into the campaign, Macdonald revealed the "treason": printers' proofs of a pamphlet by Edward Farrer not just arguing for annexation but showing precisely how America could squeeze Canadians into surrender. Since Ned Farrer edited the leading Liberal newspaper, the link to Laurier hardly needed to be made.

Laurier was not helpless. In Quebec, Mercier gave his full support. In Ontario, Mowat was staunch and as unquestionably pro-British as Macdonald. The Grit farmers liked the Liberal trade policy. So did Quebec farmers, for all the warnings from their bishops that annexation might result. On March 5, the great loyalty campaign ended. In Quebec, Laurier took 37 seats to 28; in Ontario, Macdonald emerged with a mere 4-seat margin. It was the rest of Canada – the "shreds and patches," as Cartwright called them – that settled the outcome: for Macdonald, 121 seats, for Laurier, 94. The margin came not only from the CPR-dominated regions but also from the Maritimes, where the call of British loyalty had worked.

Three months later, Macdonald was dead. The campaign had killed him. He died believing that he had saved the country he had created. Many of the nation's three-quarters of a million voters felt that they knew him, with his huge nose and his flying hair, his wit and his patient cynicism. "You'll never die, John A.," the crowds had shouted and now that he was suddenly gone, without an obvious successor, it seemed possible that the young Dominion might die with him. It dismayed his contemporaries and later generations that the undoubted first Father of Confederation could never provide uplifting moral lessons for the young. In fact, Macdonald had shown how Canada could be managed; with infinite cunning and patience, by bold visions and an infinity of small compromises, and by remembering that every enemy might someday be needed as a friend.

Macdonald had also taught patience. "A week is a long time in politics," said a later British prime minister. Macdonald knew it well. Riel, equal rights, Jesuit estates, had barely mattered in 1891, and with luck they might vanish forever. The census of that year furnished all the statistical evidence of depopulation critics of the NP desired, but the election was over when the figures appeared, and prosperity was building. British markets absorbed the wheat excluded by the McKinley tariff and asked for more. In the Kootenays of British Columbia, a mining boom began to roar, worrying only because it was American-financed. Talk was heard of a new railway through the Crowsnest Pass.

As Canadian self-confidence recovered, the Liberals could question themselves and their new leader. The 1891 session brought some comfort. J. Israel Tarte, the Quebec Tory organizer and Chapleau's ally, had slowly exposed the corrupt tangle of contracts and kickbacks in Langevin's Department of Public Works. Now, as a Liberal convert, Tarte forced the new Parliament into a session of scandals. One MP and a cluster of officials went to jail. Langevin might well have joined them but for a timely resignation. Liberal rejoicing was premature. Suddenly, Honoré Mercier's own corruption lay exposed in the scandalous finances of the Baie des Chaleurs Railway. All Canada could know how his luxurious journeys to Paris and Rome had been financed. Provincial Conservatives swept the discredited regime from office and then settled down to the dry, unpopular business of restoring Quebec's financial credit. Mercier countered Langevin. All politicians were tarred with the same brush.

Liberal troubles were not over. Blake and even Mowat had seen the annexationist implications of Laurier's policy of unrestricted reciprocity. Both men had loyally kept silent, but now, with the election over, Blake explained in a public letter why he had not stood again in West Durham. His letter virtually accused his fellow Liberals of plotting treason. It was all that Macdonald could have wished.

Blake himself never expected the devastating consequences of his letter. After every general election, the parties laid a host of challenges for electoral malpractice. Always, party managers had met, traded off cases and settled on a few to be fought through the courts and in by-elections. This time, with their coffers bulging, the Tories insisted on trying every charge. The Liberals, penniless, had no means to defend themselves. In a flood of by-elections, the West Durham letter sent the party to defeat. By 1895, the Tory majority had climbed from thirty-one to sixty-three. To many Liberals, it was proof enough that Laurier's leadership had been a sad mistake. Even without the Old Chieftain, the Tories seemed unbeatable.

Appearances deceived. One small nagging issue slowly tore the government apart: the Manitoba schools.

Macdonald had put off the issue, as he had so much else. A strong successor could have made a decision, confident that the inevitable turbulence would have settled in the four or five years before another election. No competent lawyer could question the issues. As a province, it was obvious that Manitoba could enact its Schools Act. Under the remedial sections of the Manitoba Act, Ottawa was equally obliged to take action to restore the rights of the French and Catholic minority. The questions of majority rights, Protestantism, or a mythical compact of founding nations were not at stake: the only issue was the political will to enforce the law.

Macdonald had no strong successor. Instead, a cabinet of feeble ministers chose old Sir John Abbott, the one-time annexationist of 1849, because he was "not particularly obnoxious to anybody." If Abbott had then promoted the ambitious Joseph Chapleau to be his lieutenant he might have found himself a new Cartier, but he would also have hurt poor Sir Hector Langevin's feelings. Abbott did nothing, and by November 1892 he was gone, fed up with politics.

Abbott's successor was inevitable: Sir John Thompson. Rarely had a more decent or honourable man come to Ottawa. His wisdom and ability were apparent in the Criminal Code and his other reforms as Minister of Justice. Dignified, an able debater, widely knowledgeable, Thompson had one political affliction, his conversion to Catholicism. As prime minister, he could never rise up and flatten the bigots who called him "pervert." He would not promote Chapleau because the Orangemen would have protested, so the last great *bleu* left for gilded retirement as lieutenant-governor of Quebec. Thompson was left with the extremes, F. A. Angers, an ultramontane *Castor* whom Chapleau had despised, and N. Clarke Wallace, past grand master of the Orange Lodge.

For all his sober virtues, Thompson was not the man to solve the Manitoba issue. Instead, he sent it back to the courts for two more years, forcing the Manitoba minorities to wait and showing even the most patient French Canadian that Ottawa would do almost anything to avoid upholding equality of language and religion in the West. Only a month before the judicial committee decided the obvious – that Ottawa had the right to impose remedial legislation – Thompson suddenly died at Windsor Castle while visiting Queen Victoria.

By rights, Sir Charles Tupper should have become prime minister but in the cabinet some ministers shuddered at the thought of the decisive, bullying "War Horse of the Cumberland." They were saved by an unexpected ally. Lord Aberdeen, a Scottish Liberal, was now governor general, but it was the formidable Lady Aberdeen who was in charge. Like many others, though for obscure reasons, she detested Tupper. Left to herself, she might have summoned Laurier, but her husband compromised. Another ancient veteran, Senator Mackenzie Bowell, an honest but indecisive Orangeman, followed Thompson. All hope of firm action on Manitoba faded. First Angers and then Wallace left the cabinet. Canadians, once again in a state of gloom after a new world-wide economic crash in 1893, could divert themselves with the government's fumbling.

First, Bowell politely asked Manitoba to mend its ways. Clifford Sifton, the province's able attorney-general, waited eight months before saying no. Seven federal cabinet ministers, in January 1896, resigned in a body to force the hopeless Bowell to quit. First Bowell branded them a "Nest of Traitors"; then he took them back. Parliament, nearing the end of its five-year term, set out to debate remedial legislation for the Manitoba minority while the Liberals held up proceedings with endless speeches. In May, the session expired.

Manitoba was as dangerous to Laurier as it was to the Tories. The Liberal leader had fumbled his first test; the second seemed even harder. In 1893, the Liberals met in Ottawa in their first national convention, buried "unrestricted reciprocity" and came up with a compromise. They did not resolve the Manitoba issue. Laurier was caught between the Protestant Liberals of Ontario and Manitoba and the pledge, brought by the great missionary from the Northwest, Father Lacombe, that Quebec's bishops would rise as one man to support remedial legislation.

Canada in the 1890s seemed aflame with religious conflict. The fires set by the Equal Rights Association had not gone out. In 1894, a Protestant Protective Association in Ontario had elected fourteen members against Oliver Mowat. In Quebec, the old

Holy War against the Liberals was being fanned into life. What could a French-Canadian Catholic with a following in Protestant Canada do?

The answer was that he would do nothing. It was the first proof that Laurier was Sir John A.'s true disciple. Israel Tarte, the ex-*bleu*, was now his closest confidant. In Quebec, where the turncoat had applied his remarkable talents to building a Laurier machine, Tarte made a crucial discovery: ordinary French Canadians knew little and cared less about Manitoba. They did not intend to go there. They did not care much for the few who had. On the other hand, with both Macdonald and Mercier gone, and a colourless Conservative government in Quebec City, *Canadiens* yearned for a real political leader. Wilfrid Laurier was the only candidate.

Faced with this shrewd analysis, Laurier's course was clear: silence and inaction. It was, after all, the ultimate privilege of an opposition leader. Forced to speak, Laurier recalled the old French fable of the man who had shed his coat for the sun, not the wind. Coercion, he warned, would never work: "If it were in my power, I would try the sunny way." It was a message that Tarte could sell on Laurier's behalf; he believed in it himself. Outside Quebec, Laurier could preach provincial rights. It was now a safe doctrine everywhere.

On April 23, the 1896 election campaign began. By prior agreement, Tupper took over as prime minister, the fifth in five years. Everywhere in Tory ranks, he found division and defection. Chapleau refused to help the party that had ignored him; secretly he sent *bleu* supporters to Laurier. In Ontario, Tory candidates preached hostility to the remedial legislation they had supposedly spent months trying to push through Parliament; in Quebec, the Conservatives proclaimed their devotion to minority rights. Above all, they counted on the bishops. When the bishops met, they proclaimed it "a great wrong" to back any candidate who refused to back remedial action. Promptly, all but eight of Laurier's Quebec candidates swore their support for remedial legislation. Only Bourget's disciple, Bishop Laflèche, issued his customary flaming denunciation of the Liberals. He was echoed by some Ontario Protestants. A Liberal vote, warned one Methodist preacher, "would stare the voter in the face at Judgement Day and condemn him to eternal perdition."

Despite the air of religious intolerance, clerical threats had surprisingly little effect in 1896. In fact, it was Sir Charles Tupper who was his party's chief asset. The dogged old man, tirelessly bullying his worn-out party machine into action, could not deliver a victory; he certainly prevented a rout. Though both D'Alton McCarthy and N. Clarke Wallace campaigned as hard for Laurier as they did for themselves, Tupper revived the old issues of industry and tariff protection. When the polls closed, Laurier's Liberals had won 118 seats to Tupper's 88. The Patrons of Industry, rustic pioneers for the third parties of the future, elected three members from Ontario.

In an election full of ironies and reversals, the greatest was in Manitoba. Only with great difficulty could the two Protestant champions, Sifton and McCarthy, get themselves elected. Manitobans voted forty-seven per cent for the party of remedial legislation, and only thirty-five per cent for the Liberals.

A political revolution was complete. Canadians in 1896 could not know it, but the Liberals would prove even more durable in office than the Conservatives. Neither period of hegemony was unbroken. Macdonald had lost to Mackenzie; Laurier would lose to Robert Borden. Yet both parties would regain power and cling to it because Macdonald and Laurier each mastered the compromises that made Canada possible.

Like most revolutions, the political upheaval that occurred in Canada between 1886 and 1896 changed symbols, not substance. The Liberals had won and would continue to win if they remembered their core of support in Quebec, the firm guidance of the business community, and the scattered, contradictory grievances of the rest of Canada. Sir John A. Macdonald had found his successor at last.

PART III

"THE CENTURY OF CANADA"

I

Flourishing

Later, Canadians would know that 1896 was one of the decisive years of their history. At the time, they barely noticed. Of course politics and the election were national preoccupations. On the other hand, few Canadians were bothered by a dispute between Venezuela and British Guiana that almost brought Britain and the United States into war – with Canada as the inevitable battleground. Apart from buying a few rifles and machine guns for her ill-equipped militia, the Dominion did nothing. In Britain, as we shall see, the consequences were much more profound. History rarely shows its significance all at once.

Canadians also ignored other vital events of the year. Washington announced the end of homesteading on public lands. Manitoba offered William Mackenzie and his burly partner Donald Mann $7000 a mile to build a line from Gladstone to Dauphin. They agreed. In August, a man known as "Lying George" Carmack, with two Indian companions, Skookum Jim and Tagish Charlie, discovered a little gold near the Klondike River.

All three developments were probably as important to Canadians as Laurier's 1896 election victory. So were others. Gold, pouring out of South African mines by the 1890s, would send prices for food and other natural products climbing. Shipping rates stayed low, continuing the slow strangulation of an old Maritime industry but making it feasible again to pour wheat into the European market. At Niagara Falls in 1895, workmen began the first hydroelectric installation. When Canadian engineers had solved the problem of winter freeze-up, "white coal" would provide a basis for dramatic industrial growth.

Instead of hope, most Canadians in 1896 shared a durable gloom. The Bank of Commerce reported in June on a year "of constant anxiety and almost unexampled difficulty in making profits and avoiding losses." Farmers grumbled at the McKinley tariff. Worse would come when the Republicans, as now seemed inevitable, returned to power. A promising cattle trade with Britain ended abruptly with severe quarantine regulations.

Meanwhile, Laurier's victorious Liberals took power. The hand-over was graceless. Tupper had made a post-election bid to cram every vacant judgeship and Senate seat with a Tory. The Aberdeens refused to sign the appointments, and the old man resigned in a snarling constitutional fury. Most Canadians were amused at Tupper's failure to fill jobs before voting day, when the patronage might have won him votes or campaign funds.

The new prime minister would make no such errors. Laurier looked frail, but he had grown tougher with age. Voters and even colleagues knew him as an elegant, courtly man, with an aura that could inspire love but never familiarity. Laurier had no taste for laborious detail; he could be captivated by ideas and he had the language to captivate others. His ministers sometimes came to believe that Laurier was a charming lightweight, to be used for their purposes. Such men were dismissed with swift, icy ruthlessness; they found themselves so isolated that they could not even avenge themselves. On the low road of politics as on the high, Laurier was a consummate expert.

He showed his skills immediately. The new cabinet was the ablest Canada had yet seen. William Fielding, one of three provincial premiers brought to Ottawa, took finance. Cartwright, still the unrepentant free-trader, was relegated to trade and commerce. The tariff would be safe with Fielding. Old *rouge* comrades were set aside. Tarte, the link with the *bleus*, would wield the immense patronage of public works. To settle Manitoba, Laurier adopted more than "sunny ways." To earn his cabinet post, Clifford Sifton helped talk Thomas Greenway into a compromise. Manitoba's minorities could go to school in their own language if they could form classes of ten or more students. Religious instruction would occur at the end of the day. Catholic bishops threatened new holy wars at the inadequacy of the settlement, but a papal envoy insisted on restraint. The old, dangerous issue vanished and the bishops found some pleasure in dealing with a French and Catholic prime minister.

Laurier took office with no real policies. He simply inherited the old NP. History played into his hands. Essentially, the National Policy had rested on false assumptions. In the 1880s, Canada was not yet an east-west economy. Her products went to Britain, the United States, or stayed home unsold. Immigrants would never go to the Northwest while good American land remained. Macdonald's policy flew in the face of facts. Suddenly, the facts changed. American public land was closed in 1896. The Canadian prairies became the "Last Best West." Rising world prices and cheap shipping created a world market for the hard spring wheat from Canada. It was now Laurier who could claim that "this scientific tariff of ours" safeguarded a booming western market for Canadian manufacturers.

Laurier's good fortune was as much an accident as was Carmack's discovery of gold, with the resulting fever that summoned swarms of prospectors to the Yukon. The Klondike made few durable fortunes and established no permanent industry. By 1899 the bonanza was over. The gold rush poured a brief but dramatic economic stimulus into British Columbia and Alberta, and it drew a flood of attention to Canada. The photographs of sourdoughs and the Chilkoot Pass did not dispel the Dominion's image of "Our Lady of the Snows": they did replace the impression of stagnant decay absorbed by Engels in 1888 with a vision of dynamism and wealth and of firm law and order enforced by scarlet-coated policemen.

As Macdonald's heir, Laurier responded to the Klondike discovery much as the Old Chieftain might have. Mounted Police, then troops, were sent because order was vital, not merely for its own sake but to give Americans in nearby Alaska no pretext for intervention. A railway link was considered but abandoned as too costly and slow. By 1899, when many of the thirty thousand people began thinking of leaving, a Yukon territorial government was in place.

It was probably Canada's good fortune that so many Americans had always believed that the northern prairie was as cold as the Yukon. This illusion had discouraged neighbourly covetousness. Now, with no other outlet for the younger sons who had always gone west to homestead, Americans came to see for themselves. Clifford Sifton, minister of the interior, had the happy historical role of presiding over the inevitable. He did so with flair. Editors and farm leaders joined guided tours. Lush prairie produce was sent to win prizes at agricultural shows. The claims of Red Fife wheat were trumpeted until it was supplanted, in 1903, by an even finer product of the Dominion's experimental farms, Charles Saunders' Marquis. Visitors revelled in Sifton's philosophy. "One of the principal ideas western men have," he boasted, "is that it is right to take anything in sight provided nobody else is ahead of them."

American homesteaders, often with an Ontario ancestor or two, made an easy transition. Most had experience in dryland farming and the backing of a family farm in Kansas or Minnesota. Sifton, however, was not content to wait. Bales of pamphlets and speakers armed with magic lantern slides set off for the traditional recruiting territory of Britain. Colonization agents waited at Hamburg and Bremen, where European immigrants would set sail for America. In his aim of populating the Canadian West, Sifton was bluntly indifferent to the old limits of race and language. Instead, he welcomed "stout, hardy peasants in sheepskin coats," who could endure pioneering hardships and make the prairie prosper. If they were Poles or Germans or Ukrainians the "national schools" he had won for Manitoba would turn their children into good Canadians.

The newcomers justified Sifton's expectations. The North West Mounted Police, whose systematic patrols and hard-headed welfare programs were as vital to prairie homesteading as railways and land offices, judged "Sifton's sheepskins" with a stern but practical eye and found them acceptable. Others did not pass their test. Keir Hardie, the Scottish socialist, was shocked to find that English labourers were among the least favoured species of settler. Employers complained that they often brought trade union ideas with them. Meanwhile Canadian labour protested immigration policies that undermined their wages with floods of cheap labour.

With or without Sifton, the Canadian West's time had come. Between 1896 and 1911, more than a million people poured into the region. Wheat production rose from 29 to 209 million bushels a year. A spider web of railway branch lines spread across the prairie, built mainly by homesteaders eager for cash between seeding and harvest time. Ten miles was as far as any settler could haul wheat in a horse-drawn wagon. Where rail lines crossed, towns grew up. In the Sifton free-enterprise spirit, land speculators were free to build costly dreams of future metropolises on local pride and cupidity. Sometimes the land speculators struck paydirt. In 1900, Saskatoon was a general store. In 1902, it was hard to find twenty houses to make it a village. Three years later it was a city, and the 1911 census found twelve thousand people, a university, and two transcontinental railways.

Prairie settlers had little in common with the self-sufficient backwoodsmen in Upper Canada or the *habitants* of New France. Beyond turf for their first leaky sod hut and a flurry of birds and small animals for the pot, the land provided nothing but a cash crop. Pioneers were consumers. To build homes, they needed lumber from British Columbia and nails, glass, and furniture from the East. Even fuel for the long prairie winter came from coal mines that Sir Alexander Galt's sons had profitably developed in the foothills of the Rockies. It was all very much as Sir John A. Macdonald would have predicted, with the infuriating exception that Liberals were in power, taking the political and (in Sifton's case) the personal profits.

In 1897, for example, it was perfectly in the NP tradition that the CPR would receive a handsome subsidy for pushing a line through the Crowsnest Pass to Vancouver. This restored a Canadian presence in a region American mining companies were treating as their own backyard. The CPR gained subsidies, a new region, and an unexpected dividend, the rich Sullivan mine at Trail. In return, the railway agreed to a perpetual freeze on the freight rates for wheat heading east and manufactured goods heading west. In an age of stable prices, the Crowsnest rate seemed like a fair deal.

Meanwhile, in 1898, unremarked by most Canadians, the Intercolonial Railway finally reached Montreal in its long struggle to become profitable. In its patronage-ridden career, the ICR had served its region as best it could. Unlike the CPR, which thirsted for profits, the ICR wanted political friends, and it had found them by cutting its rates. It did so still. Maritime producers got rates as much as fifty per cent lower than in central Canada – and even lower ones could be negotiated. While the Maritime age of wood, wind, and water was ending, industrialism had already taken its place. In 1870, New Brunswick's per-capita manufacturing had been as high as the national average, and it kept on growing. From 1900 to 1920, manufacturing grew four-fold in Nova Scotia and five-fold in New Brunswick. Two iron and steel complexes developed; so did sugar refining, clothing and shoe factories, and a host of engineering and hardware manufacturers. Thanks to the ICR's favours, even prairie residents used Simms's brushes, ate Ganong's chocolates, and spread Crosby's molasses. The Maritimes grumbled and prospered, a satisfying combination.

At times, Laurier could even improve on Macdonald. Caught among his party's protectionists and free-traders, with a rising chorus of imperialists in Toronto and English-speaking Montreal, a fumbler might have failed. Between them, Fielding and Laurier united such disparate forces by proclaiming, in the 1897 budget, a unilateral "imperial preference." The tariff reductions hurt few entrenched interests, pleased tariff cutters, and helped Laurier cut an imperial figure when he went to London for the Diamond Jubilee of the venerable Queen Victoria. British audiences delighted in the frail, eloquent French Canadian. Private sessions were a little different. The colonial secretary, Joseph Chamberlain, found the newly knighted Sir Wilfrid obdurate in resisting British schemes to win Canadian commitments to imperial defence.

This, too, was in the Macdonald tradition. The old man had despised "over-washed Englishmen." D'Alton McCarthy's "imperial federation" Macdonald had dismissed as nonsense. British overtures for military aid in 1885 during the Sudan crisis had been politely rejected. Militia colonels "anxious for excitement or notoriety," according to Macdonald, would not speak for Canada.

In 1891, when Macdonald had proclaimed "a British subject I was born, a British subject I will die," he had meant no more than had Laurier in 1897, when he declared to London audiences, "I am British to the core." Neither man could contemplate being an American; the alternative was to be British. The English were something else.

Among some English-speaking Canadians, the British connection was becoming more important. To McCarthy and imperial federationists in the 1880s, being British had also been an alternative to the shame of being merely Canadian, the people of a failing country that still refused to be American. Now, in the post-1896 prosperity, the Canadian mood was vastly more positive. British imperialism, in its sensationalist heyday, offered the vulgar conceit of racial superiority. Its American counterpart, triumphant in Cuba and the Philippines in 1898, offered the same appeal. Sprayed by the same effusions, many Canadians accepted a flattering new kind of "imperial nationalism." If, as British and American imperialists insisted, northern races would dominate those in warmer climates, who could be more northerly than Canadians? In no distant era, Canada would dominate the British Empire. Meanwhile, in the novels of Gilbert Parker and the Rev. C. W. Gordon (writing as Ralph Connor) they could rejoice in the fictional triumphs of physical and moral courage. They could yearn for Canada to be summoned to play a heroic role.

Such dreams, fostered by an outspoken English-Canadian elite, were not universal. Imperialism was as absurd as ever to families with their roots deep in Ontario or Maritime soil and their minds preoccupied with economic realities. *Canadiens* remembered Mercier's warning that the imperialists would conscript their sons and send them to perish on the burning Sahara. On suitable occasions it was polite to attribute *la survivance* to British justice; most French Canadians naturally preferred to keep the credit themselves. The clergy might preach a dutiful allegiance, but they could not urge love. No more than English Canadians did the *Canadiens* know or care what their partners in Confederation really felt.

Sir Wilfrid was almost uniquely knowledgeable. Years before, he had given Toronto his most memorable image of Canadian duality. Recalling the waters of the Ottawa River and the Great Lakes, meeting below the island of Montreal, he had declared: "There they run parallel, separate, distinguishable, and yet are one stream, flowing within the same banks. . . ." Under Laurier, pure luck had given Liberalism an almost mystical association with prosperous times. It was Laurier himself who committed his party to the holy grail of national unity.

His test came in 1899 with the crisis in distant South Africa. Two tiny Boer republics had concluded that preservation of their Old Testament lifestyle compelled them to drive the British into the sea. In ordinary times, Britain would have met the challenge alone but her own diplomacy had isolated her from the European powers. The approaching war might even be deterred if self-governing colonies voluntarily displayed their solidarity; at the very least, Europe would be impressed. Laurier cheerfully won unanimous Canadian parliamentary approval for Britain's opposition to the Boers. An official contingent was another matter. If Britain were in real danger, Canada would respond with utter devotion. The Boers posed no such threat. Of course the British were perfectly entitled to recruit soldiers in Canada. Alternatively, the outspoken Tory MP and imperial loyalist Colonel Sam Hughes promised to raise thousands of volunteers. Neither arrangement met Britain's need to display imperial solidarity to a hostile world.

Laurier's cautious policy collapsed within two weeks of the outbreak of war in October 1899. In Toronto and Montreal, concerted press campaigns by Tory and popular newspapers demanded action. Embarrassing leaks in Ottawa about a planned contingent suggested government duplicity. Some Liberal ministers pressed for an official force. On October 14, Laurier gave in. In an unexpected display of efficiency, a battalion of a thousand volunteers was recruited, equipped, and despatched to Cape Town by the end of the month. Another contingent left early in 1900. Donald A. Smith, now Lord Strathcona and Canadian high commissioner in London, sent a mounted regiment at his own expense. Though the British paid almost the full cost of the troops in South Africa, the men served as Canadians, performed well, and incidentally, came home with a stronger sense of national identity than stay-at-homes would have expected. Under Colonel William Otter, the Canadians had been trained and disciplined like regulars, not like wild colonials. The precedent would stick.

The warlike experience might have united Canadians in a new pride, as it did Australians. In fact, it added a new cause for division. In Montreal, news of a British victory led to boisterous fights between French- and English-speaking university students. In Ontario, Tories insisted that Laurier had been controlled by the wicked J. Israel Tarte and that French Canadians had proved their disloyalty in Britain's hour of need. As usual, one extremism called forth its counterpart. Jules-Paul Tardivel, the Kentucky-born convert to Quebec ultramontane nationalism, offered his readers new and more passionate arguments against Canada in his Montreal-based journal, *La Vérité*.

Those were not the arguments of the bearded young MP for Labelle. Henri Bourassa, Papineau's grandson, was a lifelong admirer of Laurier but he was too intelligent, too logical, and too proud to be anyone's disciple. The despatch of an official contingent had shocked him and he forced Parliament to debate the issue. Had Laurier bowed to imperial coercion? Had he set a fearful precedent for future British wars? If so much had been done against two tiny, distant nations, Bourassa asked, "how many men shall we send, and how many millions shall we expend to fight a first class power or a coalition of powers?" From Laurier, there came only denials that any precedent had been set.

Bourassa was no threat – yet. As the 1900 election approached, it was Ontario that threatened Laurier's majority. Across Canada, poor Tupper's collection of government scandals and misjudgements dwindled to absurdity in such unexpected prosperity. It was no real argument to claim that the Liberals had stolen Conservative policies: political larceny was no crime. Ontario Tories, left to their own devices, could exploit only the old racial and religious hatreds. The Liberals cheerfully ensured that *Canadien* and Irish voters were listening. A phrase of Tupper's, "Laurier is too English for me," was torn from context and blazoned across Ontario by the Liberals – admittedly to little effect. Tupper took Ontario but little else. Laurier held 133 seats to the Conservatives' 80. The Tories had become what the Liberals had been, a party of outsiders, tied to the prejudices of Ontario. An Ottawa editor mourned that his party had "Francophobia on the brain."

The need for national unity had persuaded a reluctant Laurier to send troops to South Africa. So had a more pragmatic concern: British diplomatic leverage was needed for Canada's final boundary dispute. In 1898, a joint high commission had left two painful issues of Canadian-American relations unsettled: reciprocity and the Alaska boundary.

Until the Klondike discoveries, no one had bothered about the vague, straggling line down misleading maps of the Alaska Panhandle, or about the 1825 Anglo-Russian treaty that had placed the line there. Surely British pressure would help the Americans to be reasonable. Nothing was more unlikely. President Teddy Roosevelt, in the full flush of American imperialism, was in a bullying mood. Businessmen in Seattle and Tacoma were eager for northern wealth. Britain had decided its North American course in 1896: war was not an option. Moreover, three-quarters of a century of neglect had enfeebled a weak Canadian-British case. On October 17, 1903, the British delegate, Lord Alverstone, refused to cause "an international calamity." He sided with three partisan American commissioners, leaving two equally partisan Canadians to cry foul. Roosevelt's view of the Alaska boundary prevailed. Canada was shut out from access to the Yukon.

More fortunate than Macdonald in 1871, Laurier was free to blame the British for the Alaska boundary fiasco. It is still hard to see Lord Alverstone's crime. He had avoided a war for which Canadians were as unprepared as the British and in which they would have suffered vastly more. Economics, not boundaries, had already condemned the Yukon to be bypassed for another forty years. That barely mattered. The Boer War had fostered Canadian military nationalism. The Alaska disappointment prodded Canadians to demand diplomatic independence and a new, purely

Canadian nationalism. This was now Henri Bourassa's ideal. He was echoed and joined by John Skirving Ewart, a Winnipeg lawyer who had helped defend Riel in 1885 and Manitoba's Catholics in the 1890s. In *The Kingdom of Canada* (1908), Ewart first argued the disturbing new notion that Canada might stand on her own as a fully sovereign state. "How are we to unify Canada?" he asked, and answered himself. "Make her a nation in name as well as in fact."

Few Canadians would follow Ewart and Bourassa. Only a minority cared about such matters, and most of those felt happier with Laurier's vague bid to the British to "call us to your councils," or his insistence that Canada would not be sucked into "the vortex of European militarism." In the wake of South Africa, Joseph Chamberlain had no plans for formal military commitments. By taking over British dockyards and fortifications at Halifax and Esquimalt in 1905, Ottawa sought to preempt pressures at home or from London for more adventurous roles in imperial defence.

Imperialism and nationalism were distractions from the main business of Canadians and immigrants alike. Both were eager to get rich, and Laurier approved. Much as he had once taken up unrestricted reciprocity to distract attention from divisive issues of race and religion, the Liberal leader perceived that prosperity and national unity went together. In his first term, Laurier had simply inherited and refined the National Policy. Safely reelected, he added a grandeur all his own.

By 1900, it was obvious that a single transcontinental rail line would not suffice for the expanding West. In 1901, bad management and lack of freight cars kept the CPR from moving more than a third of a bumper crop before freeze-up on Lake Superior. Angry farmers launched the Territorial Grain Growers' Association to protest the blockade and even took the railway to court. Expansion was the answer. "We want all the railways we can get," declared the Manitoba *Free Press*; farmers, promoters, contractors, politicians, and assorted boodlers agreed.

In the West, the CPR had a dangerous competitor in William Mackenzie and Donald Mann's Canadian Northern Railway. Its jerry-built tracks, laid by farmers in the spirit of an old-fashioned barn-raising and equipped with second-hand rolling stock, ran in a network north of the CPR line, heading west to Edmonton and east to Port Arthur to compete with the CPR terminus at Fort William. Lake ships had barely ten weeks to rush the western harvest down the lakes and canals to Montreal. In eastern Canada, the Grand Trunk was excluded from the western bonanza. Its new American-born manager, Charles Hays, finally admitted what most people had long suspected: the Chicago-to-Portland route would never pay a dividend. His long-suffering shareholders needed a true transcontinental to prosper.

The solution was obvious. The Grand Trunk and the Canadian-Northern should merge. Laurier even presided over a few meetings which unfortunately failed. Confident of prairie support, Mackenzie and Mann demanded control. Hays disparaged "that little bunch of lines up around Winnipeg" and reminded Liberals of past political services. Laurier might have tried a shotgun marriage, but he had no such intentions. The visionary and the politician took over. In 1903, Laurier unveiled his program. If the Tories had boasted of the CPR, the Liberals would do even better. If Sifton was right, the West would have twelve million people within one generation. Boldness was justified. A government-built National Transcontinental would start from the Intercolonial headquarters at Moncton, cross the St. Lawrence at Quebec City, and traverse the clay-belt region of northern Quebec and Ontario on the way to Winnipeg. The Grand Trunk would lease the line for ninety-nine years and construct its own Grand Trunk Pacific line to Prince Rupert on the Pacific coast. As for Mackenzie and Mann, they were free to come east whenever they were ready.

Canadians gasped. Hardly an interest was untouched, from bankers and contractors to Quebec clergy and *nationalistes*, guaranteed new space for their dreams of colonization. Only the minister of railways, A. G. Blair, was angry, partly because he had never been consulted, partly because he favoured Mackenzie

and Mann. Laurier got rid of him. The opposition protested too –
with little more effect. Tupper's heir was an honest, unflamboyant
Halifax lawyer named Robert Borden. He was dismayed by the
folly of a scheme that left taxpayers to carry nine-tenths of the
cost while the Grand Trunk was almost guaranteed its profits.
Canadians, if they had paused to reflect, might have agreed.
Instead, Laurier cheered them on with a logic suited to a school
playground. "I am aware that this plan may scare the timid and
frighten the irresolute," he admitted, "but I may claim that every
man who has in his bosom a stout Canadian heart will welcome it
as worthy of this young nation. . . ."

Railway development pushed Canadians, for the first time,
toward their northern frontier. The National Transcontinental,
the Canadian Northern, and the Grand Trunk Pacific cut across
the Canadian Shield and the park belt that fringed the prairies. If
colonists faced a grim future farming the clay belt, a pulp and
paper industry would grow up from the now-accessible forests. So
would a mining industry. Its harbinger was the great complex
Francis Clergue had built with American capital at Sault Ste.
Marie. Ships of his Lake Superior Consolidated Corporation
brought iron ore, and trains of his Algoma Central hauled timber
and nickel ore to the mills and smelters Clergue housed in
impressive stone factory buildings. Tourists and promoters marvelled – until 1903 when the whole grandiose enterprise collapsed. Ontario's Liberal government glumly assumed the debts
and persisted in its dreams for what people called New Ontario.
Later that year, as the province's Temiskaming and Northern
Ontario railways pushed north, miners uncovered the richest silver deposits in the world at Cobalt. Other provinces envied and
imitated their neighbour.

Never in their history had Canadians experienced such a run of
prosperity. In 1904, they could re-elect the architect. Only a
scheme by the bitter A. G. Blair (backed by Mackenzie and Mann)
to buy up Liberal newspapers and turn them Tory briefly troubled
the Liberal chieftain. Laurier disposed of the plot by threatening
exposure, then he travelled the country with a message that set
rafters ringing. "Let me tell you, my fellow Canadians," the prime

minister told a packed audience in Toronto's Massey Hall, "that all the signs point this way, that the twentieth century shall be the century of Canada and of Canadian development. For the next seventy-five years, nay for the next hundred years, Canada shall be the star towards which all men who love progress and freedom shall come."

Torontonians cheered (though they voted Conservative). Even Laurier now accepted that old habit. He had rich compensations. Not since the Pacific Scandal election of 1874 had any party won such a majority of seats or votes; 138 Liberals to only 75 Conservatives. In Nova Scotia, every Tory – including Robert Borden – was beaten.

Prosperity certainly had its rewards.

2

Questioning

Voters rewarded Laurier as the political designer of their prosperity, but businessmen were the real heroes. This was a novelty. Canadians had never before attributed omniscience or patriotism to their industrial and financial magnates. For the most part, business leaders had led decorous, frugal lives, working long hours and deferring gratifications for the hereafter. They and their families ate much the same monotonous meals as humbler Canadians (though even the lower middle class expected to be served by a maid). They dressed for respectability, not the climate, and suffered without complaint.

The gulf between rich and poor was now opened wide. Aristocratic visitors to Canada marvelled at the vulgarity of the wealthy, not at their seeming absence. Huge and sometimes hideous new mansions sprouted in major cities. Elegant automobiles, often worth more than the prime minister's annual salary, stood at the front doors. Americans referred to their post-Civil War era of corrupt and speculative wealth as "The Great Barbecue." Laurier presided over the Canadian counterpart. Some of its leading beneficiaries "helped" Liberal ministers with their investments.

Businessmen also expected their desires to be respected. The righteous might grumble about cartels and the "trusts"; no serious corrective legislation was enacted. British Columbians clamoured against Oriental immigration, but so long as Sir James Dunsmuir, the province's chief coal-mine owner, wanted cheap labour for his mines, the Chinese suffered no more than a discriminatory head tax and a ban on bringing their wives. In

Ontario, small businessmen demanded publicly owned hydro-electricity delivered at cost instead of having the power of Niagara Falls left to an avaricious Toronto-based monopoly. When provincial Liberals backed the private monopoly in 1905, their scandal-ridden government lost power to the Tories. By 1907, Ontario's publicly owned hydro system, commanded by the autocratic Adam Beck, demonstrated the blessings of business socialism. In Quebec and Manitoba, the hydro developers wisely made peace with business critics.

Business sometimes had reforming instincts. Sir Clifford Sifton, a millionaire as well as a politician, turned the Canadian Commission of Conservation into a powerful if short-lived force for environmental improvements. He opposed power exports to the United States; worried publicly about pollution, drainage, forest fires, and migratory birds; and promoted town planning. Canada's cities, slum-ridden and mortally dangerous to small children, cried out for reform. In 1901, mayors Oliver Howland of Toronto and W. D. Lighthall of Westmount formed the League of Canadian Municipalities with the virtuous goal of eliminating politics and making city government "a business proposition."

Even in prosperity, businessmen grumbled endlessly about unions, anti-tariff farmers, politicians, and the relentless struggle for "a living profit." The strain of competition, some feared, led to "dyspepsia of the mind." It also led to a dramatic growth in joint stock ownership to finance the expensive new machinery, and a wave of mergers and consolidations after 1909 that fully justified the fears of enemies of "trusts" and critics of unearned wealth. A young Max Aitken, fresh from New Brunswick, earned $1.5 million in common stock for organizing Canada Cement and almost as much for creating the Steel Company of Canada. The fortune launched a British publishing and political career. Aitken would live much of his life as Lord Beaverbrook.

Admiration for businessmen and the affluence they had apparently created was widespread but not universal. Whether or not business methods could reform cities, industries helped to make them grimy, overcrowded, and slum-ridden. Electricity now lighted main streets and the wealthier districts of major cities, but the poles marched past the poorer streets without connections. Herbert Ames, a Montreal businessman-reformer, explored and dutifully catalogued incomes and living conditions in working-class wards of his city. Officials, clergy, and journalists did much the same work in Toronto, Winnipeg, Halifax, and Vancouver. Perhaps it was a sign of prosperity that anyone cared, even though investigation did not usually lead to substantial action.

The plight of the poor had an old and easy explanation. Men were masters of their fate – though it troubled softer consciences that women and children usually shared a man's misfortune. The Rev. E. H. Dewart in the Methodist *Christian Guardian* offered a brisk dose of the conventional wisdom: "The best anti-poverty society is an association of men who would adopt as their governing principle in life, industry, sobriety, economy and intelligence." In so hard-drinking a society as Canada, sobriety needed extra help. Temperance, transformed slowly into total abstinence and prohibition, had been the single most powerful social reform crusade in nineteenth-century Canada. Most Protestants and even a few Catholics endorsed it like an extra gospel, though it would not have been Canada if the French had not differed markedly from the English on the question. In 1898, when a national referendum favoured prohibition for Canada, Laurier had politely ignored the vote, ostensibly because less than half the population had voted, or because Quebec had been stoutly opposed.

The prohibition cause drew women into political life as defenders of the sacred institution of the family. Only rare eccentrics like Toronto's superintendent of schools, James L. Hughes, Tory, Orange, and educational reformer, insisted on the fundamental equality of men and women. More universal was a faith in "maternal feminism," the divinely sanctioned role of women as wives, mothers, and guardians of social convention against those heedless brutes, their husbands. The nurturing role grew as Victorian Canadians came to see their children not as undersized adults but as beings in a key stage of development. Nursing, teaching, perhaps even medicine, became logical extensions of the maternal role. So did social reform.

Canadian women went into politics not to win theoretical equality but to gain specific goals. The Women's Christian Temperance Union (founded at Owen Sound in 1874), in conjunction with broader organizations like the Dominion Alliance, attacked liquor. Adelaide Hunter Hoodless crusaded for pasteurization of milk and for university-based training in domestic science. Her Women's Institutes became another of the organizations which Canada has given the world. The National Council of Canadian Women, launched in 1893 by the redoubtable Lady Aberdeen, denounced liquor, divorce, prostitution, profiteering, and "the modern cult of self-indulgence and its god, pleasure."

Dominated by the wives of the elite, the Council insisted that women would do more good by gentle persuasion than by thrusting themselves into the corrupt world of politics. Not all agreed. Emily Stowe, Canada's first woman doctor, had pioneered the women's suffrage issue in Toronto in the 1880s. Her daughter, Amelia Stowe-Gullen, continued the crusade, but it was characteristic of the new Canadian West that the flame burned most brightly in the prairie cities. Nellie McClung, a novelist and ingenious publicist, burlesqued Manitoba's all-male legislature and its pompous premier, Sir Rodmond Roblin. Cora Hind, a brilliant Winnipeg crop-forecaster, and Emily Murphy, later an Alberta judge and a novelist whose best-known work dealt with drug addiction, were powerful allies. So were leaders of the West's agrarian movement. E. A. Partridge of the *Grain Grower's Guide* wondered pointedly why the vote was available to "the lowest imbruted foreign hobo" but not to Canadian women.

Though the National Council grew to two hundred fifty thousand members – about half as many people as backed Laurier in 1904 – the majority of Canadian women remained collectively silent. So did the mass of Canadian workers. Prosperity was by no means evenly shared. It dribbled slowly across the widening gulf between employer and employee. A powerful, if misleading, impression that the wealthy were self-made men was an effective antidote for egalitarian yearnings. The flood of immigrants, most of whom entered into direct competition with Canadian workers in factories and construction camps, was a more practical weapon against employee militancy. Devotion to the protective tariff and foreign investment coincided, in business ideology, with faith in a free labour market and abhorrence of foreign labour agitators. In 1903, a bill sponsored by Senator James Lougheed of Alberta would have sentenced such union organizers to two years in jail. It passed the Senate but the lower house was too busy to debate it.

In 1900, as a bid to win and organize workers' votes, the Liberals created a small Department of Labour. A promising and dependable young graduate student, William Lyon Mackenzie King (a grandson of the Upper-Canadian rebel) was put in charge. Among King's duties (executed by loyal Liberals in the tiny union movement) was collection of the first statistics on employment and cost of living. For the first time, labour union memberships were also counted. A statistic that business leaders did not cheer during the century's first decade was union growth; from twenty thousand in 1900 to a hundred and twenty thousand by 1911 – eight per cent of the entire labour force, male and female.

Organized labour was a feeble, divided critic of a prosperity that gave most Canadian workers no more than a mean and precarious subsistence. From Charlottetown to Vancouver, skilled workers joined international affiliates of the American Federation of Labour. When Ralph Smith, the Liberal president of the Trades and Labour Congress, tried to kick the internationals out of the organization, the TLC convention at Berlin, Ontario, in 1902 gave him the boot instead. Employers were left to run their own anti-AFL crusade, borrowing the approved American tools – strike-breakers, calls on the militia, and "yellow dog" contracts (solemn oaths extracted from employees never even to contemplate union membership on pain of fine and dismissal). From 1902, union growth was painfully slow; strikes grew longer and more bitter.

In Europe and even in the United States, the early twentieth century saw the emergence of powerful labour and socialist movements, strong and even violent challenges to business power. By contrast, Canada was really a backwater of radical and union activity. The small, doctrinaire Socialist Party of Canada actually won a few seats in the British Columbia legislature and an occasional municipal election across the country. A lengthy Alberta coal strike in 1906, just before the coldest winter in Western memory, publicised Mackenzie King's growing talent as a conciliator and led to the Industrial Disputes Investigation Act of 1907. By publicising issues and forcing negotiation, the IDI Act was probably more useful than its labour critics have ever admitted but neither King nor business could concede that unions had a right to exist as such or that workers had a right to bargain collectively. Long, violent, often unsuccessful strikes were waged over union recognition. In 1909-1910, most of Canada's tiny regular army stood guard over Cape Breton coal mines until starvation forced miners to abandon the international union of their choice.

Distance, small numbers, and divisions, not ideology, kept labour from becoming a national force. Skilled workers in craft unions had no links with the unorganized, unskilled majority. Only radical unions like the Western Federation of Miners and, later, the Industrial Workers of the World tried to organize the migrant army of "bunkhouse men" in construction, logging, and mining camps. They had meagre success. In Quebec, clergy and *nationalistes* did their best to shield *Canadiens* from socialist and materialist influences.

Where labour votes could be concentrated, they could elect populist candidates like Médéric Martin, the cigarmaker who became mayor of Montreal, or Alphonse Verville, president of the Trades and Labour Congress. In Toronto, Horatio Hocken, a Tory Orangeman, used his past leadership of a printers' strike to win labour votes. In return he gave the city parks, playgrounds, public baths, free milk for slum children, and a municipal abbatoir and cold storage to fight the meat trust. Infant mortality fell sharply, Toronto became more habitable, and its workers embraced the charms of Tory democracy.

Farmers rediscovered their political influence too. It was not easy. First the Grange of the 1870s and then the Patrons of the 1890s had collapsed in a wreckage of mismanaged co-operatives and political sell-outs. Only the grievances survived – the tariff, a weak bargaining position, rural depopulation, and jarring reminders of a disgraceful disrespect for the nation's primary producers. Canadian farmers grew sensitive to "Hey Rube" jokes and taunts.

In the West, farmers developed a heightened sense of exasperation. Eastern farms had diversified sufficiently that no climatic or market disaster was total. The western monoculture of wheat (in an unpredictable and often merciless climate) and the exactions of railways, elevator, and milling monopolies, and the Winnipeg Grain Exchange could easily reduce prairie farmers to penury. Rainfall, frost, soil conditions, and insects could not be helped, but once a farmer had hauled his grain ten miles to the only available elevator, he could hardly take it home again. The only answer to arrogant and dishonest elevator agents or to mysterious fluctuations of the commodity markets was political action and co-operation. The message might be preached by cautious Liberals like W. R. Motherwell, founder of the Territorial Grain Grower's Association, or passionate socialists like E. A. Partridge, editor of the influential *Grain Grower's Guide.* Farmers soon understood. So did governments. Across the vast West, farmers were the only voters in sight, and, unlike workers, their minds were not easily distracted.

A federal Grains Act in 1900, imposing regulations and inspectors, proved ineffective but instructive. Partridge successfully promoted a Grain Growers' Grain Company and a reluctant Manitoba government finally coerced the Grain Exchange into granting it a seat. Farmer-owned elevator companies spread across the West. So did farm organizations and subscriptions to Partridge's *Grain Grower's Guide.* At least some readers absorbed his view that the story of the West was "a history of heartless robbery . . . by the Big 'vested' interests – so called from the size of their owners' vests."

One prairie issue was the political future of the North West Territories. By 1897, a long campaign led by a Regina lawyer, Frederick Haultain, won responsible government for the Territories. In 1904, both parties promised provincial status, and a year later Laurier was ready to act. By creating the two provinces of Alberta and Saskatchewan, split at the sixtieth meridian, he separated Haultain, the grand old man of territorial politics, from most of his supporters, and he launched both new provinces with strong Liberal governments. By keeping federal control of land and resources, Laurier also guaranteed continued free homesteads and a friendly climate for investors. A generous financial settlement, soon extended to other provinces as a "final and unalterable" resolution of old fiscal arguments, guaranteed political peace and economic prosperity for the prairies.

There was one small problem. The new provinces assumed that they would continue their Ontario-style system of schools; even Protestants were reconciled to some minority Catholic rights. Privately, however, Laurier had promised Catholic bishops a return to their full equality of 1875. In the draft autonomy bills, he had quietly inserted an appropriate guarantee. An astonished and furious Clifford Sifton resigned. Fielding threatened to follow. Bitter at the "betrayal" by his Protestant colleagues, Laurier compromised. The conflict became public. Richard Bedford Bennett, the Alberta Tory leader, tried to light the Ontario heather with speeches against Catholic-inspired coercion. More savage by far was the anger of men like Bourassa. By retreating, Bourassa insisted, Laurier had made the West "a land of refuge for the scum of all nations." Armand Lavergne, once Laurier's friend and now Bourassa's chief supporter, went farther. "In constituting the French Canadian . . . the equal in rights and privileges to the Doukhobor or the Galician who had just disembarked," he declared, "we have opened a gulf between eastern and western Canadians which nothing will fill."

One might argue, of course, that French Canadians showed little sign of wishing to share the West and that Laurier's leadership was enough evidence of their influence. The phenomenal birthrate, sustained since 1760, a provincial government, a self-confident Catholic clergy, and a proud culture should have been protection enough for the French fact in North America. Instead, French Canada in the 1900s experienced an acute crisis of self-confidence, aggravated by Liberal policies and the Laurier prosperity.

The West had few attractions for the *Canadiens* but they could see the floods of immigrants hurried through Quebec by Sifton's agents. Many of them halted in Montreal to create Jewish, Greek, and Italian ghettoes with customs and languages even stranger

and more unwelcome than the English and Irish. British Canadians might grumble about foreigners but they were as confident
as Sifton that assimilation would come. French Canadians saw
only the menace of people who neither knew nor respected the old
racial compact and compromises.

Some French Canadians, like Rodolphe Forget, J. D. Rolland,
and François Béique, became millionaires in the resulting business bonanza; but most shared only the jobs created by English-
speaking employers. Montreal, once half-English, now was filled
with rural French Canadians. Quebeckers no longer fled to New
England; instead they crowded into the slums of an alien city. As a
French tourist complained, one could live for weeks in Montreal
without seeing or hearing any language but English. The Quebec
government, Liberal since 1897, saw its role as the fervent
promoter of private development of natural resources as much as
factories. Only if English and American capital expanded the provincial economy could Quebec afford the costly and futile colonization projects favoured by the Church and *nationalistes.*

Bourassa himself, fleeing the futility of federal politics to turn
his fire on the provincial Liberal regime, toyed with a more progressive version of the nationalist program. Errol Bouchette, Quebec's first economist of note, pleaded with Quebeckers to regain
control of their own resources and industries, by public ownership
if necessary. Opinion-leaders recoiled at such socialist heresies.
Bourassa recommended control of trusts, Catholic unions for
Canadien workers, even the municipal reforms urged by Montreal's civic-conscious business leaders. No more than his grand-
father Papineau could Bourassa emancipate himself from a
traditional, rural view of French Canada's future. The problems of
colonists tilling the thin soils of northern Quebec would be
blamed on politicians. The hardships depicted in Louis Hémon's
Maria Chapdelaine must be endured, and, like Maria, French Canadians must reject the easy life of assimilation to remain true to
their traditions. "It is not necessary for us to possess industry and
money," declared Jules-Paul Tardivel. "We would no longer be
French Canadians but Americans like the others. Our mission is
to possess the soil and to spread ideas."

Such notions might have limited impact on the hard-headed and sometimes hedonistic *Canadiens*. The preaching of clergy and intellectuals should not be confused with public opinion, but at intervals the two connect. If Bourassa and his youthful followers increasingly saw Laurier as a sell-out to imperialists, materialists, and exploiters, ordinary French Canadians had less reason than their English-speaking neighbours to revel in Laurier's economic achievements. Nor were those achievements always apparent.

By 1908, the federal Liberals looked shopworn and dirty. The country had survived a short but sharp recession in 1907, the harbinger of worse to come. Robert Borden, still the Tory leader, had chosen that year to unveil his Halifax Program, a reaffirmation of the National Policy spiced by calls for public ownership of telephones, telegraphs, and railways, an efficient and reformed civil service, and a ban on election contributions from corporations. Laurier introduced a civil service commission and waited patiently while Tories predictably denounced their leader's proposals as intolerable socialism. As voter bait, Conservatives were left with what contemporary Americans had christened "muckraking." Admittedly the scandals were rich and redolent, from Sifton's corrupt old Department of the Interior to the supply contracts for the government's Arctic voyages of explorations. The government replied in kind and the resulting campaign in 1908 was as sordid as any Canadian election in history. On election day, the Liberals retained 135 seats to the Conservatives' 85.

The Liberals had urged voters to "let Laurier finish his work." Probably Laurier's work was done. In 1909, Mackenzie King, elected to Parliament in 1908, became minister of a full-fledged Department of Labour. A tiny Department of External Affairs opened over an Ottawa barber shop. Its task was to cope with what Laurier never quite managed, systematic replies to the relentless flow of British memoranda on diplomacy, defence, shipping, and utter esoterica. Few Canadians cared, but diplomacy had done well for them since the Alaska dispute. In 1904, the French had forsaken their old, troublesome landing rights on the Newfoundland shore. Tribunals accepted Canadian views of a controversy over the Bering Sea and the ninety-year-old fisheries disagreement with the Americans. Laurier could have left with his country prosperous and respected. Instead, he looked at his aging colleagues, found no successor, and carried on.

Old issues such as imperialism took new shapes. In Europe, Britain had ended her old hostility to France and Russia because an old friend had suddenly become a dangerous new threat. Germany's industrial power had given her the world's best army. Now battleships poured from her dockyards to challenge the Royal Navy's supremacy. Wealthy and aristocratic British taxpayers, asked to finance a modest new welfare state as well as a massive expansion of their fleet, threatened rebellion. Canada and other dominions received urgent invitations to help. Laurier saw the political trap and seized a solution. Launching a small Canadian navy would look helpful, but both control and spending would remain at home. To his delight, an appropriate Conservative-sponsored resolution passed Parliament unanimously.

Then the compromise fell apart. Within a year both imperialists and Quebec nationalists had savaged the new Naval Service Act. Laurier offered a "tin-pot navy," the imperialists argued, when Britain needed battleships. Bourassa, in his newly launched newspaper, Le Devoir, insisted that the navy was a subterfuge for committing Canada to imperial wars and the conscription of young Canadiens. What enemy would distinguish between British and Canadian warships bearing identical White Ensigns? A symbolic by-election in rural Quebec in the autumn of 1910 showed the nationalistes that they had finally found a popular issue.

Laurier was unafraid. He spent that summer in a triumphal visit to the West. With his own eyes he saw the vast fields and the booming cities. The 1907 recession had been a mere hiccup in the process of endless growth. Homesteaders poured into the West in ever greater numbers. With too few misgivings, officials sent them to till the Palliser Triangle. Heavy rains in the Triangle in 1910 seemed to confirm their wisdom. Of course, there were discontents. Delegations met the prime minister to repeat old grievances about tariffs, freight rates, and land policies, but as ever, Laurier pursed his lips, shared his deep concern, and promised action. That fall, a thousand farmers staged the first "March on Ottawa," coming, like most of their successors, by train and not on foot. Again Laurier promised action.

Thanks to Washington, this time he delivered. By signing the Payne-Aldrich Bill, which sent American tariffs to new heights, President William Taft had finally provoked a free-trade revolt in a mid-term election year. Taft hoped that dusting off the old Canadian Reciprocity business might regain western support. With astonishing speed, an agreement was signed and despatched to both Canada and the Congress for approval. In Ottawa, a Tory politician later confessed that his heart sank to his boots. After half a century of trying for Reciprocity, it was Laurier who could claim the coup. Then politicians went home to their ridings and got another shock: Canadians were displeased. After years of prosperity and east-west trade, Canadians no longer cared about Reciprocity; in fact, for millions of them in business, factories, and transportation it represented a deadly threat to jobs. In Toronto, eighteen prominent Liberals, led by Clifford Sifton and Sir Edmund Walker of the Bank of Commerce, publicly broke with their party. In Montreal, Sir William Van Horne of the CPR brusquely commanded his business associates "to bust the damned thing."

Neither Borden nor Laurier immediately grasped their altered fortunes. Exasperated by a Tory filibuster on the Reciprocity Agreement, Laurier called an election for September 1911. In Quebec, Tory businessmen now funnelled cash to Bourassa and the *nationalistes*, leaving them to veto candidates and manage the Conservative provincial campaign. In return, the *nationalistes* hoped, Bourassa's followers would hold the balance of power. Elsewhere, anti-Americanism and Reciprocity were the real issues, with a flood of money and smooth provincial organizations in Ontario, Manitoba, and British Columbia to support Conservative fortunes. By the end, Laurier glimpsed defeat. Rowdy mobs in Montreal drove him from his platform to seek refuge in a railway car. On the night of September 21, Conservative candidates swept 107 seats outside Quebec, 4 short of a majority. Quebec gave

Borden 27 more (mostly from rural counties) for a total of 134. Laurier salvaged only 87, and most of his ministers, Mackenzie King among them, were gone.

The *nationalistes* had miscalculated. Robert Borden could now manage without them, though some secured minor portfolios. Like Laurier in 1896, Borden sought compromise and moderation. Thomas White, a defecting Liberal from the Toronto financial community, became Minister of Finance, while George Eulas Foster, scourge of the Liberals in the opposition years, had to settle, like Cartwright in 1896, for trade and commerce. Reluctantly Borden accepted Sam Hughes, the favourite of Orangemen and imperialists, as Minister of Militia, an obscure enough portfolio in normal times. With a suitably new broom, Borden set reforms afoot in the civil service, proposed a commission to set a "scientific" tariff, and launched an investigation of the scandalously mismanaged and overdue National Transcontinental. Manitoba's northern border, a vexed issue for three years, climbed north to join its neighbours at the sixtieth parallel, and both Ontario and Quebec expanded to include the vast Ungava district around Hudson Bay. An exasperated Borden complained that he could have done a great deal more if his colleagues had not spent so much of their time with quarrels over political favours. Borden's distaste for patronage was only one of the things that distinguished him from Laurier and Macdonald.

Another was his view of empire. The Tory-*nationaliste* alliance on the naval question had been based on self-deception. Like old Joseph Howe but unlike Laurier or Macdonald, Borden believed in some form of imperial federation. Some day, colonies would sit as equals with the mother country, but they would have to earn their places by honourable sacrifice. Such an opportunity had come. After direct consultations with the British admiralty, Borden announced that Canada would send $5 million to buy three of the most advanced battleships. At once, his Quebec lieutenant, Frederick Monk, demanded a referendum. The request refused, Monk resigned. The Liberals filibustered, dragging the debate into 1913. Then Borden's brightest recruit, Arthur Meighen, devised a closure motion to cut off debate. This first use of closure did not save Borden's naval policy. A Liberal-dominated senate bluntly rejected it, and, for good measure, his tariff commission and a federal highways law as well.

The Senate could do so cheerfully because Borden's government was now in deadly trouble. The long years of prosperity were over. By 1912, a world-wide depression was taking hold. Immigrants, arriving in greater numbers to escape economic woes at home, joined growing armies of unemployed in Canadian cities. In 1913 and 1914 the prairies suffered their first widespread crop failures in a decade. The ecological folly of farming the drought-prone Palliser Triangle was exposed. Close to completion, the new transcontinental railways found themselves in a desperate credit squeeze. Hardest hit was the Canadian Northern, its eastern route authorized by Laurier in 1908 and financed by Toronto's Bank of Commerce. Promoters who had paid lavish favours to the Liberals now had to plead for Tory sympathy. The thirst for political revenge had to be resisted by an argument as old as the Grand Trunk and the 1850s: railway bankruptcy would destroy Canadian credit with foreign investors.

Beset by problems it had not caused, Borden's government faced new problems from its Ontario stronghold. Urged on by Michael Fallon, Roman Catholic bishop of London, and by fears of French-Canadian settlement in Ontario's eastern counties, Sir James Whitney's provincial government issued Regulation 17, curtailing the education rights of Ontario's French-speaking minority. For Fallon, Regulation 17 was sweet revenge for his dismissal years before by French-speaking clerics at the University of Ottawa. Franco-Ontarians knew they were victims of raw prejudice and opportunism. In Ontario's 1914 election, Liberals vied with Tories in backing Regulation 17. The Tories won in a landslide.

For Canada as a whole, Regulation 17 was another brutal, needless confrontation between French and English at a moment when Canadian unity would be tested as never before.

3

National Crisis

Suddenly, Canada was at war. The crisis that bubbled out of the Balkans in the summer of 1914 had looked no worse than half a dozen predecessors. Inexorably, alliance systems and mobilization plans clicked into place. Serbia, Russia, and France ranged against the Austro-Hungarian and German empires. At midnight on August 4, the British ultimatum to Berlin expired and another empire joined the war.

In Winnipeg, J. W. Dafoe told readers of the *Free Press* that Canadians would make their own war on Prussian militarism. In Ottawa, Sir Wilfrid Laurier was more conventional. In Britain's hour of danger, Canada's only possible answer was "Ready, Aye Ready." Crowds in Montreal, Toronto, and Quebec bellowed their support.

Canada was a little better prepared than she knew. Since 1897, defence spending had grown six-fold. In 1913, sixty thousand militiamen had drilled in camps. Since 1909, most provinces, including Quebec, had imposed military training in their schools. Pre-war planning even safeguarded ports, canals, and bridges from surprise attack. A detailed scheme would have despatched a twenty-five-thousand-man Canadian Expeditionary Force within a month. Other preparations were less helpful. In 1902, at the behest of Colonel Sam Hughes, Laurier's government had adopted the Ross rifle. It was a fine target rifle, and it could be made in Canada; experience would reveal few other virtues.

The war crisis excited Canadians. When Parliament met, a Liberal insisted that Borden's emergency legislation "omit no power that the Government may need." The War Measures Act met that test. Experts universally agreed that the war would be short. If massed armies did not settle the issue, economic collapse certainly would. As Minister of Militia, Sam Hughes scrapped mobilization plans designed by his professional soldiers, summoned volunteers to a brand new camp at Valcartier, near Quebec, and went in full uniform to sort out the confusion he had caused. By early October, a vast convoy had left for England with thirty-two thousand ill-trained soldiers. Canadians marvelled.

They also poured out their patriotism in voluntary effort. A Canadian Patriotic Fund collected donations for soldiers' families. A Military Hospitals Commission created facilities for the sick and wounded veterans. The pre-war militia organization and patriotic civilians recruited close to half a million men by early 1916 with scarcely a penny of government money. Churches, charities, the Red Cross, and women's organizations found interesting and often useful ways to "do their bit," from buying machine guns to distributing white feathers as symbols of cowardice to healthy young civilian men. Patriots also forced the dismissal of Germans and Austrians from public employment, banned the teaching of German in schools and universities, and pressured the city of Berlin into renaming itself Kitchener. Miners in British Columbia went on strike to prevent the hiring of "enemy aliens," and by April of 1915, public clamour had forced the government to intern more than seven thousand largely harmless people.

From the first, the frugal practices of peacetime public finance were forgotten. At the best of times Sam Hughes was a spender and the war gave him and a growing entourage of cronies all the excuse they needed. By 1915, the militia department was swallowing more than the entire government had spent in 1913. Less public but almost as serious was the financial appetite of the transcontinental railways. Cut off from traditional money markets by the war, with facilities badly needed to ship men and supplies, the Grand Trunk and the Canadian Northern left Borden's government no choice but to support them.

As Minister of Finance, Sir Thomas White was no innovator. Only a horror of raising taxes and a faith in a short war forced him into the first heavy Canadian borrowing in New York. Financiers universally believed that Canadians would never lend money to their government. They were wrong. Desperation drove White in 1915 to seek $50 million in a special domestic war loan; Canadians gave him $100 million. Further loans in 1916 and 1917 were also over-subscribed. Victory Loans, directed at humbler citizens and backed by floods of advertising, delivered $400 million in 1917 and $600 million in 1918. While government revenue rose from $126 million to $233.7 million between 1913 and 1918, mostly due to higher tariffs, the national debt climbed from $434 million to $2463 million. By then, White and his colleagues had to argue that the cost of a war to end all wars might fairly be shared with later generations.

The burden would have been far greater without massive exports of wheat, timber, and Canadian-made munitions. At first, the war only aggravated the prevailing depression. Hunger as well as patriotism drove thousands of young men into the Canadian Expeditionary Force. Industrialists, eager for business, got Hughes's backing to form a committee to bid for British artillery shell contracts. By the summer of 1915, the Shell Committee had orders worth $170 million but greed, confusion, and the problems of learning by doing allowed them to deliver only $5.5 million's worth. The British, beset by their own comparable problems, insisted on reorganization. The solution was an Imperial Munitions Board, officially a British agency, headed by a talented and hardheaded Canadian manager, Joseph Flavelle. By 1917, Flavelle had turned his skills as a bacon exporter into making the IMB the biggest business in Canada with a quarter of a million workers and a turnover of $2 million a day. In 1917, when the British, desperate for foreign exchange, could no longer afford to buy in Canada, Flavelle neatly switched his market to a rearming United States. By the war's end, the IMB's own factories and its contractors were producing ships, aircraft, chemicals, and explosives as well as shells.

The war also ended the depression in agriculture. With huge conscript armies trapped in the trenches, and Russia's wheat exports stopped by the war, Canada's allies needed all she could produce. Nature obliged with an unprecedented fifteen million bushels of wheat in 1915. Prices soared and the caution which might have returned the prairie dry belt to grazing was forgotten in the rush for profits. Yields fell in the later war years but farm profits climbed, and consumers accepted higher prices and shortages as the cost of war. Manufacturers shared the benefits as farmers spent their new wealth on cars and furniture as well as more land and machinery. Employers and farmers soon regretted that so many men had been encouraged to go to war.

Manpower had become the crucial resource of the war effort. By the end of 1914, the government had authorized fifty thousand men for the Canadian Expeditionary Force. By the summer of 1915, the target was a hundred and fifty thousand. A visit to England shocked Borden with both the magnitude of the struggle and the ineffectiveness of British wartime leadership. As if to set them an example, he raised Canada's manpower commitment to two hundred fifty thousand, and in January 1916 he doubled it to five hundred thousand.

At the outset, Henri Bourassa had backed the war, but he added a prescient warning. The government, he suggested, should "ensure our own internal security before starting or pursuing an effort that it will perhaps not be in a state to sustain until the end." The government's own chief military advisor, Major General Willoughby Gwatkin, cautioned in 1915 that Canada might have trouble finding men for even two divisions in the trenches. Instead, by 1916, Hughes had committed the Dominion to four divisions with the promise of many more.

In fact, men were found. When the old militia had exhausted its influence, politicians, businessmen, and local patriots accepted colonelcies from Hughes and raised still more battalions. Appeals to civic pride, sporting links, and the passion for wearing Highland regalia drew recruits. Clergy preached on Christian duty and women wore badges proclaiming "Knit or Fight." Medical officers sometimes accepted the young, the old, and the physically or mentally handicapped. Barriers of racial prejudice were lowered to admit Indians and Japanese Canadians, though most black Canadians were funnelled into a construction unit.

Even when backed by acute social pressure, voluntary recruiting was highly selective. Most of the men of the early contingents were British-born recent immigrants to Canada, with close ties to their homeland and harsh experience of a country where employers often advertised "No English need apply." In cities like Winnipeg, Toronto, and English-speaking Montreal, recruiting pressure was more powerful than in rural districts or in regions like the Maritimes where roots went very deep. In French Canada, the pressures were weak indeed. No one distributed white feathers in Quebec City. The agencies that recruited in other provinces – the militia, local leaders, imperial patriots – were, in French Canada, weak or otherwise engaged. Historians often repeat a myth that a Methodist was put in charge of Quebec recruiting. In fact, no one was in charge of recruiting in Quebec or anywhere else until 1917. Lies, however widely spread and innocently believed, remain lies.

It was easy to blame Sam Hughes and the Borden government. No man was less fitted to understand French Canada than the tempestuous minister of militia. Though most of Borden's *nationaliste* colleagues loyally backed the war, they had won election by passionately opposing such imperial adventures. Quebec Liberals enjoyed their discomfiture and Bourassa, rapidly losing interest in the European conflict, dismissed his former colleagues as traitors. Ontario's Regulation 17 was a convenient distraction. The real enemies of French Canada were not Germans, insisted Bourassa, but "English-Canadian anglicisers, the Ontario intriguers, or Irish priests." As if to confirm the point, wartime nativism drove the western provinces to annul French and minority education rights conceded years before.

In fact, French Canadians did not need Bourassa's speeches to convince them to stay out of uniform. When Quebec's famous Twenty-second Battalion, the "Vandoos," was authorized in October 1914, it had difficulty filling its ranks. So did most of its many successors. Few Quebeckers were moved by loyalty to Britain or France; unemployment or an urge for adventure and escape were the usual goads for recruiting. For the vast majority, the ordered familiarity of the farm or home town, well-paid work in the new munitions factories and textile mills, and a comfortable sense of isolation from a dangerous world were reason enough to stay home.

Those Canadians who did enlist became part of the British army. Not even the assertively nationalistic Hughes claimed to control "his boys" in action, though he lustily condemned British tactics. Hughes's zest for chaos and croneyism complicated Canadian administration in England. By 1916, three rival Canadian generals each claimed Hughes's full authority. Hundreds of CEF battalions arrived in Britain only to be broken up for reinforcements. The embittered soldiers blamed unfeeling military bureaucrats. The staff, more knowledgeably, blamed Hughes.

No more than in 1812 or 1885 were Canadians natural-born soldiers. They learned their business in the daily misery of trench warfare and in bloody battles made more dangerous by inexperienced officers and bad equipment. After the second Battle of Ypres, where a raw First Division counted 6035 casualties, soldiers abandoned their useless Ross rifles. At the St. Eloi craters in 1916, the Second Division suffered a painful setback because its commanders could not locate their men. The remorseless test of battle eliminated the hopelessly inept and persuaded the survivors that precise staff work, painstaking preparation, and sensible but uncompromising discipline could both win battles and save lives. The clearest evidence came on the Easter weekend of 1917. After weeks of stock-piling, tunnelling, rehearsals, and bombardment, Sir Julian Byng sent forward all four divisions of the Canadian Corps to take Vimy Ridge. In five days, the seemingly impossible had been done. It was one of those great deeds, done together, which have created nations. French and English could take equal pride in the victory.

Byng was British but his ways were inherited only weeks later by his Canadian successor. Sir Arthur Currie was a pear-shaped figure with a slightly shady pre-war record as a Victoria real estate speculator. The war proved him to be a cool, methodical soldier, with a fondness for unconventional tactics and an openness to innovation. That summer, instead of squandering men in an attack on Lens, as his British superiors wanted, he captured nearby Hill 70. Then, when the Germans, as he had predicted, desperately tried to retake the position, Currie used his artillery to destroy them.

Currie's authority was all the stronger because, after 1916, Canada had assumed effective control of her overseas forces. In November of that year, after a tempest of rage and threats at his loss of power, Hughes finally resigned. Sir Robert Borden created a new Overseas Ministry in London to manage Canadian forces in England and France. The chaos and conflict that affected every branch of administration, from chaplains to veterinarians, slowly vanished. By 1918, the British retained little more than tactical control of the Canadian units in France. Brilliant soldiers like Brigadier General A. G. L. McNaughton, a chemistry professor before the war, pioneered innovations in gunnery and military engineering. In military terms, if not yet in constitutional law, the war had transformed Canada from a colony into a junior but sovereign ally. Both administrative efficiency and hard-won military prestige had achieved the change.

Canadians also won a reputation in the air. By war's end, almost a quarter of the pilots in the Royal Air Force were Canadians, many of them trained at British flying schools in Canada. Two Canadians, Major W. A. Bishop and Major Raymond Collishaw, ranked third and fifth among the air aces of the war. They and many others established a remarkable Canadian reputation in the air, in part because of superior training methods. Having deplored a distinct Canadian navy, Borden's government approved an independent Canadian air force only in the last months of the war. It never saw action. At sea, a few Canadians served with the Royal Navy but Canada's own tiny navy was allowed no greater role than patrolling for German U-boats outside Halifax harbour.

Experts have long debated alternatives to the Allies' blood-soaked strategy of seeking victory on the Western Front. Not even skill, experience, and careful preparation prevented heavy casualties. Taking Vimy Ridge cost 10,604 dead and wounded. Ordered to finish the grim British offensive at Passchendaele in October 1917, Currie protested that he would lose sixteen thousand men.

The toll was 15,654. Keeping each of the four Canadian divisions in action required twenty thousand new soldiers a year. By 1917, they were no longer coming.

A year earlier, the patriotic leagues had warned that their recruiting efforts were failing. To soften Quebec's rising hostility to the war effort, prominent Torontonians launched a "Bonne Entente" movement. Banquets and speeches failed to soften the bitterness of French-English relations. Soon, many of these same men began to demand conscription. The arguments became familiar. Volunteering took too many of the bravest and best young men of English Canada. Industry suffered when skilled workers joined up. Acutely aware of its 1914 promise of voluntary recruiting, the government tried to keep faith. Borden finally put Quebec recruiting in charge of a prominent French-Canadian drug manufacturer. One of his Quebec cabinet ministers set out (vainly) to raise a battalion. Borden also launched a voluntary scheme of national registration to identify potential recruits. Though suspicious that the scheme was a mere prelude to conscription, both the Quebec Catholic hierarchy and the Trades and Labour Congress urged compliance. A fifth of the registration cards were never returned. Of the registrants who seemed eligible, almost none volunteered.

Save for his short, discouraging visit to London in 1915, Borden knew no more about British policy and strategy than he could read in the papers. Once, in January 1916, frustration and ill-health provoked him to write that Canadians would not put five hundred thousand men in the field "and willingly accept the position of having no more voice and receiving no more consideration than if we were toy automata." He tore up the letter and spent that year struggling to reform his creaking war administration and, in spare moments, urging sympathetic Americans to forsake their neutrality.

In London, December 1916 brought dramatic shifts, partly engineered by the expatriate Canadian, Max Aitken. David Lloyd George, a former Welsh radical and the only man in the British government Borden had really respected, headed a new coalition. Faced with hostile officials and a war effort sadly awry, Lloyd George summoned the dominion premiers. "We want more men from them," he bluntly explained. "We can hardly ask them to make another great recruiting effort unless it is accompanied by an invitation to come over and discuss the situation with us." On March 2, Borden and his fellow prime ministers met to hear the dreadful news. Russia was collapsing. The French army had mutinied. Germany's submarines would bring Britain to starvation. The Americans had finally entered the war, to Borden's profound delight, but years might pass before American military strength was mobilized. Lloyd George's purpose was served: Borden worked hard on developing a new consultative Imperial War Cabinet, but the manpower message sunk in.

Visits to Canadian camps confirmed the need for men. Without reinforcements, wounded men would be returned to the fighting until they were dead or too terribly mangled to be useful. Canada's honour depended on keeping her Corps at full strength, though Borden halted Hughes's former policy of expanding it. The bitter victory of Vimy Ridge in April 1917 only confirmed the prime minister's resolve.

Later, Liberals would pretend that Borden dreamed up conscription to save his party. This was absurd. Certainly the Tories were in trouble. A 1914 political truce had long since ended. Conservatives had lost every provincial election since then. A wartime record of fumbling and ill-concealed scandals seemed to promise Laurier's comeback at the next election. Borden was not fooled by the patriots; conscription would be unpopular across Canada. In Australia, voters had rejected it already and would do so again. But Borden saw no choice. With all the earnestness that drove him, Borden would keep faith with Britain and with Canada's own young soldiers. On May 18, 1917, he announced that men would be selectively conscripted for service overseas.

Almost inevitably, conscription became a French-English debate. Opponents in English Canada – farmers, trade unionists, pacifists – had few outlets for their views; French Canada was virtually unanimous in opposition, and Bourassa provided ready-made arguments. Borden, he insisted, was a mere imperialist, pouring out Canadian lives and money at Britain's command. Canada's front line was Canada, not France and Flanders.

Canadians should use the war to get rich by supplying the food and shells the belligerents needed. Such arguments enraged English-Canadian patriots. To Borden, they were servile and unworthy. Despite their image as a cold, materialistic people, Borden wanted to lead Canadians to a higher destiny. His reputation would perish in the attempt.

On the means Borden was very flexible. He would form a coalition with Laurier. He would delay conscription until a general election. The Liberal leader refused. Sensing imminent victory over the Tories, Laurier's party would surely stay loyal. If Laurier joined Borden, he would again lose Quebec to Bourassa. Liberal party meetings in Toronto and Winnipeg trounced advocates of conscription.

Despite the evidence, Laurier was wrong. Especially in Ontario and the West, the war had become a crusade, as Dafoe had proclaimed in 1914. Out of the terrible fiery furnace of sacrifice, surely a new and purified Canada must come, purged of corruption and selfishness. It was a conviction which Liberals could share more easily than Tories. It lay behind the sudden, overwhelming triumph of reforming campaigns across the West in 1915 and 1916, such as prohibition and women's suffrage. By 1917, women in provinces from Ontario to British Columbia had won the right to vote though both sexes had also lost the right to drink. Both causes remained frankly repugnant to Laurier, Quebec Liberals, and, for that matter, to Bourassa and the *nationalistes*. Hate the Tories as they might, reforming Liberals like Newton Rowell, the party's Ontario leader, and Manitoba's J. W. Dafoe could see that Borden was in earnest about the war, and Laurier patently was not.

The prime minister was also a shrewder, abler politician than Laurier would ever admit. Reaching out to second-rank Liberals, Borden found them sympathetic but nervous. With help from Arthur Meighen, Borden gave himself two more weapons. A Military Voters' Act would enfranchise soldiers; a Wartime Elections Act gave votes to soldiers' wives, sisters, and mothers and took it away from Canadians of enemy origin naturalized since 1902. The women, Meighen explained, would speak for men who had lost their lives; disfranchised aliens would also be spared from conscription. It went without saying that they had also voted Liberal. It took closure to end the debate. Almost at once, sensing that Laurier was lost, the Liberal defections began. On October 6, Parliament dissolved, and the long-postponed election could take place. Five days later, Borden announced a coalition Union government pledged to conscription, wartime prohibition, and the elimination of political patronage. It was a pledge Borden could never have won from his own party. The man who had grown to despise partyism could finally lead a government based on talent and patriotism – as he saw it.

The brand-new Union government expected an easy victory with endorsements from eight out of nine provincial premiers (Quebec's Sir Lomer Gouin was the obvious exception) and almost every English-language newspaper. Outside Quebec the Liberal leadership was shattered. Unexpectedly, in the Maritimes and parts of the West, rank-and-file Liberals began to revive their party. Struggles to compress Tory and Liberal ambitions into a single Unionist candidacy provoked exasperating squabbles. On a western tour, Laurier drew large crowds. At Kitchener, with its German-speaking population, an anti-conscriptionist crowd howled down Borden. By late November, nervous ministers had persuaded Borden to announce that farmers' sons and soldiers' brothers would be exempt from conscription. At last the Union campaign got going. While Quebec extremists exulted at British defeats, respectable Ontarians' newspapers insisted that a vote for Laurier would allow Bourassa to rule Canada and set the German Kaiser rejoicing. By election day, English Canadians could almost believe that conscription would fall exclusively on "slackers" and French Canadians.

The result split Canada as no election ever had before: Borden took 153 seats, only 3 in Quebec, Laurier won 82, only 20 of them outside Quebec. As usual, seat totals could be deceptive. Without the military vote, Laurier had only a hundred thousand fewer supporters than Borden. The soldiers gave the government 14 more seats and two hundred thousand votes.

During the months of campaigning, from October to December, the Military Service Act had been in abeyance.

Devised by Arthur Meighen, it was not a monument to his usual lucidity. Conscripts, selected on the basis of age and marital status, had three separate stages of appeal. Of 404,395 called in the first class, 380,510 appealed. When the men were called for training, less than twenty thousand appeared. "Freely denounced as an engine of oppression," one commentator observed, the Act "contained so many safeguards against oppression that it had been made in no small degree inoperative." Quebec conscription tribunals, duly composed of a Conservative and a Liberal, granted blanket exemptions to *Canadiens* but, according to the central appeal judge, "applied conscription against the English-speaking minority in Quebec with a rigour unparalleled."

The new government was soon busy with its program. Early in 1918, regulations prohibited the import, sale, and distribution of liquor for the duration of the war and one year after. On May 24, the federal franchise was open at last to women as well as men. The coalition made it a little easier to settle one part of the long, agonizing railway problem – Mackenzie and Mann's now-bankrupt Canadian Northern. In December 1917, Borden finally achieved the solution he had advocated as long ago as 1904: public ownership. In return for money to rescue the Canadian Northern's heaviest investor, the Bank of Commerce, the railway vanished into a new Canadian Government Railways system. The Grand Trunk would have to wait.

So would much else. In March of 1918, disaster struck the Allied cause. German armies, redeployed after the collapse of Russia, smashed through the British lines. The entire British Fifth Army dissolved. By coincidence, anti-conscription riots broke out in Quebec City on the Easter weekend. They ended only when soldiers, rushed from Toronto, fired on a furious crowd, killing four civilians. Future protesters, warned Ottawa, would be conscripted on the spot. To meet the likelihood of heavy losses in France, the Union government also cancelled all exemptions under the Military Service Act. At the onset of seeding time, farmers watched their sons depart to the military depots and cursed the lying Unionist politicians.

More than farmers and French Canadians were bitter now.

Thousands of families mourned soldier-sons and husbands. Inflation, moderate until 1916, soared out of control in 1917. Wages could not keep pace and more workers than ever turned to unions and to strikes. Suddenly, the violence of war came home to a peaceful country. On December 6, 1917, the blast from an exploding munitions ship devastated the working-class end of Halifax, killing 1630 people. Dazed survivors faced the worst blizzards in years. In that winter, German U-boats started patrolling near Halifax, surfacing to sink and capture merchant ships.

Amateurism and voluntarism had run their course. Behind the façade of business-dominated committees like the Patriotic Fund, it was government that controlled, regulated, and provided the money. Food and fuel controllers preached conservation, sought ingenious ways to increase production, and hunted for boarders. Called on to conscript wealth as well as men, the finance minister, Sir Thomas White, cautiously imposed a Business Profits Tax and a War Income Tax. In 1918, only 31,130 Canadians were paying taxes through their new T-1 forms, for a total of $8 million. An "anti-loafing" regulation threatened jail for any man, sixteen to sixty, who was not gainfully employed. For the first time, the government authorized its federal police forces to hunt for sedition. Radical unions and foreign-dominated socialist parties were ordered suppressed, and, after years of patriotic pressure, publications in "enemy" languages were at last outlawed. A wartime labour code was more permissive, at least for employers. Collective bargaining and equal pay for men and women were recommended but the right to strike was banned for the duration.

Overseas, the mood of exhaustion and despair was far heavier, but the Canadian Corps was exempt. By amazing luck, it had escaped the major German offensives, and Currie grimly insisted on holding it together. The 5th Division, held in reserve in England since 1916, was finally broken up for reinforcements despite election promises that it would serve as a formation. The extra men made the Corps the strongest organization of its size on the British front.

Borden came back to England that spring, angry at the waste of Passchendaele, furious when he learned from Currie of the sloth, mismanagement, and lack of foresight of British generals. "Let the past bury its dead," he stormed at Lloyd George and his fellow prime ministers, "but for God's sake let us get down to earnest endeavour." Through the summer Borden finally got a share in the British planning for a war which it seemed might well drag on to 1920. Somehow, the British army must be husbanded and rebuilt. Perhaps the Russian front could be revived with Canadian help. Then, in mid-August, he headed back to Ottawa, trapped by the practical dilemma of imperial federalism – Canada could not seem to manage without its prime minister; no one else could represent it effectively in London. If anything, the war had shown Borden the limits of Empire and the surprising convenience of dealing with wartime Washington. When the diplomats could be side-stepped, Americans talked business and made decisions as the British never would. It was a disturbing thought in what might be only the middle of an interminable war.

Then, in a sudden, unexpected development, the war rushed to a conclusion. On August 8, 1918, a Canadian and Australian attack near Amiens smashed through the German lines. Tanks, aircraft, and infantry worked with new efficiency. Before the assault bogged down, Currie insisted on switching fronts. Again and again Canadian troops attacked, suffering huge casualties but driving deeper than ever before imaginable. The conscripts were needed as the Corps rolled forward, passing still-green fields and undamaged towns. Retreating Germans fought dangerously well to the final day at Mons, where the war had begun for the British in 1914. On November 11, at 11 A.M., it ended for everybody.

The Canadians had lost 60,661 dead; as many more would return hopelessly mutilated in mind or body. During the autumn of 1918, almost as many Canadians may have died from a strange, virulent influenza epidemic. Both tolls had taken the young and the talented. For the survivors, nothing would ever be quite the same again.

4

Dead Ends

Two contradictory hopes sustained most Canadians during the war years: on the one hand that they would find a new and finer world; on the other that they would return to the old one. Reformers could take heart in women's suffrage and prohibition. Reform-minded books ranged from Mackenzie King's turgid tract on labour relations, *Industry and Humanity*, to Stephen Leacock's essay, "The Unsolved Riddle of Social Justice," with its surprising conclusion that the government "ought to supply work and pay for the unemployed, maintenance for the infirm and aged and education and opportunity for the children." The conservative view was less literary: its proponents were too busy running businesses and the country to write much.

Reformers were also audible. Backed by a resolution adopted in Calgary in February 1919, a quarter of a million veterans and their supporters demanded a $2000 re-establishment bonus. It seemed a fair return for years of earning $1.10 a day while civilians prospered safely at home. Profiteers like Sir Joseph Flavelle, with embarrassing gains of $1.7 million from his bacon business, could pay the bill. The Union government offered a flinty resistance. Ministers insisted that Canada had done more than the Americans for war widows, orphans, and the disabled. Money for the able-bodied would only reinforce the paternalism of army life. Warned that "full re-establishment" would cost $1 billion, politicians, business, and even some veterans' leaders turned against the bonus. When the pressure collapsed, the government seized the moment to "tighten up" pensions and retraining as well.

Organized labour looked tougher and better organized. The war years saw union ranks grow from 143,200 in 1915 to 378,000 by 1919. The expansion concealed sharp splits. In 1918, conservatives recaptured the leadership of the Trades and Labour Congress from the radicals who had wielded it since 1912. The angry minority, mostly from the West, swore to meet in Calgary in March 1919, to plot their strategy. By the time they met, an even more militant caucus, drawn from western cities, notably Vancouver, had taken over the meeting. The excited majority called for a proletarian revolution in Canada, cheered the Bolshevik Revolution in Russia, and so frightened a timid Sir Thomas White in Ottawa that he proposed summoning a British cruiser to Vancouver harbour. Delegates dispersed to plan a "One Big Union," an industrial organization of workers, to challenge the craft-based conservatism of the Trades and Labour Congress.

None of this, beyond steaming rhetoric, had much to do with the Winnipeg General Strike. In fact Bob Russell, prime architect of the One Big Union, worked in vain to prevent the outbreak among his fellow machinists. The trouble was that a general strike in 1918 had won collective bargaining rights for Winnipeg's civic workers; now it must be tried again to help the employees of Winnipeg's obdurate factory owners. On May 15, after an overwhelming vote of support from its twelve thousand members, Winnipeg's Labour Council proclaimed a general strike. An astonishing thirty thousand Winnipeggers walked out, from waiters to telephone operators. Other general strikes spread from Vancouver to Amherst, Nova Scotia.

Strike organizers never understood that it was their angry speeches, not their cautious deeds, that Winnipeg's nervous middle class noticed. After a month without strike pay, most Winnipeg workers had had enough. Strikes elsewhere had collapsed. The words on both sides got angrier. Winnipeg's civic leaders, convinced that labour was plotting its own Bolshevik Revolution, got automatic backing from Arthur Meighen, Manitoba's cabinet representative in Ottawa. Persuaded that "enemy aliens" were behind the strike, Parliament swiftly amended the law to allow easy deportation. Dawn arrests of strike leaders promptly followed. This gave a dying strike a last, tragic rally. On Saturday, June 21, crowds filled the street in front of the city hall to protest the arrests. Mounted police charged the throng and special constables attacked with clubs. "Bloody Saturday" and the ensuing trials of the strike leaders (British or Canadian to a man) gave Winnipeg's workers a long, bitter memory of their ordeal. Driven back to the city's north end, they gave their neighbourhoods a durable allegiance to labour and socialist politics.

In the wake of the strike's collapse and the trial of leaders for sedition, the attempt to create a One Big Union was doomed. Employer resistance, counter-attacks by the craft unions, and bitter disputes among the OBU's own leaders left only fragments of its bold vision. The split was also a foretaste of divisions to come. Within a few years, the TLC drove out its biggest Canadian affiliate, the Canadian Brotherhood of Railway Employees, because it rivalled an international union. A tiny Communist party, organized in a barn near Guelph in 1921, obeyed Moscow's orders to "bore from within" the labour movement with divisive consequences. By 1927, the Communists had begun to build their own labour organization, the Workers' Unity League. In Quebec, years of sermons and editorials combined with the resentments of the war years to produce a small Catholic union movement. In 1921, the Catholic "syndicates" took public shape at a congress in Hull. The dream of a strong, united, and radical Canadian labour movement was buried for the next thirty years.

Only businessmen seemed to win their post-war demands, largely because they already dominated politics, media, and opinion. Manufacturers were determined to safeguard the tariff; merchants aimed at wiping out government controls; financiers insisted on ending inflation at once. They all succeeded. Within days of the Armistice, Sir Joseph Flavelle had closed his munitions factories and put their assets on sale. That might have been sound if bankers had not clamped on their favourite weapon of deflation, high interest rates. Capital to readjust industry to peacetime purposes vanished. So did jobs. In due course, so did inflation, but not before farmers and small businesses had suffered financial disaster. Bankers and their admirers found such policies excellent. Fiscal righteousness had been profitable for them.

In 1917, the government had closed the Winnipeg Grain Exchange and created a single Wheat Board to market grain. Farmers first grumbled and then rejoiced as prices soared to a record $3.15 a bushel. After the 1919 crop, the Wheat Board dissolved and free enterprise returned. The earlier rural grumbles salved the politicians' consciences; faith in the market did the rest. Despite a serious crop failure on top of years of declining prairie productivity, wheat prices plummeted forty-five per cent in two years. Farmers who had invested in land, machinery, and comforts in the confidence of high prices now had real reason for lamentation.

Unlike veterans and labour, however, they still had the strength to be influential. In the war years, farmers had confirmed the political independence of the Canadian Council of Agriculture by endorsing a Farmers' Platform in 1916. In 1918, furious at the cancellation of their sons' exemption from conscription, farmers had marched on Ottawa. Many endorsed an even stronger platform, deliberately titled a "New National Policy," loaded with familiar demands for reciprocity, lower freight rates, and bank reform, and fresh planks insisting on railway nationalization and a graduated income tax. In T. A. Crerar, minister of agriculture for the Unionists, the farmers had a leader who even wrote his ministerial letters on United Grain Growers' paper. When White's 1919 budget fell short of farmers' wishes, Crerar quit.

The prime minister seemed far removed from the domestic turbulence of 1919. Even before the Armistice, Borden had left for Europe to achieve the war aims he had set for Canada. So far as Sir Robert was concerned, his country had just won her War for Independence. Inside or outside the Empire – Borden was no longer as sure as he had once been – Canada must emerge from the war a sovereign power with her own signature on the peace treaty and her own seat in the new League of Nations. Borden's powerful patron, David Lloyd George, had no real objections. Once it was clear that the great powers would dominate both arrangements, Canada's concern could be met. It was the Americans who resisted, outraged that the devious Lloyd George would use mere colonies to win extra votes for Britain. Finally, on May 6, 1919, President Woodrow Wilson glumly withdrew his objections, but Americans on the whole did not. Canada's full membership in the League of Nations became an added argument for American isolationists, who protested British dominance in the organization. The United States stayed out, Canada remained, but the League was crippled. Borden's international dreams had reached a dead end.

Even in Canada, Borden's hard-won overseas triumphs were seen as merely symbolic and perhaps even dangerous. The prime minister's insistence that Parliament vote on the German peace treaty was dismissed by a leading Liberal, William Fielding, as "a colossal humbug"; Article x of the League Covenant, pledging members to mutual defence, was seen by a French-Canadian MP as putting Canada "at the beck and call of a Council not responsible to the nation." Borden's own colleagues bitterly resented his absence in the midst of so many crises and at a time when the post-war fate of his Union coalition was so obviously in doubt. For all his earnestness and sense of duty, Borden seems to have lost interest in politics. In July, he sailed down the St. Lawrence in a bold bid to win over Quebec's premier. Sir Lomer Gouin was tempted; he had been running the province for Ottawa since the 1918 riots. Electoral common sense hauled Gouin back, and Borden went home. By the autumn, the prime minister was too ailing and exhausted to postpone any longer a long-awaited rest cure in the United States.

Borden's colleagues, buffeted from all sides, welcomed the rest cure because they knew they could not agree on a replacement. They were not idle. A Royal Commission on Labour Relations collected a long list of useful reforms, most of which would wait a generation to be seen again. A civil service reform removed forty thousand government employees from patronage (and robbed Unionists of that much more influence). Titles of nobility, discredited by wartime profiteering and scandals, also ended (with a brief revival in the 1930s). As cynics might have expected, the income tax survived the war and grew dramatically in size and bite. One legacy of the influenza epidemic (and fears of wartime

venereal disease) was a small Department of Health. Even after
"tightening up," the government had to treat eight thousand sick
and wounded veterans and maintain eighty thousand pensioners.

No problem had bigger economic or political impact than the
railways. In 1919, the Grand Trunk followed the Canadian Northern via receivership into nationalization. This time, there was no
Bank of Commerce to guard its interests; $180 million in watered
shares simply evaporated, mostly at the expense of English investors. Politically, the real issue was a plan by Lord Shaughnessy of
the Canadian Pacific to lease the entire national railway system,
run it under the CPR, and charge its losses to the taxpayer. In this
fashion, free enterprise would prevail and the CPR (with its eager
partner, the Bank of Montreal) would profit immensely. Arthur
Meighen bluntly rejected the scheme. Lord Shaughnessy was
beside himself with rage and Montreal's powerful financial and
business community dutifully echoed his fury. Most Canadians
came to see Meighen as an austere, even frigid exponent of free
enterprise: to Montreal business, he was a rabid socialist. His
party, denounced by the Quebec electorate for conscription, lost
access to its richest financial sources. Henceforth, the party of the
Canadian rich would verge on penury.

The government's railway policy had other consequences. In
November 1918, the old, patronage-battered Intercolonial was
drawn into the new system, christened the Canadian National
Railways in 1919. The ICR headquarters left Moncton for Toronto
and then Montreal. To meet the appalling debt charges for the system, rates were immediately raised to central Canadian levels
and, in September 1920, subjected to a drastic, system-wide forty-
per-cent increase. Maritime protests were dismissed as the familiar whining of a too-favoured region. In fact, Maritimers were
right. The ICR was *their* railway. Its regionally-based rates were
not only vital to local manufacturing, they had produced a regular
profit. By 1925, the Maritimes' national market was gone. British
Empire Steel Company, owner of Cape Breton's steel and coal
industry, reeled towards ruin amidst wage-cuts and long, violent
strikes. In half a decade, a hundred and fifty thousand Maritimers
left the region. Lack of hydroelectricity, a lower coal tariff,

and greedy profit-taking were all factors, in the first great era of Maritime decline, but the loss of the ICR was decisive.

Perhaps, as Dafoe had predicted in 1918, no one in power in the post-war years could have made friends. In October 1919, veteran politicians got a shock even opposition parties had to heed: Ontario provincial voters handed the legislature to the United Farmers and a clutch of labour members. With a premier, Ernest Drury, who had not even run in the election, a new farmer-labour government took office. In February 1920, Crerar emerged as leader of a National Progressive party. By 1921, farmers held power in Manitoba and Alberta. In Saskatchewan, a foxy Premier C. A. Dunning made his Liberals look so much like Progressives that no one bothered to try telling the difference. Far more than veterans or labour, farmers were the force that rolled out of English-speaking Canada like a juggernaut, sweeping up more Liberals than old Tories.

On February 17, 1919, the venerable Sir Wilfrid had died, confident as ever that he would have regained power. To his French-Canadian followers, Laurier's ghost would be their guide to a successor. Lady Laurier sensibly thought that William Fielding might be the man to reunite a shattered party but he had deserted in 1917. Young William Lyon Mackenzie King, too brash and ambitious to win the living Laurier's approval, was now the beneficiary of the ghost. Had he not run as Laurier's candidate in 1917 and lost? When Liberals gathered in a sweaty Ottawa exhibition hall in August 1919 for Canada's first leadership convention, they agreed King was a bearable alternative. His youth and his contact with modern notions like unions and management efficiency might help him. King won on the third ballot.

King's antagonist would not be Robert Borden. The old prime minister had returned to Ottawa in the spring of 1920 still sick and indecisive. Colleagues urged him to stay on. Meighen, bluntly, advised him to go. A weary Borden, dutifully trying to preserve Unionism, preferred Thomas White, perhaps even Sir Lomer Gouin, as his successor. Both refused. The Tory backbenchers wanted Meighen, and, on July 10, 1920, they got him. "The only unpardonable sin in politics," claimed the new prime minister, "is lack of courage." He had plenty. He was tough, hard-working, brilliant in speech and grasp. He was also as utterly inflexible in his political principles as the plump and prolix King was adjustable. When Progressives continued to win by-elections, Meighen ended the suspense and ordered the longest federal election campaign in history – from September 1 to December 7, 1921.

Meighen wanted time because he had a message. The tariff, he believed, could be as clear and successful an issue as it had been in 1911. While King treated Progressives as "Liberals in a hurry," Meighen flayed them with all the brilliance of his tongue. Crerar campaigned in Ontario and the West but experience had shown that farmers would organize themselves. As for King's campaign, Meighen's description was not misleading: "Protection on apples in British Columbia, Free Trade in the Prairie Provinces and rural parts of Ontario, Protection in industrial centres of Ontario, Conscription in Quebec, and Humbug in the Maritimes." In a sense, it worked. Humbug and Conscription gave King almost all his 116 seats. Outside Ontario and British Columbia, where he collected 50 seats, Meighen was routed. Farmers in Ontario and the West gave Crerar 65 seats. Winnipeg and Calgary each elected a labour member. One of these, J. S. Woodsworth, a former Winnipeg clergyman and editor of a strike newspaper, insisted that for the first time Labour would sit as a separate party.

Canadians in 1921 had voted in distinct regional patterns, and they had elected their first minority Parliament. King now proved to have an acute and single-minded commitment to compromise. The prospect was daunting. On tariffs, railways, and much else, his conservative Quebec caucus had more in common with the Conservatives than with the Progressives with their Protestantism, their economic fancies, and their wartime espousal of conscription. Liberal ranks included both Laurierites and conscriptionists. As a labour negotiator, resolving opposite viewpoints with no visible opinions of his own, King had acquired the experience he now deployed.

King found the little that united farmers and Quebeckers and swiftly exploited it. Both *Canadiens* and farmers hated militarism. Defence would be cut to the bone. Both despised

imperialism. With J. W. Dafoe and his new under secretary of
state for external affairs, O. D. Skelton (Laurier's biographer),
King would be properly escorted to London to put Canada's blunt
veto on any schemes for consultation or imperial collaboration.
Nationalists and *nationalistes* might not cheer but they would
take quiet comfort. Lloyd George's appeal for aid in a possible war
with the Turks at Chanak in 1922 inspired Meighen to utter an
instinctive "Ready, Aye Ready." From King, it drew resentful
silence. The League of Nations, with its dangerous Article x,
would be reminded by Senator Raoul Dandurand, president of its
Assembly in 1925, that "Canada is a fire-proof house, far from the
source of any conflagration." If more public gestures were
needed, King sent another *Canadien*, Ernest Lapointe, to Washington in 1923 to sign the Halibut Treaty without the proffered
assistance from Great Britain.

If this seemed little, at home there was less. Not until 1924 was
the tariff even modestly reduced – on items that exclusively troubled Tory Ontario. The Hudson's Bay Railway, a prairie dream for
thirty years, would come – but only when King got a majority. The
Crowsnest Pass freight rate, suspended during the war, was
restored – for wheat only – in 1923. In the Maritimes, solid for King
in 1921, there was very little, for surely the region was as Liberal
as it needed to be. It was the West that needed pleasing and
patience.

In 1923, the Ontario farmer government was utterly defeated.
Its reforms counted for little in the face of internal divisions and
voters eager to sneer at rural earnestness. Those weaknesses
could be exploited. Pragmatic farmer-politicians like Ernest
Drury and Thomas Crerar were driven half-mad by rural ideolo-
gues, determined that farmers form a movement, not a party.
Alberta's Henry Wise Wood preached that government must be
based on groups like farmers, business, and labour, not on political parties. This brand of social corporatism did not fit practical
politics. Nor did farmers like what their representatives were
doing for them. The Progressives, on the dubious principle that
they were not really "politicians," forbade Crerar from becoming
leader of the opposition in 1922. Thereafter, their movement fell

apart. Radicals debated freight rates and such monetary theories as Social Credit; the pragmatists plotted how they could safely make peace with King.

By 1925, some were ready for a switch. So was Meighen. In opposition, he had worked ingeniously and well. The Maritimes had risen with one voice in a Maritimes Rights movement that just happened to be managed by Tories. By 1925, all three Maritime provincial governments had fallen to Conservatives. Elsewhere, Meighen could count on the recurrence of hard times since the war and what seemed to him the transparent futility of King's government. About Quebec, Meighen could do nothing nor would he even try to buy votes in the West. If anyone really wanted the Hudson's Bay Railway, he promised $3 million and no more. The outcome of the election, on October 29, 1925, was as good a victory as Meighen could have hoped to get: forty-seven per cent of the votes to King's forty per cent, and 116 seats to 99 for the Liberals, with the Progressives cut to nine per cent and 24 seats.

Yet King did not resign. Liberals raged privately at his "vanity and pomposity," his "predilection for strange and unworthy favourites." When Meighen and King each presented the Progressives with their programs, seven switched back to King and his majority held. Defeated in his own seat, King went west to win Prince Albert, and he brought Saskatchewan's C. A. Dunning back with him to the cabinet. A new finance minister gave Canadians a "prosperity budget" of tax-cuts and giveaways, an experience few of them had had since 1906. Meighen's near-victory in 1925 forced voters to realize that the Progressives were through and that the next contest would be a Liberal-Tory run-off. J. W. Dafoe was typical. In three elections he had avoided voting Liberal: now he saw no alternative.

First, there would be an unpleasant test. Prohibition, dead in most of Canada by 1924, persisted bravely south of the border, imposing a strain on the morality of customs officers and their elected superiors that natural avarice could not resist. The result, exposed by a vigorous Tory MP, Harry Stevens, was an odorous scandal of kickbacks, cover-ups, and bribes reaching all the way to the minister of customs, a French Canadian. King swiftly hoisted the guilty minister to the safety of the Senate and offered no signs of repentance. Tories raged, and pure-minded Progressives squirmed. The upshot, after much uproar, was a vote of censure on King's government which it would surely lose. But first, King won a weekend adjournment. Next, he headed to the governor general, Lord Byng of Vimy, to seek a dissolution, thus avoiding formal censure. Byng, shocked by the impropriety, refused. An equally shocked King urged him to check with London. Byng refused so colonial a gesture. King indignantly resigned. Meighen, against good advice but out of loyalty to the governor general, an honourable British soldier, accepted office. Then, when the Liberals orchestrated their own vote of censure, Byng gave Meighen the election he had denied King.

Meighen never could understand it. His opponent, the man who perennially insisted that "Parliament would decide," had been caught trying to run away from Parliament's decision. The man of insistent legalism had defied constitutional convention. King, too, may have been nonplussed by events, but luck was with him. In English-speaking Canada, the election issue had already been settled by the prosperity budget and Meighen. The customs scandals might arouse loyal Tories, but, in good times, muck smells like fertilizer. In Quebec, Byng could easily be portrayed as a British colonial governor, bullying the great rebel's grandson. And many of the Tories' customs house villains had been *Canadiens.* Meighen added Nova Scotia to his majorities in Ontario and British Columbia but his 99 seats could still not match King's 128 nor the remnant of 20 Progressives and 3 Labourites. Meighen suffered the ultimate humiliation; defeat in his own riding.

In memory, the twenties would shine as a golden era suspended between the Great War and the Great Depression. Only the last half decade actually qualified as golden, but economic growth was steady and remarkable. American prosperity poured over the border in the form of investment in branch plants, able to serve a British Empire sheltered behind an empire-wide tariff. Automobile, rubber, chemical, and clothing factories grew up around the lower

Great Lakes in industrial cities like Hamilton, Oshawa, Windsor, St. Catharines, and Montreal. To supply both Canadian and American markets there was a prodigious prodding and digging away at the minerals of the Canadian Shield, from the Noranda copper properties in Quebec to the gold of Kirkland Lake and the nickel of Sudbury. When King finally launched the promised Hudson's Bay Railway in 1927, it fulfilled an old tradition by opening up Flin Flon and the area beyond for the exploitation of its mineral wealth.

In 1920, the CNR earned $234 million, spent $231 million, and had the balance to retire its $1311-million debt. Instead of collapsing under the impossible debt load, the CNR staggered into the new decade.

An American-born, British-seasoned railroader, Sir Henry Thornton, cheerfully accepted King's invitation to run the system. Thornton was not original in his insistence that salvation lay with expansion, but he certainly expanded with a flair. The CNR added five thousand miles of track, built new locomotives, cars, and the grandest hotels the country had seen, from the Nova Scotian in Halifax to Jasper Park Lodge in the Rockies. The CNR bought ships to service the West Indies, experimented with air service, and created a transcontinental network to send programs to "radio cars" on its luxurious passenger trains. It was the golden age of Canadian rail, and of all the potential dead ends in the decade this was the most certain.

The twenties brought American investment and American markets, and these would make Canada a north-south nation once again. British economic influence had slipped with wartime liquidation of investments; now it fell consistently. The routes of the new transportation network would be highways, barely two-lane and winding at the beginning of the decade; a spreading telephone system; and the air itself, now spotted with the frail aircraft sent out by the British after the war as a gift to an infant Canadian air force. Even before its official birth in 1923, the Royal Canadian Air Force had shown how planes could be used to spot forest fires, deliver treaty money, and even catch smugglers. By surmounting the barriers of distance and mountain ranges to deliver prospectors and supplies to the far North, bush pilots managed to make northern isolation easier to bear. To the south, cars and trucks were having an even greater economic impact. Just as Canada's costly railway system had begun to rationalize and reform itself, road traffic had arrived as its most devastating competition. Canadians with $3250 to spend on a McLaughlin roadster or $850 for a Model T hardly worried. Provincial treasurers certainly did.

Almost every development of the twenties contradicted national unity. Ottawa had always managed railways; roads had been left under provincial control as unimportant. Now they mattered. The expansion of secondary education, and new allowances for widows, the blind, and the disabled were paid for from provincial coffers. Sir John A. Macdonald had planned an east-west country; now the branch-plant factories, the mineral exploration, the floods of American films, magazines, and radio programs were switching Canada to a north-south axis. Perhaps that was why Meighen's 1911-style nationalism grew fainter and more shrill.

With new responsibilities, provinces needed more revenue. Eager for allies, Mackenzie King tried to oblige, restrained only by his concern for the national debt. In London, the judicial Committee gave a hand. Lord Haldane, as its spokesman, administered a final kick to the once-sweeping claim that Ottawa was responsible for "peace, order and good government." In yet another decision about the regulation of booze, Haldane's Committee ruled that Ottawa's sweeping powers were restricted to periods of emergency. Otherwise, it was the provinces, with their control of "property and civil rights," which had the sweeping powers. As a further boost to provincial rights and revenues, King gave the prairie provinces full control of their natural resources.

Under duress, the federal government took a few initiatives. In 1929, over opposition from Ottawa and Quebec, the courts reinterpreted the British North America Act to say that women, as well as men, were "persons." Its responsibility for veterans had kept Ottawa slightly involved in health policies and a national employment service. In 1925, in exchange for supporting King, J. S. Woodsworth of the tiny Labour Party extorted a promise that old-age pensions would be established. The promise was kept in 1927 – Ottawa would meet half the cost of a meagre, means-tested pension for those over seventy. The provinces, compelled to pay the other half, hesitated. Nova Scotia found a novel way to raise its share. It legalized liquor, sold it profitably in government-run stores, and helped its elderly. Other provinces followed suit. By ending prohibition, Ontario's new Tory government bounced from deficit to surplus budgets.

Even when Britain, through the Statute of Westminster, granted Canada and her four other dominions formal independence in the world, Canada's provinces interfered. Before the Statute could be passed, Canada needed a formula to amend her constitution, the British North America Act. Not even the euphoria brought on by the country's diamond jubilee in 1927 could bring the premiers and Ottawa to agree on such a formula. While the British waited impatiently to adopt the Statute of Westminster, premiers Howard Ferguson of Ontario and Alexandre Taschereau of Quebec imposed their conditions. Canada's constitution, they insisted, would stay in London. Independent they might be, but Canadians could not yet trust themselves to alter their own system of government fairly.

The diamond jubilee year generated some tinselly nationalism, but nothing could hide the raw racial intolerance that had flourished since the war years. A Manitoba author had tried to create a more positive image of Canada's racial diversity by describing the provinces as a mosaic of cultures, but the diversity of languages and cultures seemed to give no pleasure. Bishop G. E. Lloyd of Saskatchewan, a colourful prairie pioneer, publicly denounced the "mongrelization" of Canada. It was Lloyd who provoked an aging Sir Clifford Sifton to deliver his tolerant, if condescending comments about "peasants in sheepskin coats." Later in the decade, the white hoods and flaming crosses of the Ku Klux Klan invaded western Canada, symbols of hatred of Catholics and "foreigners." Within a year, the Klan promoters had absconded with a hundred thousand dollars in membership funds, but their ugly message remained. In 1929, Saskatchewan voters chose a Tory government headed by J. T. M. Anderson, a respected educator whose book,

The Education of New Canadians, had demanded firm assimilation with "a true Canadian spirit and attachment to British institutions."

Nationalism and anxiety about alien forces had made the West a natural birthplace for the interdenominational movement that ended in 1925 with the formation of the United Church of Canada. Methodists, Congregationalists, and all but a sturdy core of Presbyterians joined the new organization. Enthusiasts had seen the new church as specifically Canadian and a challenge to a secular age. Others, with less idealism, saw it as a sensible business merger or as an answer to the numerical challenge of the Catholics. The first Moderator, George Pidgeon, firmly suppressed any vestiges of the old Methodist radicalism; wealthy contributors might be upset.

Not even Church Union could rescue Canadian Protestantism from the challenge of fundamentalists on one side or of rationalism and secularism on the other. Nothing could save the churches from paying the price of two great but divisive crusades: the War and prohibition.

Quebec had resisted both crusades and would fight until 1940 against a third: votes for women. In the post-war world, French Canada's leaders felt their people to be more isolated and endangered than ever. The conscription crisis had not been something as remote as Riel or the Ontario schools. The Canadian majority had imposed its will on Quebec; had taken Quebec's sons into an English-speaking army. Henri Bourassa, back in Parliament after 1921 as an independent, pleaded still for his bilingual, bicultural Canadian compact but he also grew conservative, abandoning forever the few radical ideas that earlier had inspired him.

In this, Bourassa was following a new intellectual fashion. The leader of the newest nationalism was Abbé Lionel Groulx, a tireless elf of a man who taught the history of Quebec to generations of students at the new University of Montreal. Only within Quebec, argued Groulx and his disciples of the *Action Française,* could a French and Catholic nationality be preserved. This preservation would demand rejection, even in the cities, of the external taints in films, books, and magazines. On Sunday, January 9, 1927,

Montreal's Laurier Palace cinema burned, killing seventy-eight children. Groulx's campaign to ban youngsters from movie theatres (and thereby the influence of American and British movies) was won.

Yet the triviality of the reform underlined the mean-minded limits of the *Action Française* program. Montreal was an ugly, unhealthy city for too many of its people, and by 1931, two-thirds of the 818,377 Montrealers were *Canadiens*. But, for them, as for most Canadians, the cities seemed bright, more lively, crowded with the material rewards of the era. In good times Groulx's austere, moralistic nationalism commanded disciples, not a mass following. In the thriving twenties, Groulx himself knew that his cause had stalled.

The twenties was really the first decade of mass-produced culture. Films, magazines, gramophones with "hit" records, professional sports, all promised a lifestyle ordinary people might soon enjoy. Intellectuals could read *Canadian Forum*, debate the merits of the Toronto-based artists, the Group of Seven; they might even have heard of Emily Carr's lonely work. Others could boast of the sailing feats of the *Bluenose* or hum the songs of the Dumbells, the soldier-entertainers who sustained what little remained of wartime nostalgia.

Canada was producing respected actors, musicians, and singers, but their renown was earned in New York, Paris, or London. The country's own frail culture was shrinking before the excitement and prosperity of the United States. No cultural force broke down the international barriers more swiftly than radio. By the mid-twenties, powerful American stations carried signals into most populated parts of Canada, and the technology of a crystal set receiver was not beyond a dexterous youngster. Canada, with its frugal comforts, its low wages, its backwater vision of itself, had never been more immediately or more dangerously challenged. Perhaps the inspiration would do some good.

5

The Depression

Great events have complex causes. Few now would date the Great Depression of the thirties from the Wall Street crash of October 1929. And, although the slump was a symptom of a much wider sickness, there are not many who would still believe those contemporary preachers who blamed it on falling morals, rising skirts, and self-indulgent insistence on living beyond one's means.

In 1929 it cost over ten thousand dollars a year to live the resplendent life depicted in the rotogravure supplements; only 13,477 Canadian families admitted to such an income. The federal Department of Labour insisted that a family needed $1200 to $1500 a year to maintain a "minimum standard of decency." Sixty per cent of working men and eighty-two per cent of working women were earning less than $1000 a year. By any definition, most people were as poor as Canadians had been for generations. Depressions did not occur because ordinary people lived beyond their means. In fact the British economist, John Maynard Keynes, would soon point out that the economy shut down because too many people had no means to buy what it could produce. Most Canadians qualified for this category.

The immediate cause of the Depression in Canada was not the Wall Street crash but the enormous 1928 wheat crop. A decade of immigration had filled the last, most infertile prairie land. As well, western farmers had forgotten politics as times improved. They listened instead to a persuasive American lawyer named Aaron Sapiro. Rather than going to the Wheat Board or the Grain Exchange, Sapiro said, why not pool the wheat harvest and sell it with the united bargaining power of any good cartel? Thousands of farmers joined the wheat pool, prospered, and added to their acreage. The idea worked brilliantly – as long as there was no glut and no serious competition. By 1928, there were both: 567 million bushels at a Pool-guaranteed price of $1.28 a bushel, to be sold in a world that could now buy much more cheaply from the United States, Argentina, Australia, and even the Soviet Union.

Of course, no one worried too much in 1929. Prosperity now seemed permanent, but perhaps, as brokers warned their clients, the market needed just a tiny "correction." Inventories had become too large. Capital investment was a trifle optimistic. Salesmen on the prairies confessed that orders were down. Business prophets cautiously reminded their customers that economies, like workers, needed an occasional rest. Slowly, and then irreversibly, an economic system based on credit, confidence, and massive resource exports began rolling down the cycle. Distant buyers cancelled orders for timber, fish, and base metals. Construction stopped. Industrialists checked their shrinking order books, and commanded wage cuts, half-time work, or even a temporary shutdown. There should be no astonishment; depressions had already occurred twice in that prosperous decade, in 1920 and 1923.

Politicians in Canada did not face much annoyance from economic indicators or unemployment statistics. The few available figures were collected by the Department of Labour in a somewhat haphazard system of local reports and published in its *Labour Gazette*. In 1929, the *Gazette* found about three per cent of its sample looking for jobs; a year later, the total had reached eleven per cent, or 530,000 men and women. That was alarming but not unprecedented. Provincial governments, pestering Ottawa for relief measures, were undoubtedly playing politics. They were also dodging their constitutional responsibility for social welfare. Mackenzie King, proud of his soberly balanced budget, was outraged that Tory premiers should mine votes from an unpleasant but short-lived down-turn. He would not give one cent, he told the House of Commons on April 3, 1930, "for these alleged unemployment purposes." He might confer with the more respectful and needy prairie premiers, but as for provincial governments that diametrically opposed him, "I would not give them a five-cent piece."

Such blunt comments were out of character, but the prime minister felt quite removed from the economic calamity that was beginning to preoccupy Canadians. He had determined on a 1930 election long before his current spiritualist added her blessing, and his new finance minister, C. A. Dunning, duly cut the federal sales tax to one per cent. The prairies could thank the Liberals for giving them control over their natural resources. Nationalists could applaud the promised Statute of Westminster, and Quebec would always remember the Tories and conscription. A royal commission on broadcasting, headed by Sir John Aird, had recommended a BBC-style safeguard for Canada's invaded airwaves, but discussion of a publicly owned broadcasting system could safely be postponed. Who knew what Quebec sensitivities it might arouse?

King felt all the more secure because of his opposition. In 1927 the Tories had followed the Liberal example with an American-style leadership convention in Winnipeg. The winner was Richard Bedford Bennett, a New Brunswick-born corporation lawyer who had waged his party's hopeless battles in Alberta before his friendship with the heiress to the fortune of the Ottawa Valley's E. B. Eddy lumber company brought him a vast inheritance. As a youth Bennett had pledged total abstinence, and he fought temptation with candy and sugar. He was a big, plump man with a booming voice, a domineering manner, and a capacity for kindness that he kept utterly secret. Like King, a lonely bachelor, Bennett carried an aura of the business competence that the era already worshipped. King considered his opponent far inferior to Meighen. About Bennett's intellect, King was right. In electoral terms, King was wrong.

The Depression was Bennett's chance. The "five-cent piece" speech was soon burnished in memory as proof of King's callousness. "Mackenzie King promises you conferences": trumpeted Bennett, "I promise you action." Quebec farmers were told to blame their miseries on imports of New Zealand butter. Bennett would save them. The Liberals had allowed a one-sided imperial preference; Bennett would demand full reciprocity. In the crisis, the United States had led the way in hoisting tariffs. Bennett would do so too, but in his hands, protection would "blast a way into the markets of the world." Even doubters stayed to marvel. After the years of anaemic compromise and shuffling evasion, here was self-confidence and dynamism. As a businessman rich enough to finance his party's entire campaign, Bennett would resolve the Depression. On July 28, Bennett won the kind of triumph Tories had not seen since the days of Sir John A. Macdonald: 137 seats to 91 for King and a rump of only 12 for the Progressives. Among the Tories, to prove that this was the age of miracles, were sixteen French-Canadian rural members.

If vigour could have demolished the Depression, it would have vanished within a year of the election. Bennett summoned the new Parliament for September 1930, forced through the biggest tariff increases since 1879, passed $20 million in emergency relief, and boasted that added protection would guarantee twenty-five thousand industrial jobs. In London for the Imperial Conference of 1930 – and to supplant King in signing the Statute of Westminster – Bennett joined his old friend, Lord Beaverbrook (the former Max Aitken) in a vain crusade for an Empire-based exclusive trading system. Two years later, after Britain's own efforts for free trade had utterly failed, an Imperial Economic Conference in Ottawa gave Bennett his belated victory. Desperate for any agreement, the British lowered their tariff barriers to Canada and received no more than Bennett's pledge not to raise his fifty per cent protection any higher. Canadian financiers and industrialists had good reason to rejoice. British politicians grumbled that Bennett had bullied them mercilessly.

While Canadians found themselves in a trade war with a steadily more protectionist United States, Bennett made a determined bid to launch the long-contemplated St. Lawrence Deep Waterway project. A treaty with President Herbert Hoover's Republican administration passed all the way to the American Senate. Senators from the Atlantic states, worried about the waterway's effect on trade in their harbours, promptly killed it. Thousands of potential jobs vanished, but Bennett poured still more money into provincial relief projects, adding close to a billion dollars to the national debt. The Wheat Pool, utterly ruined when its advance payments to farmers far exceeded the price it received for their wheat, staggered on only because Bennett provided secret subsidies. Canada's chartered banks preened themselves on surviving without a bankruptcy, but Bennett finally forced them to accept a central Bank of Canada – though the government held only a minority of the shares.

Bennett's most unexpected creation was the Canadian Radio Broadcasting Commission. Prodded by young enthusiasts in the Canadian Radio League who insisted that it would be either the State or the States, Bennett had taken up the Aird Commission report with unexpected interest. A Judicial Committee decision, surprising only because of the Committee's past practices, confirmed that broadcasting was in the federal domain. Born in 1932, in the depth of the Depression, the CRBC was a sadly underfinanced compromise. It was also a Canadian stake in public broadcasting in the decade when radio became the mass medium that mattered to almost everyone.

Radio mattered because, as the Depression deepened, radio sets became the only escape from a besetting hopelessness for many people. This was no ordinary depression in which savings vanished and countless city families slipped home to the security of the farm. As J. S. Woodsworth told Parliament, "If they went out today, they would meet another army of unemployed coming back from the country to the city." People in Ottawa, he reported, took refuge in garbage dumps. Bennett's own files bulged with reports of misery. Even the aged daughter of a former prime minister was reported to be on the verge of starvation.

Unemployment insurance had been a Liberal policy in 1919. Only unions now pleaded for it: experts and politicians claimed that it would subsidize idleness. Instead, they insisted, wages must fall until everyone would find work. It took time. By 1933, the government's crude statistics reported twenty-three per cent out of work. A third of Canada's manufacturing jobs had vanished. Net farm income fell from $417 million in 1929 to $109 million in 1933.

Those with jobs found some compensations. Prices fell faster than wages until 1932-33. A fifteen-per-cent wage cut imposed on civil servants by Ottawa and imitated by most provinces and other major employers still left living standards undamaged. The prosperous few could enjoy themselves with an obliviousness to wider suffering that wealth seems to confer. Newspapers and radio helped. Media in the thirties seem to have accepted a solemn duty to trivialize or ignore the misery of millions. Lush Hollywood musicals and adventure films filled neighbourhood movie theatres. Air races, professional sports, and the exotic junketing of reporters such as Gordon Sinclair gave the public an escape. The birth of the Dionne quintuplets on May 28, 1934, at Callander, Ontario, provided some reporters, politicians, business promoters, and members of the medical profession with a special chance for fame and fortune.

The unemployed would eagerly have shared in the escape, but relief procedures, designed to force the idle to work, crushed self-respect. Relief officials insisted that cars, telephones, pets, ornaments, comfortable furniture, and all but a single bare light fixture be sacrificed. Recipients collected food vouchers, sought medical care from an over-worked contract doctor, and visited a municipal depot for issues of used clothing. Men shovelled snow, chopped wood, or pulled weeds for their relief benefits. Since women did not work, often no provision was made for their clothing or personal needs. The new social work profession sold its services as "experts" in detecting fraud and waste.

Misery on relief was deliberate public policy. Even at the depths of the Depression, editors and business leaders insisted that jobs were available if men would only hunt for them. One result of this was that single unemployed men were sent packing by relief officials. Thousands rode boxcars to British Columbia. Some froze to death or were murdered on the way. Provincial governments established work camps for single men. In 1933, Bennett's government followed suit, using the Department of National Defence to run camps behind a discreet façade of civilian administration. On paper, men hacking at bush or restoring historic fortifications cost a dollar a day. After their expenses had been deducted, twenty cents remained as their actual pay.

Those who held jobs knew that thousands were waiting for a chance to replace them. Some employers fired women because men needed work; others replaced men with women because they would accept lower pay. There were few strikes. Only the Communist-led Workers Unity League organized vigorously, and its efforts often ended in bloodshed and failure. Bred in the doctrine of self-help, individual Canadians seemed almost pathetically willing to accept responsibility for their plight. Some literally died rather than accept relief. Only slowly did guilt turn to despair and then to deep resentment as the depth and duration of the Depression exceeded every memory. When urban politicians like Montreal's Camillien Houde or Vancouver's Gerry McGeer sought votes by helping the unemployed, their cities risked bankruptcy.

Nowhere was destitution greater than across much of the prairie West. In eastern Canada, farmers suffered falling prices and occasional foreclosures, but there was food to eat, and the rural population actually increased. In the West, where Canadians had boasted of the greatest farmland in the world, the thirties brought literal starvation.

The collapse of world grain markets would have been catastrophe enough, but people would have eaten. In 1929, drought devastated much of the harvest, and not for another ten long years would weather or crop conditions give the prairies a satisfactory harvest. In 1931, the wind began lifting the topsoil in great black clouds. The next year brought the first great plague of grasshoppers, which devoured every green thing and clothing and tool handles besides. In 1933, drought, hail, rust, and frost joined the grasshoppers, as though all nature's forces had united in giving prairie settlers a notice to quit.

Thousands obeyed, fleeing the region in despair or hauling their families and remaining livestock to the parkland belt or the Peace River country. A battered remnant stayed and, in a rare collaboration of farmer and scientist, learned to fight the encroaching desert with trash cover, contour ploughing, and new strains of wheat. Huge acreages, sold for cultivation through the greed of governments and railways, were finally returned to the grazing role for which they were appropriate.

The prairie West had been Canada's proudest achievement. In 1928, only British Columbia had boasted a higher per-capita income than Alberta's $548. At $478, Saskatchewan had stood fourth. By 1933, at a mere $135 a person, Saskatchewan was the poorest province in Canada. Her government was bankrupt and her people turned gratefully to the trainloads of food and used clothing sent as charity from other regions. Even Depression-battered Newfoundland sent salt cod; the poor Westerners, not knowing how to use it, soaked it, boiled it, and finally used it to plug holes in their roofs.

Bennett's bold speeches and dynamic policies provided no solutions to the spreading misery. Within the narrow available orthodoxies, no government could. By espousing protection, Canada merely added to the beggar-my-neighbour policies that deepened the world-wide depression. In opposition, the Liberals provided no alternatives. Their defeat in 1930, they soon discovered, had been another stroke of luck. The Tories were in trouble and Mackenzie King had no intention of helping them out with his own ideas. King's fourteen-point program of 1933 set high standards for vagueness and contradiction. The Liberals, King claimed, would "liberalize internal trade"; they would create "a more equitable distribution of wealth." Such phrases were almost deliberately meaningless. At heart, King seemed satisfied that the economy was working as badly as could be expected when Liberals were out of power.

Bennett would have been unlikely to take King's, or anyone else's, advice. A lonely, domineering man, inhabiting an extensive suite in the Château Laurier, Bennett was portrayed by cartoonists as conducting cabinet meetings with himself in every chair. By now his wealth and corpulence inspired more loathing than reassurance. Goaded by his own sense of failure, Bennett's reaction was to strike out.

The labour crises of 1919 had added Section 98 to the Criminal Code: a sweeping description of sedition accompanied by savage prison terms and possible deportation. In 1931, the government seized leaders of the small Communist party. Chief Justice Sir William Mulock (a Laurier minister and King's first patron) condemned the men with every appearance of relish. Bennett's pledge to crush communism "with the iron heel of ruthlessness" was remembered. Book censorship became a duty of customs officials. The Royal Canadian Mounted Police, expanded in 1920 from the old Royal North West Mounted Police, now served Bennett as a secret service and riot police. Though Communists *were* involved in much of the unrest that accompanied the Depression, some Canadians saw the strikers, hunger marchers, and even rioters only as fellow human beings, fighting for jobs, a living wage, and a little dignity.

There had to be alternatives, but few were emerging. Among the country's intellectuals, the University of Toronto economic historian Harold Innis lectured his junior and more radical colleagues against venturing to mingle their ideas with contemporary politics. The United Church of Canada, heir to a reforming Methodist tradition, worried about its dwindling finances and prudently proclaimed moral depravity a greater evil than economic misery. J. W. Dafoe, editor of the influential *Winnipeg Free Press*, urged Liberals to find new ideas and then damned anything that strayed from his *laisser-faire* individualism.

The ferment came, as had almost every radical idea of the twenties, from Calgary. One doctrine was already familiar, thanks to the advocacy of William Irvine, Woodsworth's Labour partner in the 1921 Parliament. Social Credit, brainchild of an English engineer, argued that the difference between the return to a producer and the final price of a product created "poverty in the midst of plenty." In the 1920s it was theory. In 1932, it was harsh reality in Alberta when a Calgary high school principal and fundamentalist radio preacher named William Aberhart took up the Social Credit message. Rarely had medium and message been better combined. A gospel-reared audience, frightened by debt, insecurity, and sudden poverty, responded to simple economics taught with the imagery of thieves, money-lenders, and social dividends. The radicalism of overthrowing the entire financial system seemed less when the temples of Canadian banking would crash in the distant east. Besides, Mr. Aberhart of the Prophetic Bible Institute was a man of God, not a politician like the corrupt opportunists in Ottawa, Toronto, and Edmonton.

Social Credit mingled radical and conservative messages in brilliant counterpoint. Another idea was less ambiguous, if more complex. Canadian socialism had shattered on the Bolshevik Revolution of 1917. The Communists had become the disciples of Lenin and Stalin and servants of Soviet policy. The remnants shared little more than a commitment to democracy. The craft unionists of the Trades and Labour Congress had fled politics in the 1920s and nothing in the 1930s would entice the TLC's aging, frightened leaders back. The wreck of the federal Progressives had left a radical remnant, the "Ginger Group," more correctly called the "co-operating independents." Among them, only the slight, bearded ex-clergyman and pacifist, J. S. Woodsworth, had both a strategy and patience. Someday, Canada would have its own version of Britain's Labour Party, complete with intellectuals, riding associations, MPs, and trade union affiliates. The Depression might be Woodsworth's opportunity to build such a party.

In 1932, a few academics ignored Innis's prudent advice and formed the League for Social Reconstruction. Woodsworth was made honorary president. That summer, at Calgary, delegates for the regular meeting of western labour parties found that the economic crisis had attracted members of farmer and socialist parties and even a solitary eastern unionist, A. R. Mosher from the nationalistic All-Canadian Congress of Labour. The result, with Woodsworth's shepherding, was the proclamation of the Co-operative Commonwealth Federation (Farmer Labour Socialist). A year later, a first national convention of the CCF met at Regina and, after laborious debates, adopted a manifesto and a constitution. Apart from a conclusion tacked on to add spice, the manifesto was an academic and sometimes technocratic document befitting its chief author, Professor Frank Underhill of the University of Toronto. The conclusion, appended at Regina, promised rather more than the body of the document would have justified: "No CCF government will rest content until it has eradicated capitalism and put into operation the full programme of socialized planning which will lead to the establishment in Canada of the co-operative commonwealth." Woodsworth, more cautiously, reminded listeners that socialism came from "the good old Latin word for 'friend,'" and promised an authentic Canadian version.

Unlike Social Credit, whose study groups and mass radio audiences swept it almost silently toward power, the CCF was exposed and embattled from birth. By 1934, it could boast hundreds of clubs and an organization in most provinces. It had also been denounced by business leaders and editors, repudiated by the TLC, and condemned as a danger to Catholicism by the coadjutor bishop of Montreal. For good measure, the disciplined militants of the Communist party were as bent on the CCF's destruction as on that of R. B. Bennett, with rather better chances of success. Social Credit, in contrast, remained within Alberta and Saskatchewan, under the sweep of Aberhart's powerful radio message.

Third parties usually look more frightening before elections than afterwards. The CCF started strong. In 1933 it could build on an old labour-socialist tradition in British Columbia to win second place behind the Liberals. T. Duff Pattullo triumphed on a slogan of "Work and Wages." The next year, the Ontario Liberals, under an engaging young onion farmer named Mitchell F. Hepburn, won that province for the first time since 1902. This time, the CCF won a single labour seat. More predictable was the Liberal victory in Saskatchewan under the former premier, Jimmy Gardiner. This time, not a single supporter of Premier Anderson's Tory government survived. The small opposition was CCF.

Not even the Depression nor Woodsworth's saintly mien could make many Canadians embrace socialism. Small businessmen and upholders of a modified status quo found their own hero in H. H. Stevens, the British Columbia Tory who had been hero of the Customs scandal. As Minister of Trade and Commerce, Stevens had turned into a crusader. A small merchant himself, Stevens had no trouble understanding how big companies controlled or shared the market. In the Depression, they had preserved their own generous profit margins by squeezing their smaller suppliers or independent retailers. The evidence was in the price spread between the primary producer and the ultimate consumer. Stevens demanded an investigation. A parliamentary committee found all the evidence it wanted of price-gouging, starvation wages, sweated labour, and predatory behaviour, with powerful names like Eaton's and Simpson's to grace the testimony. Harry Stevens and his main backer, Toronto clothier Warren K. Cook, were delighted. Bennett was not. When the prime minister tried to suppress Stevens's opinions and drove him from the cabinet, millions of Canadians accepted the ex-minister as a crusading hero.

Canadian heroes were scarce. Until 1932, people saw no alternative leaders. Under Herbert Hoover, Americans were faring no better. Then, in developments Canadians could follow on their radios, Franklin Delano Roosevelt swept into the White House and the long drama of the New Deal began. A generation of Canadians became instinctive Democrats. The Roosevelt radio image may have been artificial but its effectiveness transcended borders. For the first time, Canadians coveted their neighbours' political leadership. Even Bennett was not immune to Roosevelt's spell. Privately he had writhed at the sneers of shantytown "Bennett-burghs" and horse-drawn automobiles called "Bennett buggies." All his life, Bennett had seen himself as a dynamic successful figure. His frustration now drove him to imitate Roosevelt. Since 1927, Canada had had a legation in Washington. Bennett had chosen his brother-in-law, W. D. Herridge, for the post. A man of ideas, Herridge now urged Bennett to adopt the style and perhaps even some of the content of the New Deal. Bennett was game. Herridge drafted speeches and Bennett demanded radio time. On January 3, 1935, he began.

Canadians listened dutifully and then with astonishment, none more so than Bennett's Tory associates. It was not the substance that was new; it was Bennett's flamboyant, uncompromising language. If the CCF's J. S. Woodsworth had seized the microphone, the words could not have been more unexpected. "There can be no permanent recovery without reform," Bennett declared. "And, to my mind, reform means Government intervention. It means Government control and regulation. It means the end of *laisser faire.*" It meant unemployment insurance, minimum wages, and maximum hours of work, marketing legislation for farmers, and measures against price-fixing. The federal trade commission Stevens had sought would now become reality.

In a few days, Bennett had regained the initiative. Then he fell ill. When he recovered, he had to hurry to England for the Silver Jubilee of King George v. By the time he returned, Mackenzie King had found his line: if Bennett's New Deal was good, it was already Liberal policy; if it was not, it was typical Tory dictatorship. In either case, King declared, most of the new program was plainly beyond Ottawa's constitutional powers. Old Tories and business interests orchestrated their opposition. By the time the Dominion Trade and Industry Commission Act appeared, Stevens had left his party. On July 7, 1935, he announced the formation of a new one. Within five days he had a program and a title: the Reconstruction party. Its target would be those thousands of Canadians who still hoped for a reformed capitalism.

By summer, Canadians wondered whether Bennett even remembered his January cry for reform. In May, Communist organizers pulled men out of the shabby, demoralizing relief camps in British Columbia. The men came eagerly. Surely there had to be more to life than labouring under army discipline for twenty cents a day. Soon, more than a thousand had piled on boxcars for an "On-to-Ottawa" trek. At Regina, Bennett ordered the march halted. He would meet the leaders. The result was a cascade of insults between a plump prime minister and the trek leader, Arthur "Slim" Evans. On Dominion Day, RCMP and city police in Regina broke up a trekkers' public meeting. A policeman was beaten to death. Even so, sympathy lay with the trekkers.

On August 22, Aberhart's Social Crediters annihilated Alberta's farmer government. The simple certainties of two-party politics had dissolved. CCFers, Reconstructionists, Communists, and Social Crediters vied with Liberals and Conservatives for votes. Bennett, pounding out the old verities of tariff and Empire, pouring his own money into the Tory campaign, seemed oblivious to all that had happened in five of the worst years his audiences had experienced. It was Mackenzie King who caught the frightened mood with his slogan, "King or Chaos." The hysteria easily captured Quebec's Premier Alexandre Taschereau. In 1930, he had admitted that Bennett might be "a safe man"; now Taschereau raged that the Tory leader had "launched into a Socialistic venture bordering on Communism."

King was confident enough not to make promises. He was right. No Parliament had ever been so lop-sided: 173 Liberals were voted in, a mere 40 Tories, and 17 Social Crediters to reflect Aberhart's provincial sweep. In contrast, with over twice the Social Credit national vote, but spread across Canada, Woodsworth led only 6 CCFers, and Stevens led only himself. In the Canadian system, third parties could mean stronger governments and bigger majorities.

Afterwards, Canadians would be accused of excessive caution in choosing King. The Liberal majority is deceiving: King gained a smaller percentage of votes in 1935 than in 1930. Canadians had so many choices they could not make up their minds.

King's luck had worked twice, with defeat in 1930 and victory in 1935. It worked yet again. In the months before the election, Bennett and the Americans had finally negotiated the Reciprocity Treaty both countries had toyed with since 1866. Within weeks of the Liberal victory, King could go to Washington to collect the prize. Its Tory origins were conveniently forgotten.

King's new government was more positive than its program. In 1937, the Bank of Canada was made a purely public institution without private shareholders. The feeble CRBC, which had enraged King by allowing Tory election propaganda, was replaced by a stronger Canadian Broadcasting Corporation. King's transport minister, C. D. Howe, launched the government-owned Trans-Canada Airlines.

Across North America, the Depression had reached bottom in 1932. Slowly, painfully, the economy was climbing from the trough. Perhaps Bennett's policies had helped. They had certainly rewarded the business and financial backers of his party. Their sectors of the economy suffered less enduring pain; it was humbler Canadians who suffered too much. After 1933, as the statistics of recovery climbed to their peak in 1937, incomes and employment lagged far behind. In the United States, more by accident than by guidance from economists like John Maynard Keynes, Roosevelt had discovered that purchasing power might be the key to recovery. In Alberta, if the British North America Act had not been used to checkmate his monetary ideas, the new premier, Aberhart, might have fallen on the same solution. Social Credit's twenty-five-dollar "prosperity certificates" were, after all, an eccentric form of purchasing power. Hidden among the better-educated young mandarins in Ottawa, similarly heterodox notions were percolating, though clad in wholly conventional language. A combination of sympathetic and unknowing Liberal ministers and the relapse of the economy in 1938 would give Canada its first Keynesian budget in 1939. Cautiously, young officials actually talked of a "stimulative deficit." Their experiment was soon obscured by a far greater event: war.

King's opposition now came from provincial premiers, not Parliament. Men like Pattullo, Hepburn, and Aberhart had broken the tradition of grey, invisible provincial leadership. In 1936, they were joined by another premier, Maurice Duplessis. Not since 1897 had the Liberal hold on Quebec been broken. On his own, as leader of the tiny provincial Conservative party, Duplessis could never have managed it, but, like Mercier, he had united the extremes. The pretext this time was not Riel but the grim, exhausting economic crisis and a provincial government too corruptly linked to the English-dominated "trusts." For Quebec, the Depression was a national as well as an economic issue. Young, nationalistic Liberals had abandoned their party. Duplessis had scooped them up in a *Union Nationale*, pledged to social reform and nationalization of the worst oppressors, such as the electricity trust. Once Duplessis was in power, the younger Liberals were set aside. Duplessis would govern in his own style, courting the Church, persecuting Communists, unionists, and even the

Jehovahs' Witnesses with an ingenious application of "property and civil rights." A "Padlock Law" allowed police to lock up premises used for "Communist" purposes. As for business, Duplessis was open to friendship, and Montreal's English-speaking leaders knew how to respond.

Duplessis's style was a variant of a new pattern. The Depression had shown the constitutional and fiscal weaknesses of the provinces. If Canada was to be a modern industrial society, drastic constitutional changes were needed. None of the new premiers agreed. They had captured the hopes of voters by arguing that style, not fresh ideas, would suffice to cure the Depression. None obliged the voters more than Ontario's Mitch Hepburn. He auctioned off government limousines in a football stadium to show that he was a man of the people. He summoned the press to watch him fire senior career officials. At the same time, Hepburn was also discovering sensual pleasures vouchsafed to few Elgin county onion farmers. Now he was the guest and confidant of financiers, speculators, and the handsome mining promoter, George McCullagh, new owner of an amalgamated *Globe and Mail.*

In 1937 General Motors employees at Oshawa contrasted soaring company profits with their own latest pay-cut and decided to organize. By summoning organizers from the bold new Congress of Industrial Organizations in the United States, the workers made Ontario that much less comfortable for American investors. When they struck General Motors, Hepburn did his best to beat the workers. In the end, it was the company that buckled. The little bridgehead of industrial unionism at Oshawa held, but Hepburn had the arguments and the money to win a smashing re-election that same year. Other premiers could take note. So could the Tories, some of whom had backed the Oshawa strikers.

The Depression forced thoughtful Canadians to realize that feeble central government had crippled their country's power to meet the crisis. Most of Bennett's five belated New Deal laws fell before the courts. Provincial premiers like Hepburn, Pattullo, Duplessis, Aberhart, and Nova Scotia's charismatic Angus L. Macdonald represented effective barriers to reform. Years of judicial reinterpretation, allied to Ottawa's fiscal caution, had left neither federal nor provincial governments with the strength to revive the economy in peacetime. Politics and the British North America Act locked Canadians into their Depression misery.

In time, Canada might have recovered. Instead, a world-wide tragedy became Canada's salvation.

PART IV

MIDDLE AGE, MIDDLE POWER

I

Mr. King's War

With passage of the Statute of Westminster in 1931, Canada could claim her full voice in the world. The 1917 experiment of a common imperial foreign policy had proved hopeless. Its major accomplishment was the end of the Anglo-Japanese alliance, demanded by Canada to placate American opinion. The British had no further appetite for sharing vital decisions; the dominions had even less taste for imperial burdens. By 1926, Lord Balfour's proposal for a "British Commonwealth of Nations," linked by no more than sentiment, tradition, and a common monarch, seemed to be the only acceptable survivor of the imperial dream. Three centuries of colonial rule ended without rancour.

Post-war Canada fled commitments in the Empire or the League of Nations. Like their American neighbours, Canadians rejoiced that the Atlantic separated them from the sordid diplomacy and quarrelsome politics of the old world. They could enjoy the luxury of near-disarmament. Under King and his isolationist under secretary, O. D. Skelton, Canada did little more than preach to the delegates who assembled regularly at Geneva for what Skelton termed "The League of European Victors." Few Canadians needed to be persuaded that the Versailles settlement had been short-sighted; even fewer wished to die to uphold its terms. Long before he re-wrote economics, John Maynard Keynes had convinced a generation that the harsh, punitive treaty would lead to a new war. He was, of course, right. Sir Robert Borden, as much as Mackenzie King, disapproved of the League's mutual security provision, Article x.

Canadians in the twenties and thirties were isolationists, indifferent to the old world. Even Canadians with strong British loyalties halted their allegiance at the English Channel. The conservative, Catholic leaders of French Canada found everything to abhor in Soviet communism and German and French socialism but much to admire in Mussolini's fascism or Franco's Spanish Falange. Both purported to be bulwarks of the Vatican. Among Canadians of neither French nor British origins, European conflicts had their own reverberations. A tiny Communist party recruited its cadre from Finns, Ukrainians, and Jews with memories of tsarist Russia. Nazi and fascist organizations sought recruits among German and Italian Canadians. Old-world divisions were too easy to import.

In the twenties, King had found that his eternal "no" in external relations and defence had provided useful common ground for his awkward coalition of prairie and Quebec supporters. He needed no reminder of the experience when he returned to power in the far more dangerous world of 1935. In 1931, Japan had invaded Manchuria; in 1933, Hitler's Germany had defied the arms limitations imposed at Versailles, and the direction, if not the horrifying extent, of Nazi policies was becoming apparent. As King took office, nervous diplomats at Geneva were devising sanctions to try to deter Mussolini from invading a helpless Ethiopia. Left on his own by the change of government, Canada's permanent official at the League, W. A. Riddell, took his chance to add oil to the list; no other commodity would more surely affect the Italian war machine.

Journalists hailed Riddell's initiative as the "Canadian Resolution." In Ottawa, Mackenzie King was horrified. Riddell had apparently committed Canada to defying Italy. He had offended influential French Canadians who saw no harm in Mussolini's imperial adventure. The "Canadian Resolution" was discreetly withdrawn. Instead, the League was treated to a homily from King on the virtues of conciliation and a reminder of the Dominion's interests: "Canada's first duty to the League and to the British Empire," King explained in 1936, ". . . is, if, possible, to keep this country united."

Canada's attitude did not cause the Second World War. Like that of New Zealand, which valiantly upheld the cause of collective security in the League, Canada's influence was tiny. It was, however, also clear. The twelve hundred Canadians who went to Spain to fight Franco were threatened with a two-year jail sentence. (A third of them did not survive service in the International Brigade's Mackenzie-Papineau battalion.) Refugees fleeing Hitler's concentration camps were rejected by Canada. Jewish immigrants were unwelcome to King's lieutenant, the minister of justice, Ernest Lapointe, or to influential anti-Semites across Canada. In the autumn of 1938, King rejoiced as much as most Canadians when Neville Chamberlain, the British prime minister, returned from Munich with the promise of "peace in our time." The crusty J. W. Dafoe of the *Winnipeg Free Press* sounded curmudgeonly when he headed his editorial, "What's the Cheering For?"

If Britain had gone to war over Czechoslovakia that autumn, King knew that even his divided country would have followed. Reluctantly, he had begun to prepare Canada for the ordeal. Fifteen years of military neglect during major change in the weapons of war had left her virtually defenceless. Rearmament might also be designed to avoid the heavy casualties that had led to conscription in the First World War. Building up the young Royal Canadian Air Force and the Royal Canadian Navy would strengthen coastal defences and avert charges of imperial subservience. The army, Canada's pride in the earlier war, would have lowest priority.

Rearmament reflected a new dimension in Canadian policy: defence links with the United States. The flood of American tourists, investment, and mass culture had accelerated the trend of Americanization, but until Roosevelt's inauguration in 1933, nothing had altered Washington's traditional indifference to Canada. As much as the dynamism of the New Deal, Roosevelt's "Good Neighbour" policy transformed Canadian-American relations. Economic links had strengthened in 1935 with a sweeping trade agreement, but more was to come. By the 1930s, it was no longer science fiction to believe that enemy bombers, refuelled at some hidden Arctic base, could sweep down on the United States. American security was affected by Canada's vast, undefended territory. Subtly, Canada now found herself sheltered behind the 120-year-old Monroe doctrine and subjected to Washington's anxieties.

At Kingston in 1938 to receive an honorary degree from Queen's University, Roosevelt assured his Canadian audience that ". . . the people of the United States will not stand idly by if domination of Canadian soil is threatened by any other empire." A delighted Mackenzie King promptly promised that Canada, too, understood her obligations: invaders must not be able to use her soil to attack the United States. It was a firmer guarantee than King had ever given Britain.

The American commitment was comforting. By early 1939, war was inevitable. Appeasement had failed. King's French-Canadian followers were sternly brought into line by Ernest Lapointe. King's adamant promise about conscription helped: "So long as this government may be in power, no such measure shall be enacted." The pledge was promptly echoed by Bennett's Tory successor, Robert Manion. In a further brilliant stroke to unite Canada, King stage-managed the country's first royal visit. In 1937, the monarchy had been shaken by the abdication of Edward VIII. In June 1939, Edward's successor, a shy, stammering George VI and his radiant queen crossed the Dominion twice. A whiff of glamour suddenly excited a Depression-weary country. The glow was still there in September, when German tanks rumbled across the Polish frontier.

By September 3, 1939, Britain was at war. Unofficially, so was Canada. Before politicians could assemble in Ottawa, the War Measures Act had been proclaimed and meagre forces had moved to war stations. King fulfilled his promise that "Parliament would decide" on the war. Only two Quebec nationalists and the CCF leader, J. S. Woodsworth, dissented. When Canada officially entered the war on September 10, she was more united than anyone could have imagined only a year before. In Montreal, a young nationalist, André Laurendeau, hunted for allies to protest the war; he found too few to matter. Across Canada the unemployed flocked to militia armouries to enlist. Montreal regiments filled their ranks first.

It was by no means apparent what should come next. A 1st Canadian Infantry Division was approved and sailed in December, but the Army's war plans suffered drastic cuts. French and British troops settled down to the "phoney war" on the French frontier. In Ottawa, the government considered how war orders might pull the economy out of a depression that was still claiming half a million unemployed. Unexpectedly, the British offered a solution. Canada's vast spaces and secure skies had been used to train flyers in the earlier war; now Canadians should contribute to a far more massive program. By December 1939, after much ill-natured haggling, King and British negotiators could announce a British Commonwealth Air Training Plan designed to train twenty thousand pilots a year. Canada would pay $350 million of the $600 million cost and provide most of the trainees. At King's insistence, the British reluctantly defined the BCATP as Canada's major contribution to the allied effort. The government could rejoice: its money would be spent in Canada. Britain would pay for the airmen once they reached England, and it seemed inconceivable that aircrew casualties could ever lead to conscription. Other countries would provide the cannon fodder.

Ordinary Canadians were also satisfied. That was the evidence of the polls. In October, Duplessis sought a new mandate from Quebec voters, offering himself as national saviour against Ottawa centralizers and conscription. Lapointe and other federal ministers criss-crossed the province, repeating pledges against conscription and swearing they would resign and leave Quebec voiceless if Duplessis won. Liberals, under Adélard Godbout, swept the province. In Ontario, Mitch Hepburn pursued his old vendetta with King by denouncing the half-hearted national war effort. Mackenzie King seized on Hepburn's attack to call a snap election. He summoned MPs to Ottawa, forced them to listen to a throne speech, and dissolved Parliament before they could reply. "Fighting Bob" Manion, out-manoeuvred and floundering, got no help by rechristening his Tories the National Government party. The CCF, divided on the war and the pacifism of their venerable leader, did no better. Voters gave the Liberals their most one-sided margin in history: fifty-one and a half per cent of the popular vote and 181 seats to only 40 for the Tories, 10 for Social Credit, and 8 for the CCF. King had a mandate for his kind of war. Manion, personally beaten, resigned.

It would be a war waged with one guiding light: avoid the errors that had destroyed the Tories in 1914-18. A Wartime Prices and Trade Board stood guard against profiteering and inflation. Organized labour, through the cautious Trades and Labour Congress, would be consulted. Every policy would be scrutinized for any possible threat of conscription. Above all, King would avoid Borden's fatal mistake of sacrificing himself and his party to the cause of allied victory. The interests of national unity and Liberalism prevented any talk of the last man or the last dollar.

Suddenly, such a negative philosophy seemed inappropriate. On April 9, 1940, Hitler struck at Norway. By June 4, the British had abandoned Dunkirk. Eight days later, France sought an armistice with Germany. Britain and her dominions stood alone against the might of Hitler and Mussolini. In Britain, the raw Canadian troops under Major-General A. G. L. McNaughton stood in the front lines against a German invasion. Behind them, a shattered British army struggled to re-arm.

Every feature of Canada's war effort was transformed. Instead of a single division, Canada's overseas army would expand to five divisions, maybe more. To combat German submarines, now free to use French and Norwegian ports, Canada must build and man scores of escort vessels to guard the Atlantic convoys. She must also build her own aircraft for the air training plan. All this had to be done with desperate haste and without experience or training.

As a measure of urgency, Parliament passed a National Resources Mobilization Act – conscription for home defence. When Montreal's tempestuous mayor Camillien Houde denounced the national registration which followed, not even Quebeckers opposed his prompt internment. Canada was in danger. Even Americans would help. On August 18, 1940, Roosevelt summoned an excited Mackenzie King to Ogdensburg, New York. A scribbled memorandum recorded their agreement: a Permanent Joint Board of Defence would "consider in the broad sense the defense of the north half of the western hemisphere." A rapturous King rejoiced that he had perhaps brought the two great English-speaking powers together. Winston Churchill, the new British prime minister, did not rejoice. He recognized that Ogdensburg represented Canada's ultimate transfer from one empire to another.

Few Canadians had the detachment or historical grasp for such reflections. The crisis of 1940 created a mood of total war, at least on the home front. Its symbol was not King but the dynamic new minister of munitions and supply, C. D. Howe. At once Howe had seen that almost anything Canada produced would be needed somewhere. An engineer and a businessman, Howe gradually won the confidence and then the devotion of able industrial leaders and businessmen. Some worked for a symbolic dollar a year, running crown corporations, controlling scarce commodities, scouring the United States for machine tools and aircraft engines. Tax concessions, credit, and $1.5 billion in direct investment unleashed the huge industrial potential that had lain idle in the thirties, and then added to it at a rate few countries have experienced in peace or war. By 1943, 1.2 million Canadians worked in war industries, mostly in factories that had not existed in 1939.

Howe and his officials worried little about costs or consequences. J. L. Ilsley, a dour Nova Scotian and King's finance minister after 1940, found the money. His own frugality coincided with the Keynesian principles of his younger officials. Remembering the war-bond experience of the First World War, this time Canada would pay its way with direct taxes and individual borrowing. The Rowell-Sirois report, published in 1940, recommended a sweeping rearrangement of federal-provincial fiscal arrangements. Premiers from the richer provinces bluntly rejected the proposals, but the war gave Ottawa all the power it needed to take over direct taxes. Provincial governments could choose between grants equal to prewar revenue or having Ottawa absorb their debt burden.

In five years, federal revenue from income, corporation, and inheritance taxes rose six-fold. Within six years, Ottawa had borrowed $12 billion, half of it from individuals. Over the first two years of the war, prices climbed fifteen per cent, but then Ottawa imposed sweeping wage and price controls, enforced by the Wartime Prices and Trade Board, and for the rest of the war, inflation was held to a mere three per cent. Donald Gordon, the hard-drinking Scot who ran the Wartime Prices and Trade Board, got much of the credit, but Ilsley's tough fiscal policies made the real difference.

Howe's massive production program helped defray the costs of war. Two-thirds of Canadian war production went to the Allies. As in the earlier war, there was a catch. By the end of 1940, Britain's reserves of gold and American dollars were gone. Not only could she not afford to buy from Canada; she could not provide the currency Canadians needed to buy vital components from the United States. For the British, Roosevelt's solution was "lend-lease," with repayment at the end of the war. For Canada, lend-lease would have meant post-war economic paralysis. Officials found an answer from the 1917 experience. On April 20, 1941, King met Roosevelt at his Hudson River estate, Hyde Park, and signed an agreement integrating the Canadian and American economies. Orders for Britain would be charged to the British lend-lease account. With E. P. Taylor, a youthful beer magnate, as his salesman, Howe soon exceeded the $250-million ceiling the Hyde Park agreement had set on Canadian munitions sales to the United States. There were no protests from Washington.

As for Britain's debt to Canada, not even the take-over of almost a billion dollars of British direct investment could meet it. By war's end, the Canadian government had approved $4 billion in direct aid and forgiven massive loans to Britain and her allies. Since almost all the money was spent in Canada, charity stayed profitably at home.

Wartime prosperity was tangible. Wages might be frozen but they were certain. More and more women joined the work force and this time the social barriers against working wives and mothers collapsed. Governments even experimented nervously with day nurseries. Full employment gave Canadians money to spend but war needs absorbed scarce raw materials, foreign exchange, and factory space. Regulations under the War Measures Act imposed exchange controls, banned non-essential imports, and ended production of civilian cars, toys, jewellery, silk stockings, and a host of hotly desired items. In January 1942, Canadians had their first experience of rationing for basic food items. By European standards, hardships and sacrifices were slight. For many Canadians, the war years were a bright contrast with the grim Depression. Discomfort and disruption contributed to the atmosphere of a common purpose and a sense that Canada had rediscovered its youth and vigour. Boring jobs or military routine had at least lifted people from pre-war ruts.

On December 7, 1941, the Japanese attack on Pearl Harbor brought the war suddenly closer. Canada declared war on Japan. Two battalions of infantry, sent to the hopeless defence of Hong Kong, were the first significant Canadian casualties of the war. Frightened British Columbians clamoured for protection. Ottawa sent thirty-four thousand soldiers, most of them conscripted under the National Resources Mobilization Act. Under the shabby pretext that Japanese Canadians needed protection from their angry neighbours, the government also interned nineteen thousand men, women, and children, auctioning off their property for derisory prices. It was an inexcusable act, born out of half a century of racial prejudice. Generals, admirals, and the RCMP protested that there was no military justification for the act. Politics sufficed.

The war with Japan demonstrated some of the realities of Canada's role in continental defence. With Alaska threatened, the United States poured men and equipment into the task of reaching the remote territory by road and of piping oil from Norman Wells to a refinery at Whitehorse to support a prospective theatre of war. Together, the Alaska Highway and the Canol project cost $270 million. At the height of construction thirty-three thousand Americans were at work in Canada, blithely indifferent to the minor details of Canadian sovereignty. Warned by an alarmed

British official, Ottawa asserted its authority by despatching a "Special Commissioner" with his own aircraft. Nervously, Ottawa paid the Americans, even for airfields and bases that were never needed. Not until the fifties did Washington concede Canada's claims to its vast arctic domain.

By bringing the United States into the war against all of the Axis powers, Japan had ensured an eventual victory for the Allies. So had Hitler, when he invaded the Soviet Union in the summer of 1941. The strength of the two superpowers was not yet apparent in 1942, while Britain was experiencing the most stunning disasters of her war, the fall of Singapore and the loss of Tobruk.

Amidst defeats and inexplicable catastrophes, many Canadians felt that they had done too little in the war. By transferring most of the British Commonwealth Air Training Plan's graduates to the RAF, King's government had deliberately sacrificed any claim to a strong, autonomous Canadian air force. Until that decision was reversed, most Canadian flyers served happily enough with the British but their contribution was buried in RAF news releases. The navy's dreary, arduous, and dangerous role of escorting Atlantic convoys attracted little publicity. King himself had refused to allow troops to be sent to the most active British theatre, the North African desert. Guilt about that decision had prodded the government into the tragic Hong Kong commitment. Contrasted with their First World War experience, in this war Canadians felt themselves on the sidelines.

In 1940, Canadians had endorsed a lacklustre war effort. By 1942, supporters of total war sensed fresh support for their views. One symbolic but fatal word summed up a Canada utterly committed to victory: *conscription*. By its own appeals for greater sacrifice, the government unconsciously fuelled a public sense that everything possible must be done for victory. Newspaper headlines, news broadcasts, and propaganda warning of the horrors of a Nazi or Japanese victory added their impact. Conservatives and anti-Mackenzie King Liberals like Hepburn seized the issue. Arthur Meighen, summoned from retirement to lead his party once again, proclaimed that he would make conscription his cause.

With deft opportunism, King acted. The issue, he announced, would be put to the people in a plebiscite. They could release the government from its pledge. Robbed of his issue, Meighen went down to defeat at the hands of the CCF in a Toronto by-election. It was a warning that although old-fashioned patriotism was the strongest political current in wartime Canada, it was not the only one. In the April plebiscite, sixty-four per cent of Canadians voted to free the government: eighty per cent of Manitobans, eighty-two per cent of Ontarians, and twenty-eight per cent of Quebeckers, the people to whom the pledge had really been made. It was the betrayal Duplessis and the nationalists had warned about. To fight conscription, a host of nationalists, young and allied, had rallied opinion. Lawyers and journalists like André Laurendeau and Jean Drapeau (a future mayor of Montreal), even Pierre Elliott Trudeau, then age twenty-three, had joined the campaign and shared the defeat. For Quebec, another bitter memory was preserved for a people whose motto was *Je me souviens.*

King had not finished, of course. The National Resources Mobilization Act would be amended but Parliament would have to vote again before conscripts went overseas. It was, he explained, "not necessarily conscription, but conscription if necessary. . . ." Lapointe was dead by now, but for Pierre Cardin, the ranking Quebec cabinet minister in Ottawa, it was conscription enough to bring his resignation. For J. L. Ralston, the dogged, honest minister of national defence, King's act was a needless obfuscation and he, too, resigned. Then he relented, and the resignation remained in King's desk.

The conscription issue of 1942 was one of those savagely divisive symbolic distractions from reality which Canadian politics so often generates. Manpower was already an issue, as a population so uselessly surplus in the thirties proved desperately inadequate to meet both military and industrial needs. A succession of councils and committees wrestled with labour shortages. By the summer of 1941, all three armed services had cautiously established women's branches. National Selective Service, established in October 1941, steadily extended its authority. By

September, no employer could hire or fire without giving notice to NSS. Men and young women were compelled to register; even those considered "underemployed" could be compelled to take a designated job.

Industrial or military conscription could allocate manpower in Canada; it could not solve recruiting problems for the armed forces. The RCAF was the favoured service for young men eager for the adventure. The needs of the Royal Canadian Navy were easily met, though there was a sometimes crippling shortage of qualified technicians. The army was the Cinderella service. Talk of a new, mechanized army fooled no one. Bitter experience had proved that front-line infantry needed high mental and physical standards to survive. To King, evidence of high rejection rates only proved that the generals were sabotaging voluntary recruiting. But the generals were doing their best. The NRMA men were encouraged by every stratagem the army could devise to "go active." Many agreed, but others refused, and eventually, a tough core of NRMA men, proof against any threat or promise, gloried in the abusive term of "zombie." Fully trained and fit, they remained in uniform because coastal communities demanded their presence and because Ralston knew they were his only reserve of infantry reinforcements.

A mixture of policy and luck had so far saved Canadians from heavy war casualties. While other Allies, including Australia and New Zealand, had borne the brunt of fighting, Canada's overseas army remained on guard in England. Air and naval losses so far were small, as King had expected, in part because it took years before trained aircrew could enter operations in strength. Canadians took enormous pride in the dramatic expansion of their fleet of corvettes, frigates, and other small warships. They did not notice that the ships were often too ill-equipped and the crews too ill-trained to defend convoys effectively. Since German U-boats concentrated on merchant ships, not on their escorts, it was civilian seamen who paid the price while the RCN learned its job. Though long-range aircraft proved to be decisive weapons against submarines, the RCAF gave low priority to coastal patrols.

Canadian admirals resented British criticism and Canadian officials usually insisted on installing inferior Canadian-made radar
and rejecting other costly electronic gear as unproven.

In the winter of 1942-43, at the crisis of the Battle of the Atlantic, failure in convoy battles forced the withdrawal of Canadian
escort groups for training and re-equipment. Canadian naval
authorities never acknowledged that humiliation, but all three
Allied partners learned from it. In March 1943, Canada was
assigned its own sector of the Atlantic under Rear Admiral L. W.
Murray. The RCAF finally acquired long-range aircraft, and Canadian ships returned to battle fit to match a wily, courageous,
underwater enemy. By war's end, Canadians could take pride in
the third largest navy in the world – 373 warships and ninety thousand men and women.

Winning the Battle of the Atlantic meant only that a massive
Allied build-up in England was possible. Allied military and political leaders differed sharply over the next step. Canadians found no
role in such decisions, and neither Churchill nor Roosevelt sought
King's advice. Unlike Sir Robert Borden, King was content to be
photographed with Allied leaders on the terrace of the Château
Frontenac in Quebec City and to leave the fate of Canadian soldiers and airmen to their decisions. With the exception of the
stubbornly independent General McNaughton, few Canadian
senior officers had their own thoughts to offer. Trained between
the wars in British military schools, veterans of the tiny permanent force accepted British leadership, even if they often resented
an unmistakable British air of superiority.

Senior RCAF officers, for example, fully shared the Royal Air
Force's faith in the bomber offensive against Germany. Belated
"Canadianization" eventually produced forty-five RCAF squadrons overseas, flying everything from Spitfires to transport planes,
but the largest RCAF formation was 6 Bomber Group. Its eleven
squadrons included only some of the thousands of Canadians who
flew and died in the most controversial major operation of the war,
the four-year bomber offensive against Germany. Even Canadianization was controversial as 6 Group struggled with its problems of
inadequate aircraft, morale, and inexperience. Like the navy's, the

RCAF's eventual achievements were won at a heavy price. Part of the cost was 9,980 young men who died in the bomber offensive (more Canadians than fell in the long advance from Normandy to the Hochwald Forest). It was an ironic comment on King's expectation that air war could never lead to heavy casualties. In all, the RCAF lost 17,101 men. It also became the fourth largest air force in the world.

Many Canadians avoided the army because their fathers remembered the First World War. Nonetheless, it became the largest of the services, with 730,000 men and women. General McNaughton eventually won his battle for a highly mechanized force. Mackenzie King had recognized the old general's passionate opposition to conscription and his conviction, inherited from the earlier war, that science and preparation could save lives. Mustering five infantry and armoured divisions in England, the army trained for long years, but still it lacked the final, vital preparation of battle experience. To the government, land operations entailed the risk of conscription. At the same time, the army's inactivity seemed to prove that Canada was not playing her part.

The years of waiting made it virtually impossible for Canadian generals to reject or even to criticize the Dieppe operation. The raid, on August 19, 1942, was the most conspicuous Canadian disaster of the war. Of 4963 troops who set out for Dieppe, 907 lay dead; 1946 remained as prisoners. Canadians have never ceased finding scapegoats, from McNaughton to the debonair Lord Louis Mountbatten. A less innocent nation might have recognized that amphibious operations are the riskiest form of war and that inexperience doubles the risk. Common sense might have argued for the kind of equipment and fire support that could have brought success. Only bloody experience at Dieppe helped convince generals and politicians that costly new resources would be needed for a real invasion of Europe.

Pressure soon resumed for further operations. To gain battle experience, the 1st Division shared in the Sicily landing in July 1943. A month of fighting turned green soldiers into effective fighting units. It also brought such public acclaim that Mackenzie King insisted on sending an additional formation – the 5th

Armoured Division – and a corps headquarters, to join the ensuing Italian campaign. Angrily opposed to the destruction of his army, mistrusted by Ralston and his British superiors, General McNaughton was removed. The symbolism of a Canadian army in the field was preserved by the promise of other Allied formations. Meanwhile, British, American, and Canadian troops crossed to the Italian mainland, ran into relentless German resistance and discovered that the war of mud, trenches, and bloody offensives had not vanished in 1918.

On June 6, 1944, Canadian sailors, airmen, and soldiers shared in the D-Day landings. The 3rd Division was one of five Allied assault formations. The Canadian price for the day was 1074 casualties. It was only a down payment. Weeks of bitter fighting followed to defend the beachhead, capture Caen, and hold the bulk of the German armies so that the Americans could break out. Savage battles in the hedgerows, aggravated by a seemingly inevitable time lag of experience, cost the 2nd and 3rd Canadian Divisions the heaviest losses of any of the formations under British command. The 4th Armoured Division, spearhead in closing the Falaise Gap, was almost as hard-hit. As the Canadians fought in Normandy, their comrades in Italy fought two brutal offensives, breaking the Hitler Line in June and the Gothic Line in the autumn. In two separate theatres, Canadians had lost twenty-three thousand men, most of them trained infantry. They would have to be replaced.

It was the crisis King had feared throughout the war. Everyone could be blamed, from staff officers who failed to anticipate casualty rates and allowed too many men to remain in support units, to generals who demanded victories, regardless of cost, to enhance their own careers. By splitting the Canadians and sending unneeded troops to Italy, King himself had aggravated the manpower problem, creating a double system of administration and reinforcements. The fact remained, as J. L. Ralston saw for himself, that the infantry reinforcement pools were empty. Canadians knew it too. Major Conn Smythe, a popular Toronto sportsman wounded in Normandy, made it his business to tell a sensational story of untrained replacements stumbling into German fire. To

Ralston, there was only one answer. Conscription was now necessary. The NRMA men must be sent.

For King, conscription was quite unthinkable. The war had virtually been won. Surely, a few thousand volunteers could be found
from so huge an army. There must be a plot by the generals, he
reasoned, or even by his own more conservative ministers, to destroy him. Resourceful as ever, he recalled both Ralston's earlier
resignation and Ralston's enemy, General McNaughton. On
November 14, an astonished cabinet learned that McNaughton
would be the new minister. Ministers sat dumbfounded as Ralston
rose, shook hands with colleagues, and silently left.

The rest was nervous anticlimax. McNaughton's charisma
had no impact on hardened "zombies." They still did not volunteer. In British Columbia, Major-General George Pearkes, who
commanded most of them, sent in his resignation. In Ottawa,
McNaughton's senior staff officers insisted that volunteers could
not be found. To the ingenious King, this represented an oppor-
tune "general's mutiny," enough to frighten wavering ministers
and Quebec backbenchers. A shaken, discredited McNaughton
confessed failure. It was left to King himself to tell a divided Parliament that fifteen thousand NRMA conscripts would be sent to
Europe. He was upheld 143 to 70, with 34 Quebec Liberals dissenting.

Neither the crisis nor the irony was over. In Montreal, there
were riots. At Terrace, British Columbia, a brigade of NRMA men
mutinied for almost a week before senior officers persuaded them
to submit. On February 5, McNaughton lost a by-election in
Ontario. The irony was that, in the end, the conscripts were hardly
needed. After the brutal battle for the Scheldt estuary in October,
Canadians went into winter quarters in Holland and Belgium. At
Canadian insistence, the two divisions in Italy were brought to the
Netherlands in a long, needless journey that nonetheless kept
them from harm. The final offensives that drove into Germany
and the flooded Netherlands cost six thousand casualties, but very
few of them were conscripts. On May 6, Germany surrendered.
Japan followed suit on August 14. As it had in 1918, pure accident
had made the bitter political crisis unnecessary.

2

Prosperity

Canada benefited richly from the war. The costs were high: forty-three thousand men and women had died; the national debt had quadrupled. Yet casualties were far lower than they had been in the First World War and they came from a larger population. Most of the money, including virtually all of the mutual aid, had been spent in Canada, doubling the gross national product and creating industries that would have a durable role in the post-war economy. Ordinary Canadians lived hard, frugal, wartime lives, but most of them always had. Wartime incomes and savings had created reserves of spending power which a previous generation could hardly have imagined. Despite wartime shortages, Canadian consumer spending rose forty per cent between 1938 and 1944.

Most Canadians both yearned for and feared the end of the war. The astonishing growth in support for the CCF was the clearest symptom of the apprehension that peace would restore the unemployment and hopelessness of the Depression. The remarkable wartime government feat of ending unemployment, stopping inflation, and redistributing income made the Depression era seem all the more unnecessary, but only the CCF promised to carry wartime planning, controls, and massive public spending into the post-war world. In 1943, Ontario voters had narrowly favoured George Drew and the Conservatives as their new government, but the CCF had come from nowhere into second place. A few months later, a Gallup Poll claimed that the CCF edged out both traditional parties in public support. In June 1944, the CCF under Tommy

Douglas swept Saskatchewan to become the first socialist government anywhere in North America.

Liberals and Conservatives felt the wartime mood. It was evident as much in innumerable earnest evening forums and debates,
in journalism and radio commentaries, as in electoral movements
or the new opinion polls. In their latest bid for electoral support,
the Tories had turned for leadership to the dry but respected Manitoba premier, John Bracken. Part of his price was the addition of
the word "Progressive" to the party name. Becoming "Progressive
Conservative" was also at least a cosmetic concession to the public demand for change. Even the Communists profited from the
ground-swell. Earlier in the war the party had been banned for
dutifully supporting Moscow's alliance with Hitler, but the line
switched the instant the Nazis invaded Russia. Re-emerging as
the Labour Progressive party, the Communists basked in the
reflected glory of the powerful Red Army. They also used their
considerable influence in the labour movement to ban wartime
strikes and to attack the hated CCF. In turn, the CCF fought back,
winning over union militants.

The real initiative lay, as always, with the government. Even in
1940, the overdue adoption of unemployment insurance had
promised at least one difference in post-war Canada. By mid-1942,
an Allied victory seemed certain. Citizens and their government
could begin to think seriously about post-war reconstruction, but
the right direction was by no means clear. One approach, represented by a committee of distinguished academics, urged the
adoption of a comprehensive system of social insurance for health,
income, and old age, and a massive program of public works. This
initiative, embodied in a 1943 report by Leonard Marsh, a McGill
University professor, was deftly gutted by the brilliant team of
civil servants that Clifford Clark, deputy minister of finance, had
gathered around him in his department.

Clark's approach was fiscally more cautious but conceptually
more radical. While Marsh had ignored constitutional obstacles,
Clark urged a restructuring of federalism to give Ottawa the fiscal
power to manage the national economy in proper Keynesian

fashion. Provinces would be financed so that the richest and the poorest could each provide a comparable level of services, avoiding the terrible inequities made apparent by the Depression. The influence of the abandoned Rowell-Sirois report was no coincidence. W. A. Mackintosh, a major Rowell-Sirois contributor, had become Clark's alter-ego. Louis St. Laurent, an eminent Quebec City lawyer and the commission's counsel, had entered King's cabinet in 1941 as successor to Ernest Lapointe. Another contributor, Brooke Claxton, became the minister of a new Department of Health and Welfare in 1944.

The "mandarins," as Clark and his able team of civil servants soon were called, gained immense influence and prestige yet their power depended entirely on the prime minister. When labour problems that had seethed for years finally burst forth in 1943, costing the economy a million days in strikes, it was King himself who engineered the government response. The problem, as Mr. Justice Charles McTague of the National War Labour Board had no trouble proving, lay with Canada's lack of procedures for union recognition and orderly bargaining. Reluctantly impressed by the argument and even more by defection of labour votes to the CCF, King approved P.C. 1003, the Wartime Labour Relations Order, in early 1944. This order-in-council gave Canadian unionists the rights to organize enjoyed by their American counterparts since 1935. It formed the basis for federal and for most provincial labour legislation when the war ended. Its immediate success was demonstrated by a dramatic drop in strikes during the balance of the war.

Another wartime measure, urged by Ian Mackenzie, the minister of pensions, by Leonard Marsh, and by McTague's board, was family allowances. For decades reformers had urged that such allowances were the only effective way to cope with the most obvious cause of family poverty, low incomes among parents. King had been horrified by the cost and the threat to individualism. He was converted by the growth of CCF support, by the desire to burnish his own self-image as a reformer, and by the arguments of his secretary, J. W. Pickersgill, that growing up as a war widow's son on a government pension had not sapped his initiative.

Characteristically, King's resolve was strengthened by discovering that the same ministers and backbenchers who demanded conscription were often as fervent in opposing family allowances. Some Progressive Conservatives tactlessly underlined another Liberal party argument for family allowances by complaining that the allowance would be a massive subsidy to the huge families of French Canada.

By 1945, King's government had acquired all the enemies ten years of power and six years of bitterly controversial decisions could have earned. If the opposition parties needed encouragement, they found it in Britain, where voters had decisively rejected their powerful wartime leader, Winston Churchill, for the untried Labour party of Clement Attlee. John Bracken and the CCF's M. J. Coldwell could each take comfort from the example. In Quebec, conscription and loyalty to Ottawa had destroyed Godbout's Liberals; since 1944, Maurice Duplessis and the *Union Nationale* had been back in power.

Yet King's infinite caution and flexibility had their rewards. Even the Quebec anti-conscriptionists who ran as independents preferred him to any other leader, especially after Bracken promised to send conscripts to fight the Japanese. King's pledge of a "New Social Order," adorned by family allowances (organized in mid-campaign) and the promise of a health insurance plan, offered security without CCF socialism. For the first time, leaders of the Trades and Labour Congress endorsed the Liberals. In more private and effective ways, so did the Communists, splitting industrial constituencies which the CCF had smugly taken for granted. An unscrupulous but effective scare-mongering campaign, financed by business, administered the *coup de grâce* to the CCF. On June 4, George Drew swept to a one-sided Conservative victory in Ontario; a week later, King led Liberals to a much narrower federal success with 125 seats against 67 for Bracken and 28 for Coldwell's CCF (almost all of them from the West). Social Credit held 13 seats, and 12 independents, mostly from Quebec, gave King his margin of safety. With symbolic fitness, soldier-voters defeated the prime minister in his Prince Albert riding. It was only a minor humiliation.

The Liberals now faced a divided opposition and the post-war challenge. It was not necessarily an easy inheritance. Whatever their promised plans and programs, cabinet members could easily recall the painful aftermath of the earlier war.

On May 6, 1945, jubilant sailors wrecked downtown Halifax. At home and overseas, soldiers and airmen demanded prompt demobilization. Britain, a major trading partner, was bankrupt. American generosity had shrivelled as the war's end approached. Roosevelt was dead; isolationist Republicans were rampant in Congress. Even by 1944, Canadian war production had eased off and some industries had switched back to civilian purposes, but the task was daunting and costly. Canadians, in their comfortable oasis, were impatient and demanding, but the rest of the world was shattered – perhaps beyond recovery – and Canada had to trade to live.

In the war with Japan, Canada played as modest a role as she could manage. Insistence that Canadian servicemen must volunteer for the Pacific led to some embarrassment when the only major Canadian unit in the war, a cruiser, effectively voted itself out of action and sailed for home. On the other hand, as long as the war continued, so did the government's limitless emergency powers. When King summoned provincial premiers to Ottawa on August 6, 1945, federal authority loomed over the meeting. Neither Drew nor Duplessis was impressed. When King, nervous enough at the radicalism of Clifford Clark's fiscal proposals, promised co-operation, not coercion, the premiers found their weapon: delay. Almost a year would pass before the finance department mandarins conceded defeat for economic centralism, but the basic rules of federal-provincial antagonism survived.

Ottawa's power and prestige remained for a time. So did its hold on tax revenue. Clark's elaborate scheme disappeared but the goal of relative equalization was soon built into complicated formulas and agreements by which all the provinces but Quebec and, for a time, Ontario, "rented" their direct tax fields to Ottawa in return for compensation. The unpopularity of being tax collector to the nation had been somewhat eased by the wartime invention of payroll deductions.

One minister at least had been utterly sanguine about Canada's post-war prospects. C. D. Howe had despised the moanings of what he called "the Security Brigade." That made him the logical choice to head a vague co-ordinating department of reconstruction. Howe accepted, but only when he retained the sweeping powers of his wartime role. Canada needed "reconversion," not reconstruction, Howe insisted. His weapons were generous credits for investment and exports, a minimum of regulations, and an ingenious tax device, "accelerated depreciation," which protected investors from loss if the economy turned sour and allowed them to turn a quick buck if it thrived. Meanwhile, Howe unashamedly cherished the crown corporations he had launched before and during the war. An aircraft industry would back up his earliest public venture in 1937, Trans-Canada Airlines. Polymer Corporation at Sarnia and Eldorado Nuclear at Port Hope would show that Canadians could work at the frontiers of science and technology. Meanwhile, as "Howe's Boys" left their dollar-a-year jobs to return to the seats of private power, they remained a loyal network and a source of funds that Howe alone could tap.

Even Howe was prudent. A government white paper by W. A. Mackintosh in 1945 had promised full employment; Howe substituted a vaguer "high and stable level of employment." Either commitment had seemed bold. It was soon apparent, though, that the post-war depression would not happen. Instead, Canada was booming. Wartime forces melted away, their transition to civilian life eased by the gratuities, grants, and educational opportunities their fathers had yearned for after the First World War. By the summer of 1947, Canada's armed forces had dwindled from a million people to only forty thousand. Barely fifteen thousand veterans were collecting out-of-work benefits. Even a limping housing industry was infected by Howe's dynamism, the insatiable post-war demand, and a National Housing Act that made mortgages available to families that would never have dared apply for them before. By 1947, builders were producing houses faster than couples were marrying, making up for years when families had been forced to double up. Three-quarters of the new buildings were individual homes, monotonous boxes scattered across cheerless suburban developments to fulfil the durable pioneer expectation that a Canadian was entitled to land and individuality.

One by-product of prosperity brought no joy to Howe and his friends, but it was as vital to continued growth as their tax concessions. In 1945, workers at the Ford Motor Company in Windsor won the Rand Formula, a uniquely Canadian basis for union security. Employees need not join a union but they had to "pay the freight" for its benefits. In 1946, the brash new industrial unions tested their wartime gains with a co-ordinated nation-wide bid for higher wages. Strikes in the British Columbia forests and in eastern Canada's basic steel, electrical, and rubber industries cost more working days than in any year since 1919, but this time there was little violence, and most unions won modest concessions. Instead of eliminating unions, employers learned to live with them. Most workers kept enough purchasing power to sustain the post-war economic boom.

More than dollars were needed. Canadians could not escape their battered world or even the disorders of their own economy. Pressed by business, the government hurried its "orderly decontrol," but meat and butter rationing returned in the post-war months. Gas and tire rationing ended, but liquor remained not only diluted (as it still is) but controlled. Farmers, harvesting bumper crops since the summer of 1939, had prospered beyond their dreams in the war years. Now a hungry Europe could no longer afford the scarce dollars to buy Canadian products. James Gardiner, the minister of agriculture, preened himself on selling a huge wheat deal to the British. Other British orders were possible only with a $1.5 billion Canadian loan, fully a third as much as Washington provided. Even this was no solution to Canada's real problem, a lack of American exchange. By 1947, King's government was reduced to drastic measures to save its dollar reserves: exchange controls, a ban on luxury imports, licensing of major purchases, and a limit on the cash tourists could take south.

Economic arguments made little impact on Washington. Congress had gone solidly Republican in 1946. Business was business again. It was another, far more frightening crisis that now seized American opinion.

Even before the Allied armies had met at the Elbe in May 1945, the wartime alliance was falling apart. Canada knew little of the details: only that, even more than the First World War, this one had been a war between the world's great powers. Canadian voters in 1945 were assured that Mackenzie King had enormous influence in the world. If so, he did not use it. Canadian diplomats, as able a team of officials as would ever serve her, struggled for the "functional principle" – Canada would demand a voice only when she had a major role to play. Occasionally, when they were asked to feed refugees or provide raw material, Canadians were actually consulted. At Bretton Woods in 1944, when bankers had launched the International Monetary Fund and the World Bank to reform the currency crises of the thirties, a Canadian delegation under Louis Rasminsky was found useful and constructive. At Dumbarton Oaks and San Francisco, where the United Nations was shaped and launched, Canadians made gains quietly. Unlike the bumptious Australians, Mackenzie King's delegation made no trouble for the major powers and kept its disquiet to itself.

Only two world powers now seemed to matter: the United States and the Soviet Union. Canada, to her acute discomfort, lay between them. Her allegiance was clear. Stalin's Russia was a tyranny as atrocious as Hitler's, tolerable only to the self-deceived or the would-be totalitarian. Russia was also a deeply wounded and profoundly frightened power. No nation had lost more in the war, but its huge armies would be no safeguard against the kind of bombs that had annihilated Hiroshima and Nagasaki and driven Japan from the war. Canadian officials were among the first to know of the desperate Russian bid to equal the nuclear balance. In September 1945, a Soviet embassy cypher clerk shared secrets of a Communist spy ring that reached into King's own office. Official Ottawa's shock was almost matched by its revulsion at having to deal with the problem. Eventually the revelations sent officials, professors, and the single Communist MP to prison. Neither King nor most of his advisers were convinced that Stalin was really bent on world conquest. The seizure of eastern European countries with all the brutal apparatus of terror and repression, they believed, merely established a vast buffer zone for a nervous but inward-looking Soviet empire.

Others did not agree. Americans had been as eager as Canadians to demobilize. Now Washington insisted that Russia posed a continental threat. The arrangements made at Ogdensburg, as Roosevelt had insisted, were permanent. Canadians found that if they were to preserve sovereignty, they would have to defend themselves or take the risk of having America do it for them. "If we do enough to assure the United States," confessed one of King's trusted advisers, "we shall have done a good deal more than a cold assessment of the risk would indicate to be necessary." On February 13, 1947, a bilateral defence agreement promised that Canadian forces would henceforth use American arms, equipment, and tactics, share facilities, and co-operate with the United States. Continentalism now had a military dimension. Another British link had withered.

In 1946, the continental threat was remote – a bogey to promote American rearmament. Western Europe was another matter. Only Britain maintained respectable military strength; her continental neighbours were now virtually defenceless against invasion or subversion. Canada's foreign exchange crisis, with its threat to peacetime reconversion, was a tenth as serious as those of western European countries. Without American credit, European recovery was hopeless. In Washington, business was business, but not if Europe fell to the Communists. Action was needed. The European Recovery Program or the Marshall Plan, launched in 1948, was a vast outpouring of American material and financial aid. To Canadian delight, American congressmen allowed Europe's Marshall Plan credits to be applied in other "American" countries. Canada's 1947 exchange crisis was over.

Europe's security crisis was not. In February 1948, Czech Communists, backed by the Soviet garrison, seized power. Days later, Jan Masaryk, symbol of Czech resistance to Hitler, fell from a window. It was "suicide," claimed the new regime in Prague. To the West, the fall of Czech democracy was a bitter reminder of the tragedy of pre-war appeasement. Next, Soviet troops blockaded the British, American, and French zones of Berlin. Stalin must be answered as Hitler had not been: by Allied unity. In western Europe, politicians struggled to fashion a defence alliance but it was a union of the weak. Canada might join; even Mackenzie King had now been shaken from his habitual caution. Not even Duplessis's Quebec could condemn resistance to communism. First, though, Canada would await the decision of the Americans. In June 1948, Congress was finally willing. Ten months later, in April 1949, the North Atlantic Treaty Organization was proclaimed. Its twelve members had pledged, at Canada's insistence, to be more than a defence league; in fact, they wanted rearmament on the cheap. Committed to buy American-style weapons, Canada, for example, could generously spare the British equipment she had stockpiled in 1945.

Canadian post-war diplomacy might be moralizing and self-important but it had finally escaped from King's management. In 1946, the old prime minister had handed external affairs to the trusted Louis St. Laurent. A conservative corporation lawyer, St. Laurent was Quebecker enough to be unimpressed by the symbols and sentiment of the British connection, but he was no provincialist. In the controversy over Clark's federal proposals, he had bluntly backed the centralizing scheme. Quebec would always complain, he explained, but Quebeckers would also admire the government that did most for them. St. Laurent was fascinated by Canada's potential role in the world. He backed officials such as his new under secretary, Lester Pearson, who insisted that Canada was now a "middle power," with influence in the United Nations, NATO, and the emerging multiracial Commonwealth. St. Laurent earned credit for persuading India to remain in the Commonwealth after 1947 when its instincts were to break all the old imperial ties. Other emerging colonies would follow that lead.

Of all Canada's connections, Washington obviously mattered most. Wartime experience had shown Canadian officials how insensitive a great democracy could be when its own interests were concerned. Moreover, rebuffs and criticism could easily drive Americans back to their old isolationism. Not only would

Europe be left vulnerable; Canadians would be left alone with their huge and often heedless neighbour. Diplomatic skill was no luxury in post-war Canada.

In June 1950, North Korean tanks rolled deep into South Korea. Canadians had little knowledge of the small peninsula with its history as a Japanese colony and its post-war partition. They saw it as a test of collective security in a Cold War turned hot. A dying session of Parliament approved the despatch of three destroyers, and, when the war went badly for troops under UN colours, the government approved a special infantry brigade recruited from veterans. Three years of fighting cost Canada 1642 casualties, 309 of them fatal. The United States and South Korea bore the heavy brunt of costs and losses.

If Korea brought the kind of response democracies should have offered Hitler, it also raised a terrifying thought: was the invasion a Soviet-ordered diversion, leaving western Europe defenceless? The fear spurred NATO rearmament. No longer could it be cheap and leisurely. Early in 1951, Ottawa announced substantial new military commitments: twelve fighter squadrons and an infantry brigade for Europe; two more brigades available as immediate support; a fleet of Canadian-built destroyer-escorts to withstand any new Battle of the Atlantic. Armed forces would grow to a hundred twenty thousand men; new weapons and equipment would cost $5 billion. C. D. Howe received fresh economic powers as Canada undertook its first serious peacetime military effort.

It was no longer Mackenzie King's Canada. At seventy-four, having served as prime minister longer than anyone in British history, he was content to go. A Liberal convention in August 1948 chose his only possible successor: Louis St. Laurent. King had been the architect of modern Canadian Liberalism, with its seemingly permanent hold on power. He retired, as he had served, with little love from Canadians and far less respect than he deserved. St. Laurent was instantly more popular: a courtly, dignified man, a permissive autocrat who left ministers to manage their departments but whose will could be inflexible. He was conservative, too, and the unfulfilled promises of King's 1945 program remained safely unused.

St. Laurent began with a bonus. In the war years, Canada had staked her claim to Newfoundland, posting thousands of troops on the island to match the American garrison. Between them, the wartime visitors had brought a brief, unfamiliar prosperity to the island, but it was the islanders themselves who would choose their fate. The British commission of government, established in 1934, was about to end. The logical choice, to almost everyone but a small, bespectacled ex-broadcaster named Joey Smallwood, was a return to responsible government. It was Smallwood, reaching past the island's merchant elite by means of the broadcast proceedings of the constitutional convention, who helped persuade Newfoundlanders to make Confederation an option. Next, after two 1948 referenda, Smallwood finally emerged with a narrow majority for union with Canada. On March 31, 1949, Newfoundland entered Confederation. Her 350,000 people had been won by social benefits, fiscal guarantees, and, above all, by the hope that prosperous, expanding Canada would haul Newfoundland from its historic poverty. The merchants and lawyers of St. John's were unpersuaded.

The details would be left for time to take care of. Proud of the overdue completion of Canada, Liberals could now seek a new mandate. The Conservatives had a new leader, their fifth in a decade. George Drew was handsome, articulate, and had won Ontario three times. Though his government had been more progressive than Hepburn's, Drew was an unabashed Tory and proconscriptionist. That gave Liberals in Quebec ample ammunition. When Drew sought an electoral alliance with Duplessis in the name of their anti-Ottawa axis, he inspired an even less scrupulous Liberal campaign in Ontario. The image of a Drew-Duplessis alliance, with Camillien Houde in the background, exploited anti-Quebec feelings. For his part, Drew played indelicately on the kind of neurotic anti-communism that was winning votes for Senator Joe McCarthy in the United States. Communism, liberalism, and the CCF were lumped in a socialist stew. Over the grubby politics of 1949 floated the avuncular image of Louis St. Laurent, addressing his audiences through their children, offering benign platitudes fit for a summer campaign in a country fully aware of its good fortune. The result was a landslide – 193 Liberals to a mere 41 Tories, 13 CCFers and 10 Social Credit. In Newfoundland, only a resentful St. John's bucked the Liberal trend.

Canadians had voted for prosperity. The Cold War rearmament and Korea had restored an economy that had begun to flag slightly in 1949. American investment had fallen off in the early post-war years, leaving Canadians to finance their own boom, but now capital poured into Canada. While corporations built or expanded branch plants to supply Canadians with the cars, radios, refrigerators, and, after 1952, the television sets they could now afford, much more foreign investment was directed at unlocking Canadian resources. Oil and gas in the Turner Valley had given Alberta a modest role in a pre-war petroleum industry, but nothing prepared the province for the huge oil finds at Leduc, outside Edmonton, in 1947. By 1956, Alberta was supplying three-quarters of Canadian needs, though as much as possible was exported to the United States and Arab oil was still much cheaper. At Chalk River, Ontario, in 1952, Canadian scientists began preliminary work on an even newer energy source: the CANDU, or Canadian Deuterium Uranium, reactor. Rearmament and the American development of nuclear weapons were creating a demand for uranium and a long list of non-ferrous metals.

Transportation had always been a major Canadian industry. New railways reached north to Lynn Lake, Manitoba, for nickel; to Pine Point in the Northwest Territories, and to Labrador's Knob Lake to reach one of the richest iron ore deposits in the world. Since the Mesabi Range deposits that had sustained American heavy industry were close to depletion, Labrador's became the best alternative. The long argument over the St. Lawrence Seaway came to an end just as Canada had decided to proceed on its own with a hydroelectric development. By 1959, after five years of building, the billion-dollar project was completed. In 1948, Ottawa had promised $150 million to the provinces to help develop a Trans-Canada Highway for an increasingly road-bound population. (It was only finished in 1965 at a cost of almost a billion dollars.) Meanwhile a new transportation technology, pipelines, carried Alberta crude oil east to the Lakehead at Superior,

Wisconsin, and west over the mountains to British Columbia. Engineers were now ready to tackle two of the great remaining hydroelectric projects of the country, Churchill Falls in Labrador and the Columbia River in British Columbia.

Critics might complain that the huge new developments fostered a continental more than a purely Canadian economy. New railways and pipelines reached into the North but their termini were often in the United States. Trade, like investment, was increasingly a bilateral affair; efforts to improve Canadian exports to Britain were dismissed as imperial echoes. As in the twenties, a few querulous academic voices complained that key sectors of Canada's economy had fallen under foreign control and that more would follow. Most Canadians were too delighted with their new prosperity to echo such worries. They certainly had no place in the minds of C. D. Howe or his associates. Even in Quebec, where Duplessis's regime was entrenched in an old-fashioned alliance of Catholicism and conservative nationalism, foreign investors formed a silent partnership. Like Liberal premiers before him, Duplessis welcomed the revenue and the jobs and let wages look after themselves. When Catholic unionists at Asbestos struck their American employers in 1949, provincial police provided management with strong-armed support. The resulting violence shocked Catholic leaders and pulled unions across Canada into unprecedented solidarity with the Quebec-based syndicates.

Later, the Asbestos strike would be interpreted by an observer, Pierre Elliott Trudeau, as the symbolic beginning of a new kind of Quebec nationalism. At the time, it was much more a reflection of a common Canadian demand to share in the new prosperity and a North American standard of living. No more than Cape Bretoners or Ontarians would Quebec workers accept deprivation for themselves and their families as the price of distinctiveness. Nor, given the cornucopia of apparently limitless Canadian wealth, did they have to. Maurice Duplessis might win votes by such symbolic acts as giving Quebec her own flag in 1948 – a blue and white emblem mythically linked to the 1758 victory over the English at Carillon. In daily life, *Canadiens* became more North American.

The 1951 census found fourteen million Canadians. It quietly revealed another fact: by the usual definitions of poverty at the time, a third of Canadians qualified, most of them elderly, rural, or tied to the have-not regions; too many of them native people and Métis. What passed without comment is that censuses from 1921 to 1941 had found that two-thirds of Canadians were poor. For the first time, the poor were a minority. Like all the best social revolutions, this one passed unnoticed. The explanation was simple: family allowances, unionization, and, above all, fulfilment of the promise of "high and stable rates of employment." Families with steady incomes and a little to spare could now break out of slum housing, find a home in the suburbs, buy a second-hand car, live healthier lives, and see their children continue a few years farther in school. They could enjoy the one- or two-week holidays that union contracts won for members and non-unionists alike. The spread of a consumer society created new sectors of service and white-collar employment. So did the growth of government.

Canadians celebrated their better life with a baby boom. During the Depression years, immigration and birth rates had both tumbled. Not since the 1880s had Canada's population grown more slowly. But by 1947, natural increase alone was adding two per cent a year. Women were leaving the work force not through coercion – that had been tried in 1919-20 and the numbers of working women had actually climbed – but through choice. The reason was apparent in maternity wards, and, by the 1950s, in a frantic demand for new schools, teachers, and, in due course, expanded colleges and universities. Prosperity not only allowed more children; it allowed them to be fed and educated to a standard no generation of Canadians had experienced.

Natural growth was supplemented by the largest flood of immigration since Sir Clifford Sifton's day. Between 1945 and 1957, a million and a half people came to Canada, including war brides, concentration camp victims, even thirty-five thousand refugees from the 1956 Hungarian uprising. Many brought industrial skills; very few came to farm. They fitted well into a Canada that was now overwhelmingly urban. By 1956, half the people of British Columbia lived in Vancouver or Victoria; a third of

Quebeckers clustered in Montreal and its sprawling suburbs. While five hundred thousand of the newcomers came from the British Isles and a hundred thousand came from the United States, many of these immigrants had no links with either founding culture or even with the eastern European roots of Sifton-era arrivals. Yet prosperity and economic growth brought racial acceptance with astonishingly little friction or cultural antagonism. On the contrary, the newcomers often made their own demands on Canada for a more sophisticated, culturally varied life. The puritan conformity of Canada began to crack as immigrants and the Canadian-born alike chafed at drinking laws, "blue" Sundays, and restaurants that served bad food and no wine. Canadian family attitudes, in turn, strained old-world traditions of parental authority and female roles.

Change was always controversial. The United Church, still dominant among Protestants but threatened by a largely Catholic influx of immigrants, defended the Sabbath and opposed liquor. Roman Catholics fought to keep birth control as an offence under the Criminal Code and deplored a soaring divorce rate. In the 1930s, the number of divorces in Canada hovered between one hundred to two hundred a year; by the 1950s, six to seven thousand marriages a year were ending in divorce. As they usually had, Canadians blamed the United States for the invasion of loose morals and permissiveness. Films, radio, and television were the obvious culprits. The Canadian Broadcasting Corporation, earnest but under-financed, developed three excellent radio networks only to be outflanked by the newer medium. By 1952, it had bravely launched Canadian television in French and English. The enormous costs of TV production compelled the CBC to buy most of its programs from American networks and to concentrate resources on a coast-to-coast microwave link-up that might unite viewers for special national occasions such as *Hockey Night in Canada.*

In 1949, a reluctant St. Laurent approved a Royal Commission on the Arts and Letters in Canada. While St. Laurent had few qualms about meddling with provincial concerns for culture, he had robust doubts about "subsidising ballet dancers." The commission's report in 1951, under the heavy imprint of its chairman,

Vincent Massey, argued forcefully that the government must do just that if Canadians were to share in performing and creative arts and to develop universities worthy of the name. The report lay where it landed, and the arts struggled on. Vancouver's symphony orchestra played in an arena. Canada's art treasures could be found behind the dinosaurs in the dusty National Museum.

Prosperity and immigration slowly built pressures politicians had to notice. In 1953, Stratford's Shakespearean Festival opened in a tent. The *Théâtre du Nouveau Monde* opened in Montreal. Suddenly, as a matter of civic pride, cities began erecting theatres. What may have been the nadir of the arts in Canada, the late 1940s, began to pass. At least some people in an affluent Canada, far from being horror-struck at the thought of subsidizing ballet dancers, began to wonder why they had not done so before. In 1957, the adventitious death of a trio of millionaires, Sir James Dunn, Isaac Killam, and Harold Crabtree, gave such a windfall of inheritance taxes that the federal government launched the Canada Council and endowed it with $100 million, half for capital grants to universities, the rest for scholarships, loans, and grants. Nervously, Canada had made itself a patron of the arts; now it awaited the critics.

Most Canadians did not seem to care. Later, they might complain that the fifties were boring, marked only by the successive fads of American popular culture. Politics, too, were predictable and routine, grey and repetitive. In a 1953 national election, the sober competence of St. Laurent and Howe, the regular government surpluses, and a discreet trickle of pre-election goodies made the Liberals proof against George Drew's bluster and evidence of scandal in the expanding defence department. The opposition parties gained a little in the election – the government lost twenty seats but the popular vote was hardly altered from 1949. Thoughtful observers assessed the results and wondered whether constitutional reforms might be desirable. Canada seemed bound for permanent one-party government.

Still, few Canadians gave any sign of caring.

3

Recession

In the fifties, Canadians could believe that they lived in a permanently prosperous, internationally esteemed, and increasingly united country. Ottawa's mandarins, their prestige undimmed from the war, skillfully applied the approved doctrines of macroeconomic management. Nationalists could be pleased that the ambitious, self-important Vincent Massey was the first native son to be governor general. Abroad, talented Canadian diplomats pursued a modest but moral path as confidants of both the Third World and the West. Even social and regional tensions seemed to be fading. The CCF was in decline. Canada's two largest labour organizations, worried by stagnant membership and the costs of rivalry, merged in 1956 as the Canadian Labour Congress. Federal-provincial conferences were decorous affairs. If few provincial premiers were now Liberals, most followed Ontario's affable Leslie Frost in a spirit of "live and let live." Only Maurice Duplessis made public war on Ottawa; privately, even he preferred compromise.

Yet problems persisted, although few of the fifteen million affluent Canadians hunted for them. Keynesian economic principles amounted to no more than Joseph's advice to the Egyptian pharaoh: run a surplus in good times to cover the deficit in bad times. In 1949 and 1953, economic down-turns had coincided with pre-election budgets. Liberal politicians and mandarins congratulated each other when re-election coincided with recovery. Yet the pharaoh had not had to manage a federal democracy. By the mid-fifties, it was the provinces, not Ottawa, that were big spenders. A baby boom, urbanization, and prosperity demanded hospitals, water and sewer systems, and highways for the two-thirds of Canadians who now owned cars. The rich provinces, Ontario and British Columbia, clamoured for money as loudly as their poorer neighbours, for they were the ones doing the most expensive growing.

Canada's post-war international role had been another Liberal bonus. Tories (and Duplessis) deplored foreign aid, and the CCF harboured a pacifist wing and condemned German rearmament. Neither approach won many votes. Most Canadians, even in Quebec, accepted commitments to NATO, Korea, and rearmament. Brooke Claxton, minister of national defence, even believed that conscription could have been possible with St. Laurent as prime minister.

But Canadian intellectuals deplored Communist-hunting by American politicians, and Canadian diplomats worried at the populist violence of American foreign policies. NATO had seemed like a way of curbing Washington's rashness, but the Republican administration elected in 1952 began to switch from reliance on costly, conscripted conventional forces to a so-called "massive deterrent" of strategic bombers. American taxpayers might like "a bigger bang for the buck"; allies like Canada worried increasingly about their power to restrain an American trigger finger. Anxiety grew as American policymakers found it necessary to persuade allies and enemies that they would, indeed, risk a nuclear holocaust to defend the United States' interests.

It was, however, two older allies who turned Canada's external policy into a Liberal embarrassment. The Anglo-French invasion of Egypt in October 1956 split the Commonwealth. Canada lined up with the newer, non-white members and, more gratefully, with the United States in deploring the Anglo-French move. At the United Nations, Lester Pearson performed diplomatic miracles in securing the UN's first peacekeeping force to cover the Anglo-French (and a simultaneous Israeli) withdrawal. His reward was a Nobel Peace Prize.

Some Canadians were not pleased. Opinion polls in 1956 showed a small majority of support for Britain. Perhaps these were the same Canadians who had grumbled as St. Laurent created a distinct Canadian citizenship, abolished appeals to the Privy Council in London, and firmly if discreetly removed crowns, Union Jacks, and other historic symbolism from the public scene. Now the Suez affair gave British sympathizers a focus for their discontent.

So did another event in an unusually active year. Bent on linking Alberta natural gas with Quebec and Ontario markets, C. D. Howe had sought fast parliamentary approval for giving a pipeline contract to a Canadian-American consortium. The project fitted national and nationalistic goals, but Tory tacticians decided that obstruction would drive Howe into one of his increasingly explosive rages. The tactics succeeded. Using their majority, the Liberals imposed closure and indiscreetly jeered when the opposition protested. A hitherto respected Speaker collapsed into partisan subservience. The ensuing parliamentary struggle lasted long enough for most Canadians to take notice. The issue itself was unimportant: the pipeline was built without further controversy. It was the arrogance of politicians like C. D. Howe that people noticed. Liberals had been too long in power.

George Drew's own public arrogance might have saved the Liberals, but, in December 1956, his ill health forced the Tories to find a successor. John Diefenbaker was quite unlike any previous Canadian party leader. First elected in 1940, Diefenbaker had held a lonely Saskatchewan seat by dint of preacher-style rhetoric and a well-publicised devotion to the underdog. He had as little in common with Tory financiers as he did with Ottawa civil servants, but his backers believed that he could find supporters in places where no one had ever voted Conservative. They were right. The Liberals also knew Diefenbaker and they dismissed him.

June 1957 was early to hold an election, but St. Laurent was now seventy-six and he could be used only one more time. This time, economic wisdom called for tight restraint on pre-election bonuses. Old-age pensioners would have to be satisfied by a six-dollar increase. Western farmers were grumbling about huge unsold stocks of grain, but surely the blame lay with the Americans' give-away export programs, not with Ottawa. Besides, the West had never voted Tory. A Liberal victory seemed a foregone conclusion. The experts and the polls agreed. The experts also agreed that Diefenbaker was impressive, reaching past prosperous Tories to voters who had missed out on wealth and power. For the first time, a Conservative leader was rallying Canadians against the smug officials with their taxes and "tight money." Even the pension increase was scorned as the work of the "six-buck" boys. Still, had voters ever shot Santa Claus?

Many Canadians went to bed on June 10 convinced, as some premature magazine headlines claimed, that St. Laurent would be returned by a reduced majority. Instead, voters had elected 112 Conservatives and only 105 Liberals. Twenty-five per cent of voters had shifted from the Liberals to Diefenbaker, incidentally boosting the CCF to 25 seats and Social Credit to 19. In Port Arthur, one of those CCFers, Douglas Fisher, defeated C. D. Howe himself.

The Liberals did not cling to power. By June 21, John Diefenbaker headed a new, hopelessly inexperienced government. The change suddenly seemed refreshing. Civil servants recalled their neutrality and dutifully faced their new masters. Suspicions were mutual and, for Diefenbaker and some of his associates, never fully alleviated. The Liberal strategy was plain. St. Laurent resigned the party leadership and his decimated caucus sat demurely silent, giving Diefenbaker time to hang himself. In January, a Liberal convention gave the succession to the Nobel Prize-winner, Lester Pearson. A world-famous diplomat with the misleading public image of a folksy, uncomplicated baseball fan seemed like a sure winner. Pearson seems to have thought so himself. Fresh from his convention victory, he demanded that Diefenbaker resign and return power to the Liberals. Even some Liberals blanched.

To his credit, Pearson saw at once that he had made a dumb move. So did Diefenbaker. Promptly he called an election. Unconsciously, Pearson had demonstrated the Liberals' unrepentant arrogance. His flood of election promises sounded phoney from politicians who had held office for twenty-two years. When Liberals tried to campaign on the harsh recession which gripped Canada by 1958, Diefenbaker presented damning evidence that the previous government had foreseen the crisis. Radio, television, and brilliantly organized public meetings, as well as Diefenbaker's spectacular theatrical skill, allowed the new prime minister to dominate the campaign. Audiences hushed as he summoned them to "catch the vision of the kind of Canada this can be." Pearson and intellectual critics could fume that it was all humbug – it worked.

Indeed, Diefenbaker's speeches were hardly necessary. Before the election, the Tory support stood at fifty per cent in the polls. Canadians were captivated by their new government. The Liberals disintegrated. Minor parties vanished in irrelevance. Waverers could scramble aboard a certain winner. Diefenbaker had paid no court to Quebec either in seeking the leadership or in the 1957 campaign. The 1958 Tory strategy was simple: "*n'isolons pas Quebec,*" said the advertisements, and Quebec would not be isolated. In 1957, Frost had ended his neutrality and delivered Ontario to the Tories. This time Duplessis released the *Union Nationale* machine. Quebec Liberal MPs who had scarcely campaigned in their careers never knew what hit them. On March 31, 1958, fifty Conservatives, many of them Duplessis nominees, swept the province's seventy-five seats. Across Canada, Diefenbaker won 53.6 per cent of the popular vote. Only Borden in 1917 had ever done better. The Conservatives held 208 seats, the Liberals held 49 (not one of them in western Canada), the CCF had dwindled to 8, and Social Credit had vanished.

The 1958 landslide was more a referendum than an election, with Diefenbaker the triumphant issue and almost no national divisions. Only Newfoundland stayed Liberal. In 1957, the four western provinces had elected more CCFers than Conservatives: nine months later they were solid for Diefenbaker – Conservative votes literally doubled. It was the kind of majority that Diefenbaker's hero, Sir John A. Macdonald, once claimed "could corrupt a committee of archangels." It evoked automatic sympathy for a tiny opposition, and it persuaded journalists, self-important by nature, to assume the role of critic. It was not hard to find things to condemn. Ministers were inexperienced and sometimes inept. Some civil servants were disloyal and many more resented that their loyalty was plainly suspect. Above all, the prime minister himself seemed nervous about his majority and eager to prove his record as a defender of Parliament even if it meant endless debate. The mere volume of sound from Parliament, liberated from the cavalier condescension of St. Laurent's ministers, persuaded Canadians that there must be much to criticize.

So there was, but much was accomplished too. Diefenbaker's "vision" had been conceived by an adviser as a development plan for Canada's northern frontier; it became a catch-all for miscellaneous but useful projects like the South Saskatchewan dam, the railway to lead-zinc deposits at Pine Point on Great Slave Lake, or the development of Frobisher Bay on Baffin Island. A procession of royal commissions, headed by impeccable Tories, produced some uncomfortably radical reports. Mr. Justice Emmett Hall provided unanswerable arguments for medicare as well as over-optimistic statistics on its costs. Kenneth Carter's commission on tax reform would infuriate the wealthy a decade later with its claim that income from capital gains should be as taxable as a paycheque. Grattan O'Leary, a veteran Tory editor, embarrassed Canadian governments and annoyed Washington with a report that proposed banning American magazines that competed for Canadian advertising.

For the first time in memory, the West was in power in Ottawa. The flood of Quebeckers who arrived in 1958 were too late for major cabinet posts. It never occurred to Diefenbaker that Tory election prospects depended on making room for them. Donald Fleming, finance minister and voice of traditional eastern Toryism, carried little weight. He had run against Diefenbaker for the party leadership in 1956. Western ministers like Alvin Hamilton, Howard Green, and George Pearkes had the prime minister's ear. So had the voices of prairie populism. Old-age pensions rose sharply. Despite free-enterprise rhetoric, the government adopted costly price supports for twenty-four farm products and kept the Wheat Board. An Agricultural Rehabilitation and Development Act (ARDA) was designed to help some farmers to prosper and others to leave the land. In 1960, Diefenbaker seized the chance to sell the huge western wheat surplus to China. Washington grumbled at Canada giving aid to the Communists, but western farm incomes tripled. With advice from a royal commission and from a new National Energy Board, the government forced Ontario to be a market for Alberta's high-priced oil. Only Quebec and the Maritimes could still profit from cheap imports.

Diefenbaker's most cherished project, a Canadian Bill of Rights, grew out of his own prairie experience and memories of the discrimination he himself had suffered, even in Tory circles, for his foreign-sounding name. Passed by Parliament in 1960 with copies immediately distributed to millions of Canadians by a sympathetic toothpaste manufacturer, the bill promised too much. It was powerless to bind provinces or even a later Parliament. It also ignored the kinds of rights French Canadians had sought for generations. To Diefenbaker, fervently preaching an "unhyphenated Canadianism," cultural and language rights were irrelevant or divisive. It was a widespread western view. Quebeckers, Diefenbaker felt, should be satisfied now that Ottawa issued them bilingual cheques.

Even with a huge majority, power gave traditional Tories far less pleasure than they had hoped. Their one major partisan bonus was the outcome of a Liberal-appointed royal commission. A 1957 report satisfied the old demand of private broadcasters that the CBC be stripped of its regulating powers. In 1958 the Conservatives established and staffed a new Board of Broadcast Governors. Among its early decisions was approval of a private network (CTV) to rival the CBC's national television coverage. John Bassett, an energetic Toronto Conservative and part-owner of the CTV network, was the chief beneficiary.

Opposition parties have always championed provincial rights. In power, Diefenbaker had costly promises to fulfil. In 1957, with the tax rental agreements ended, St. Laurent had bluntly told the provinces that, like Quebec, they could have ten per cent of federal income and corporation taxes. Ottawa would collect more, but provincial taxpayers would feel it. More was needed because by now hospital insurance had become the latest and most costly of over a dozen shared programs. Under Diefenbaker, Ottawa's share of income taxes fell from ninety to eighty-four per cent by 1962.

Federal-provincial relations grew more acrimonious. A long-awaited constitutional amending formula almost won approval until Quebec backed out – her demand to run unemployment insurance had been rejected. British Columbia's premier W. A. C. Bennett repudiated a Canadian-American agreement to develop Columbia River power and then demanded control of off-shore resources. Joey Smallwood cried betrayal when Ottawa insisted on the letter of Newfoundland's terms of Confederation in 1949 instead of Smallwood's more generous interpretation. He was furious too when Diefenbaker refused RCMP reinforcements to crush a loggers' strike in 1959.

Such battles were a reassertion of history. It was Ottawa's immense post-war power and the harmony of federal-provincial relations which had been unusual. So, too, was Canada's post-war industrial strength. A clear economic strategy with tough priorities, heavy investment, and conscious sacrifice of inefficient industrial sectors might have given Canada a durable, if specialized, industrial future. Instead, it was her defeated enemies who chose that route while Canadians prospered from a flood of foreign investment. Simply being North American had seemed guarantee enough of permanent prosperity.

It was not. Brief recessions in 1949 and 1953-54 gave warnings. Canada's return to the vulnerability of a resource-exporter was concealed by pride in her new hydro-electric projects and pipelines and in the Seaway. With the conservatism of wealth, the Liberals had reverted to the older monetarist techniques of high interest rates to curb inflation. The new governor of the Bank of Canada, James Coyne, was an ardent fan of the policy. His strategies of "tight money" provided Tories with a campaign issue in 1957, but, though recession deepened and modest inflation rates vanished, Coyne's policies persisted. Canadians, he insisted, must tighten their belts and pay their way. A professed nationalist, Coyne found arguments from the warnings in another Liberal royal commission report on Canada's economic prospects, headed by a wealthy Toronto accountant, Walter Gordon. Foreign investors now controlled key Canadian industries and resources, Gordon warned, threatening Canada's sovereignty. Yet the Bank's high interest rates attracted foreign money while they dampened Canadian business and industrial expansion. As a nationalist, Coyne did more harm than good.

Diefenbaker's government had inherited far worse problems from the Liberals than Diefenbaker or most Canadians realized, and its huge majority left it no excuses. In Europe, the new Common Market threatened old Canadian markets. Giant supertankers, developed when the Suez Canal was blocked in 1956, cut the price of oil and threatened Alberta's favourite industry. The government solution, banning imported oil west of the Ottawa river, angered Ontario. Another problem was $6.4 billion in Victory Bonds, maturing fifteen years after the war. Reconversion of the bonds at higher interest cost money. James Coyne claimed that bondholders should have had even higher rates. Canadians, believing the expert, felt cheated and blamed Diefenbaker. The prime minister blamed Coyne. The outcome was an ugly public row. Conservative politicians tried to blacken Coyne for arranging a $25,000 pension for himself, not for his policies which neither they nor most Canadians probably understood. In the end, Coyne went, but not without damaging the Tory regime with the voters and even with the mutually protective band of Ottawa mandarins.

Despite Coyne and a substantial ignorance of economic mysteries, Diefenbaker's policies were far more effective against the recession than contemporaries recognized. His spending proclivities were the despair of Donald Fleming. Regularly the finance minister promised surpluses, squeezed civil service salaries, demanded restraint, and froze hiring, only to have to confess yet another deficit. Government spending between 1957 and 1961 rose thirty-two per cent. A winter works program taught the construction industry to work year-round. Grants to universities doubled and a federal technical and vocational training program not only expanded schools but kept hundreds of thousands of students from the overcrowded labour market. Grim unemployment figures hid the fact that employment and output had both grown. Yet Diefenbaker's own political approach encouraged Canadians to look at appearances, not facts, and the image was a damning contrast to the Liberal's apparent record of efficiency and success.

Economic disorder was matched by Canada's relations with the world. With a rhetorical flourish, Diefenbaker had pledged a fifteen-per-cent shift of Canadian trade from the United States to Britain. The figure, taken from the air, was absurd. While the British took up the proposal, the new government raised tariffs instead. Diefenbaker toured the world, seeking the prestige Pearson had garnered. He revelled in the links with Britain and the monarchy. To his initial embarrassment and later pride, Canada played a major role in excluding South Africa from the Commonwealth in 1961. Alone among the innumerable repugnant policies of Commonwealth members, apartheid was deemed intolerable. Having condemned Canada's Suez role in 1956, the Conservatives took their own share of UN peacekeeping in the Congo in 1960. Through no Canadian fault, it was not a happy experience as soldiers were beaten and abused without the right of self-defence.

Whatever the dangers and attractions of the world, economics and defence had bound Canada steadily closer to the United States. China, and later the Soviet Union, might buy Canadian wheat but the bilateral trend was steady. Each year, Canadian-American trade grew while manufactured exports to other countries declined. Walter Gordon's report had helped push the Conservatives toward economic nationalism. A new law required corporations and labour unions to report their affairs so that the degree of foreign influence might at least be public.

American dependence on the deterrent and Soviet development of both nuclear weapons and the means to deliver them to American cities made continental defence a major priority. Late in the forties, the Liberals had approved a Canadian-designed fighter plane, the CF-100, and later a Canadian share in building three radar warning lines. Next, developing a newer, supersonic fighter, the Avro-Arrow CF-105, became essential, exciting, and so costly that it would probably not have survived a Liberal victory in 1957. Even plans for a unified North American Air Defence Command (NORAD) had been too touchy to be settled before the 1957 election.

Once in power and with the aged Major-General George Pearkes as defence minister, Diefenbaker acted decisively. The

North American Air Defence Command agreement was signed before officials could even warn of its dangers. The Arrow was a tougher problem. Suspicious of Liberal contractors, certain that costs would rise and that no other buyers could be found, Diefenbaker finally cancelled the project on February 20, 1959. In a day, fourteen thousand engineers, scientists, and skilled workers became unemployed. In a week, all five prototypes were demolished. Amid the bitter outcry, Diefenbaker added to the confusion. The age of the missile had arrived, he claimed, and both bombers and fighters were obsolete. The Arrow's replacement was indeed a Bomarc missile, but it was useful only against manned bombers. It had to be supplemented by F-101 fighters which the Americans had relegated to their reserves. National pride was doubly hurt. So was national security and Diefenbaker's credibility.

The Bomarcs were dubious weapons, useful only with nuclear warheads. An anti-nuclear crusade, begun in Britain, had spread to Canada to be endorsed by women's groups, professors, and by both the Liberals and the CCF. More seriously, it appealed to the rigid moralism and anti-Americanism of Howard Green, Diefenbaker's latest Secretary of State for External Affairs. Canada, the government announced, would not acquire nuclear weapons. Or perhaps it would. Or did it know? Every major weapon system the government had ordered for its NATO and NORAD commitments, from Bomarcs and F-101s to Honest John rockets, depended on nuclear warheads. Diefenbaker insisted otherwise: the weapons were non-nuclear. Only the innocent and the resolutely unmilitary could believe him. In Canada, such people were numerous.

Cancelling the Arrow was the last tough defence decision Diefenbaker was willing to make. The aftermath of confusion and deception undermined his reputation with allies and Canadian opinion-makers alike. Not even the nuclear disarmers could trust him. In Washington, Diefenbaker's contradictions and Green's increasingly evident hostility might have been tolerated by an aging, complacent Republican administration, but a dynamic new president, John F. Kennedy, viewed them differently. Diefenbaker instinctively disliked Kennedy. It was mutual. As in the 1930s with Roosevelt and Bennett, many Canadians contrasted their own leader with the handsome, articulate American and were embarrassed. The image of Camelot persuaded younger members of the Canadian elite that they were too sophisticated for the fire and brimstone or the crude evasions of their own national leader.

There were now alternatives, though none was as charismatic as Kennedy. Under Pearson, the Liberals had shed most of the veterans of the St. Laurent era. Reassured by Conservative fumbling that Liberalism was still the way to power, ambitious younger politicians emerged to rebuild party organizations, notably in the major cities. Newer Canadians, angry at sharp Tory restrictions against immigration imposed in 1957, remembered which party had brought them to Canada. Business leaders recalled the old competence of the St. Laurent-Howe era. Newer policies, some of them proposed but unnoticed during the 1958 débâcle, brightened the Liberal image.

A competitor was a regenerated and retitled CCF. The post-merger Canadian Labour Congress had settled its differences about endorsing the CCF by agreeing to form a new left-wing party. A battered CCF agreed, and, by 1961, a New Party movement was under way. With the CCF's guiding genius, David Lewis, in control, two thousand delegates met in Ottawa for a steaming August convention. It was an amalgam of new and old politics. Veteran CCF and labour organizers managed the business and delivered the leadership to the CCF premier of Saskatchewan, Tommy Douglas. A surprise delegation of left-wing Quebec nationalists committed the excited convention to a "two-nations" version of Canada. Rank-and-filers ignored their leaders' pleas for a title that could never be abbreviated. The "New Democratic Party," the delegates' choice, at once became the NDP.

Liberals and New Democrats seemed more fearsome than they were. Under Pearson, the Liberals had forgotten the rural ridings where King had patiently hunted supporters. Some CCFers warned that the NDP's labour image would be hard to sell to prairie farmers. Both parties seemed designed to split a sophisticated urban electorate that had been the most fragile and flighty element of the 1958 Tory coalition. More dangerous but unnoticed was Social Credit, not in the West anymore but in rural Quebec. A spellbinding used-car dealer named Réal Caouette had quietly created a mass hinterland movement of people angry at governments, taxes, and change. No one much cared, for there was much more exciting news from Quebec City.

In 1959, Duplessis had died. His *Union Nationale* had been a personal regime, a tight, authoritarian machine with which *Le Chef* could guard his endangered people. Even the Church, for all its seeming influence, depended utterly on Duplessis for money to run its imposing empire of hospitals, schools, and orphanages. Beyond ruthless use of patronage and an electoral machine that did not shrink from violence and fraud, Duplessis had depended on his wars with Ottawa to harvest votes. Successive Liberal leaders were dismissed as "travelling salesmen" of federalism. Now *Le Chef* was gone. Soon, so was his able and reforming successor, Paul Sauvé. By backing Diefenbaker, the *Union Nationale* had gained patronage and lost independence. The initiative now lay with Jean Lesage, once Pearson's parliamentary assistant and a man whose aloof dignity contrasted with the vulgarity of the Duplessis era.

Il faut que ça change, proclaimed the Liberal slogans, to be echoed by younger, better-educated Quebec voters, shaped by the 1950s to demand more of life and of government than the Church or Duplessis had allowed them. When Lesage won the 1960 election, most Canadians welcomed the message and saw it take shape as a superbly talented new team – Paul Gerin-Lajoie, René Lévesque, Georges Lapalme – began attracting comparable talent to the task of reform. Canadians were slower to overhear the other slogan of the 1960 victory, *maîtres chez-nous*. The state would replace the Church and the land as the fundamental instrument of *Canadien* survival. Unless something dramatic happened in Ottawa, that state would be *Québécois*; its logical direction was independence.

On June 10, 1962, Diefenbaker faced the electorate. The experts had predicted a Liberal victory, guided by polls and a mid-campaign economic crisis in which the dollar had been sharply devalued. Economists might approve, but Liberals issued a "Diefenbuck" as a triumphant reminder of Tory mismanagement and despatched a "truth squad" to report Diefenbaker's lies. The tactics backfired. It was the Liberals' own campaign that sagged. Even with warm backing, Lester Pearson did not excite Canadians. To be fair, he had a huge margin to trim. Voters elected 112 Conservatives, 100 Liberals, 19 New Democrats, and an astonishing 30 Social Crediters, all but 4 of them from Réal Caouette's grass-roots Quebec campaign. With their help, Diefenbaker could still govern. He did so now with deeper suspicions of officials and even of colleagues. Only the West had remained true and solid.

The defence issue should have gone away. After all, peacetime governments had always let politics rule military decisions. Diefenbaker listened to Howard Green and believed his anti-nuclear mail. The Bomarcs, finally inserted in their silos at North Bay and La Macaza, were armed with sandbags. The F-101s were safer unarmed. Decisions could wait.

The Cuban missile crisis ended the delay. For a few tense days in October 1962, President Kennedy waged a war of nuclear bluff against Soviet strategic will. Canada did not play. NORAD in the United States moved to readiness; its Canadian element, covering New York and Pittsburgh as well as Toronto and Montreal, did not. Whatever they might have felt later, most Canadians at the time were appalled. The polls reflected a dramatic switch in favour of acquiring nuclear warheads. Lester Pearson switched with the polls. In January 1963, a single speech in Scarborough reversed the Liberal anti-nuclear stand. George Pearkes's successor in the defence portfolio, Douglas Harkness, resigned, humiliated by his prime minister's evasions. A series of American statements, deliberate or accidental, refuted Diefenbaker's speeches. A blunt State Department release summarized American opinion and the plain facts: Canada had proposed no arrangement "sufficiently practical to contribute effectively to North American defence." It was a bombshell.

Even modest overtures to Caouette's *Créditistes* might have kept their loyalty. Diefenbaker saw no need. On February 5, they abandoned the sinking government. So did more Tory ministers. The government sank. An election followed.

Within days, the nuclear weapons issue vanished. Diefenbaker promised a full statement on defence. It never appeared. Instead, he denounced the White House for engineering his downfall. Almost no newspapers backed Diefenbaker or his Tories. In much of urban Canada, Conservatives sat out the campaign. Pearson's campaign, programmed carefully on the Kennedy victory of 1960, stumbled and backfired but this time it did not fail – quite. On April 8, Pearson won 129 seats to Diefenbaker's 95. The NDP won 17, Social Credit 24. For the first time since 1925, Liberals would face a minority government. The Mackenzie King alliance of Quebec and the prairies against Tory Ontario was gone. Of 48 prairie seats, Diefenbaker's Tories held all but 7. The two central provinces had given Pearson all but 30 of his supporters. In Quebec, two elections had cut Progressive Conservative voter support from fifty to nineteen per cent.

In five years the great national consensus of 1958 had dissolved. The old rivalries and frustrations had found new shapes, but they had all the old virulence. Once again, Canadians were face to face with their history.

4

Confusion

It had been the elite more than the ordinary Canadians who had abandoned Diefenbaker. They yearned for the effortless competence of post-war governments, the smooth relations with Washington. Some humbler voters, frightened by the recession, recalled the ancestral wisdom that "Liberal times are good times." Only in the West had Diefenbaker's times been good.

Like other Canadians, Pearson took Liberal efficiency and prosperity for granted. Few guessed his own priority: French Canada. Outside Quebec, most Canadians rejoiced at the so-called "Quiet Revolution." In 1962, René Lévesque had bullied a reluctant Jean Lesage into making hydro nationalization a provincial election issue. The outcome was a rout for the *Union Nationale*. Much of the rest of Canada approved: publicly-owned electricity would make Quebec more like other provinces. So would displacement of church control of the schools by a new department of education in 1964. Now Quebec would have a high-school system like other provinces. Surely Canada would be more united.

Diefenbaker had ignored Quebec ministers when they tried to explain the significance of such developments. In 1961 the NDP had encountered the radical new Quebec nationalism, absorbed the catch-phrases, and continued on its own familiar, centralizing way. It never regained its chance in French Canada. Only Pearson, unilingual, indecisive, and unpolitical, had a diplomat's ears. In 1962, in a speech unnoticed outside Quebec, Pearson had recognized that *Canadiens* would control their economic and cultural destiny; they must also play a full and equal role in Ottawa. In power, he launched a powerful Royal Commission on Bilingualism and Biculturalism, as much to educate as to find answers. André Laurendeau, now the cool, reflective editor of *Le Devoir*, and Davidson Dunton, a former head of the CBC, were joint chairmen. For a start, French would become a language heard in the Liberal cabinet and caucus.

Bereft of any powerful Quebec Liberals, Pearson chose his own Quebeckers: able, decent men, often with his own lack of gut political instinct. In vengeful opposition, Diefenbaker was now in his element. Too often it was Quebec ministers who were bloodied or humiliated by his shafts. An irresolute prime minister and a minority government seemed helpless in their defence.

However, Quebeckers were not alone in their humiliation. Walter Gordon, inspiration of economic nationalism in the fifties, had been Pearson's ally and financial adviser in rebuilding the party. As finance minister, he was important to Pearson's pledge that Liberals would begin with "Sixty Days of Decision." Gordon's contribution was a confused, ill-argued budget. Never before in Canadian experience had parts of a budget been hauled back for revision. Opposition parties had tasted Liberal blood, and the procession of scandals provided a national spectacle.

Pearson's insistence on a simple maple leaf flag as national emblem in place of the traditional red ensign had provoked indignant protests from the Royal Canadian Legion convention where it was unveiled in 1964. Diefenbaker's caucus rallied against the so-called "Pearson pennant." For months, Parliament was trapped in the uproar until the bland compromise emerged: red on white with a single stylized leaf. National unity was not one of the by-products.

Liberals had not restored efficiency; few people watching the parliamentary cacophony gave them credit for reviving prosperity. Economic recovery was real enough but it had begun in 1961 as Chinese and then Soviet wheat sales spread their impact. Thanks to wheat as a leading staple, Canada entered a new era of export surpluses. Liberals took credit for implementing an old and controversial solution to Canada's fading branch-plant automotive industry. The Auto Trade pact of January 1965 erased the border for firms in Canada and the United States making cars and parts. The immediate outcome was an impressive boom in Ontario's manufacturing towns.

By the mid-sixties it was rare for Ottawa to get much credit for economic achievements. The Conservatives' success with the Agricultural Rehabilitation and Development Act (ARDA) inspired a procession of acronymic programs from the Liberals. Canadians absorbed the latest American faith that costly agencies with well-paid officials could somehow lift neglected regions from poverty.

In the new decade, provinces aspired to grandeur. Quebec's huge Manicouagan hydro dam satisfied René Lévesque's claim to the obvious – that Québécois could be brilliant engineers. Toronto had acquired its first subway line in 1954 and a second by 1960; Montreal must follow suit in time for a grandiose world's fair in 1967. Nova Scotia boasted a Volvo assembly plant; Quebec matched it with Peugeot. To finish the education of the baby boom, every province expanded old universities and most added new ones. In a single announcement, Ontario created a collection of twenty-two community colleges exclusively for skills training. In British Columbia, where Premier W. A. C. Bennett's government seemed more eager to develop mountains than people, cheap Columbia power was given to the Americans so that Bennett could develop his own hydroelectric scheme on the Peace River. To the despair of Général A. G. L. McNaughton, ending his career as co-chairman of the International Joint Commission, the Pearson government limply acquiesced.

The pendulum of power had swung back to the provinces as it had before, but it would swing even farther if they could get more money. The need was clear enough. The baby boom grew more costly with age. Post-secondary education, experts now claimed, was the key to economic growth and social justice. Both seemed desirable. So was medicare. In 1962, Saskatchewan's CCF government braved financial risks and a doctors' strike to introduce comprehensive medical insurance. Liberals had promised such a plan since 1919 but had not hurried: it was a provincial matter. Some premiers, like Ontario's John Robarts, latest in an endless Tory dynasty, professed philosophical objections. Others merely shuddered at the cost.

In their campaign, the Liberals had promised a new era of "co-operative federalism" to waft away the familiar jurisdictional quarrels. Words made no difference when money and power were at stake. A major federal Liberal promise was a national scheme of contributory portable old-age pensions. Who cared that the plan invaded provincial jurisdiction? Premiers did. They also saw that a contributory plan would create a huge capital fund for years before big pay-outs began. While Ontario's John Robarts, as a Conservative, had no love for the scheme, it was actually the Liberal premier of Quebec, Jean Lesage, who was most awkward. The politics of grandeur cost money. Surpluses, squirrelled away by the frugal Duplessis, had vanished. Buying private electricity companies had used up Quebec's credit and there were still universities and secondary schools to build. Provincial voters grumbled that the Liberals were taxing too heavily. In fact, Lesage was running a staggering deficit. Rural Quebec threatened one flank; radical nationalists even in Lesage's own government cited revolutionary bomb blasts and holdups to press their case. A magazine poll in 1964 showed thirteen per cent of Quebeckers ready for independence.

When Pearson and the premiers met in Quebec City in 1964 to discuss the pension plan, the old tradition of affable federal-provincial relations ended. Behind police guards, amid bomb threats, Canadian politicians shared a revelation. The normally cool, dignified Lesage was angry and defiant (and drunk). Even more significant, the Quebec Pension Plan his officials unveiled was plainly better conceived and better argued than the federal version. Ottawa's mystic expertise had vanished. Paradoxically, the humiliation helped save the federal plan. A far-sighted John Robarts sensed that Confederation might crumble if Ottawa's plan collapsed. Ontario backed Ottawa – at a price. A new Canada Pension Plan would imitate the Quebec version. Quebec would still opt out, but the other provinces would get the CPP's funds to invest as they chose against the day when pensions would be paid. A crisis had passed but neither Pearson nor his officials would easily recover their prestige.

At least Canada's external standing should have been safe with the Liberals. With Kennedy, Pearson had already found an easy rapport; he resembled the tweedy, liberal-minded academics with whom the young president surrounded himself. As Pearson had promised, Canada at once accepted nuclear warheads for its weapons with all the safeguards Washington had promised. A white paper by Paul Hellyer, the new defence minister, reassured anti-war activists that first priority for Canadian armed forces would be peacekeeping. New equipment would be non-nuclear and military strength would be trimmed to pay for it. Allies were content. Few readers noticed a discreet but explicit promise: the armed forces would also be unified.

All was not serene. Gordon's ill-fated budget had initially included a take-over tax on foreign purchases of Canadian businesses. The O'Leary Report, shelved by Diefenbaker, led to a law discouraging Canadian advertising in foreign periodicals in order to promote the sale of Canadian magazines. Pressure from Washington persuaded the Liberals to exempt *Time* and *Reader's Digest*. More friction came from the government's reluctant decision to put the corrupt Seafarers' International Union under trusteeship and to prosecute its American ex-gangster leader, Hal Banks. When Banks jumped bail to the United States and his parent union showed no repentance for its corruption, federal officials were forced to seek help in Washington. President Kennedy, however, seemed to prefer union blandishments to Ottawa's appeals.

On the whole, though, Canadian-American relations improved. Pearson's own policies imitated the programs of Kennedy's "New Frontier." A "Company of Young Canadians" was a strife-ridden imitation of the Peace Corps. An overdue concern for Canada's blacks and Indians was a guilty reflection that Canada, too, had civil rights problems. Kennedy's assassination on November 22, 1963, was a blow an entire generation of Canadians would not forget.

Kennedy's successor, Lyndon Johnson, offered no such human rapport. At the time, few Canadians recognized the sterility of Kennedy's record or the practical idealism of Lyndon Johnson's "War on Poverty," although privately Pearson had questioned the wisdom of Kennedy's policies on Cuba and the Far East. Merely by continuing his predecessor's Vietnam entanglement, Johnson had taken the United States into a real war by February 1965. Vietnam was not Korea. Canadians, full of moral righteousness, condemned the war, and Pearson took their disapproval to Philadelphia in April 1965. It was a deed few Canadians would have welcomed from an American leader, and President Johnson was not a tolerant man. "Lester," he told the Canadian, "you peed on my carpet." His rage forced an apology from the Canadian prime minister but the era of special relationships was over.

Often, in 1965, leading Liberals reviewed opinion polls, a fractious Parliament, and their own achievements – chiefly the flag and the Canada Pension Plan – and pondered how pleasant life would be with a majority. It seemed easy. The Conservatives were preoccupied with plots against Diefenbaker. Social Credit split into English- and French-speaking factions. A July announcement of medicare by 1968 would silence the NDP. Canada was unmistakably prosperous, and even the West would be won by the latest wheat sales to Russia. Only Pearson was reluctant, but his friend, Walter Gordon, was persuasive. On September 7, uncertainty faintly sounding in his voice, Pearson made his public case for an election.

While Diefenbaker was being annihilated by Liberal voters, the prime minister decided that he would remain in Ottawa, bearing the burdens of state, safe from the electorate. It did not work out. Electioneering was Diefenbaker's delight. Reluctant Tories, dragooned to old loyalties by the party's brightest organizer, Edwin Goodman, found funds and candidates to save the party. Their leader campaigned joyfully, gleefully throwing Liberals on the defensive to the ecstasy of rural and small-town audiences. The Liberal campaign floundered and even ran short of money. As in the past, Pearson could not help it much. On November 8, voters returned a virtually identical House of Commons – 131 Liberals,

97 Conservatives, 21 New Democrats, 9 of Caouette's *Créditistes*, and a rump of 5 Social Crediters. Only Tommy Douglas found comfort from the campaign: his NDP had finally profited from disillusion to reach a new plateau of eighteen per cent of the vote. A dynamic Quebec New Democrat, Robert Cliche, had helped win support but no seats.

Cliche might have done even better without the only significant Liberal coup of the campaign. More than ever, Pearson wanted a powerful Quebec lieutenant. His choice fell on Jean Marchand, leader of Quebec's formerly Catholic unions and the man who had steered them away from both the Canadian Labour Congress and the NDP. Marchand refused to come alone. One partner, Gérard Pelletier, editor of *La Presse*, was welcome. The other, Pierre Elliott Trudeau, was not. Ostensibly a law professor, Trudeau had the reputation of being a wealthy intellectual dilettante who had edited a radical magazine and had denounced Pearson for adopting nuclear weapons in 1963. But Marchand insisted, and safe seats were found for all the "three wise men."

Marchand was indeed influential. Ever since the Conservatives had frozen civil service salaries in the struggle to balance their budget, federal employees had demanded collective bargaining. All three major federal parties had agreed. By 1965, many civil servants also insisted on the right to strike. As an ex-civil servant, Pearson was appalled. Marchand, his minister of manpower, was not. Quebec had granted that right to its provincial employees without disaster, and his own union had profited; Ottawa must follow suit. The Public Service Staff Relations Act in 1967 gave federal employees a free choice and a chance to change their minds between compulsory arbitration and going on strike.

Marchand was too sanguine. A younger generation of workers, free of Depression memories, demanded more even than their leaders recommended. A violent wildcat strike at Hamilton in the summer of 1966 was part of a year of labour turmoil. Canadians survived the first railway strike since 1950 and an illegal postal strike that drew unexpected sympathy for ill-paid sorters and letter carriers. Public opinion forced a generous settlement. For the first time, hospital workers and even teachers joined picket lines. Buying labour peace was costly. To forestall a crippling St. Lawrence Seaway strike, a government arbitrator approved a thirty-per-cent increase in wages. Without remotely considering the arguments, editorials called the settlement "the Pearson Formula" and raged at the government's folly.

Peace was needed because Montreal was about to become an international showplace. Preparing for Canada's centennial had become a sour joke. To some Canadians, part of the national identity was an aloofness to windy boosterism and flag-waving. The eager opportunism of communities, folk groups, and publishers jostling for the cornucopia of centennial grants made easy satire. One town would burn its outhouses; another would build a pad for flying saucers. No centennial project could match the magnitude of Montreal's. Almost single-handed, Mayor Jean Drapeau had dreamed up the idea of a world-class exposition, sold it to the international community, and virtually blackmailed Ottawa and Quebec City into underwriting his efforts. Despite Canada's vast empty spaces, the fair would be staged on islands in the St. Lawrence, built with earth excavated for the city's new subway line. Of all the absurdities of centennial year, Expo '67 easily took the prize. For a city with crowded slums and without even proper sewage treatment, it was an extravagance beyond excuse.

In 1966, Quebec voters rejected the Lesage version of the politics of grandeur. Under Daniel Johnson, the *Union Nationale* had recovered from 1962, shed some of its conservatism, and burnished its nationalism. Johnson's slogan was *Québec d'abord* or "Quebec first," discreetly translated for English-speaking supporters as "A better Quebec for all Quebeckers." The French was more precise. Johnson won because rural voters resented the cost of Liberal reforms, but the new government changed very little. Instead, Johnson presented Ottawa with new, uncompromising demands for fiscal transfers. He also set out to assert Quebec's role in the world. In France's President Charles de Gaulle, Johnson had an eager patron. Since the war, de Gaulle had sought vengeance for humiliations he felt he had suffered at the hands of his Anglo-Saxon allies, and it was irrelevant to him that most Quebec opinion had favoured his wartime enemies in Vichy.

Financial demands were one thing; seeking an international role was another. Pearson was furious. As usual, he also felt helpless. Even the Lesage government had argued that Quebec had a right to be involved in treaties that affected such constitutional responsibilities as education or culture, but for Daniel Johnson, external aggrandizement offered a cheap and a popular issue. The French cheerfully made life miserable for Canada's ambassador and bluntly refused to welcome General Georges Vanier, Canada's governor general.

Meanwhile, Pearson had discovered unsuspected virtues in the most dubious member of the "three wise men." As a parliamentary assistant, Pierre Elliott Trudeau had offered Pearson unexpected and welcome advice about Quebec. As minister of justice from April 1967, he showed a quite untraditional zeal for reform and an astonishing flair for handling critics. It was hardly in the tradition of Ernest Lapointe that a Quebec Liberal would proclaim that the state had no business in the bedrooms of the nation, or that divorce reform was overdue.

Even more valuable was Trudeau's hard distinction between the national and the provincial rights of French Canadians. Like Pearson, Trudeau was committed to having the federal government – and as much of Canada as could be managed – provide equal opportunities for French and English. Unlike Pearson, he had a firm, perhaps an unrealistic, idea that the functions of a federal government could be clearly defined. Years before he had lectured the infant NDP on the dangers of centralization. Yet, where the federal role was clear, he felt, provinces had no business. Trudeau felt liberated from the ancestral tribalism of Quebec nationalism and scornful of those who remained in self-imposed bondage in what he called "the wigwam." Talent, boldness, and inherited wealth had taken him to Harvard, the Sorbonne, and the London School of Economics. He had travelled the globe. If St. Laurent, Laurier, and Cartier had burst the limits of Quebec to see themselves as Canadians, Trudeau's limits were the world.

Suddenly and quite unexpectedly, Canadians too seemed liberated from parochialism. When centennial year came, the sneers and the cynicism died away. To their own astonishment, a host of Canadians looked about themselves and felt proud of their achievements. Celebrating turned out to be fun, and the organization of the celebration proved more efficient than most people had expected. To national surprise and then delight, Montreal's Expo '67 opened on schedule. Then came a suffusing glow of pride as Canadians realized that they had even helped sponsor an artistic and innovative success. For once, Canadians felt smugly superior to their American neighbours, torn with urban riots and sinking deeper in the morass of Vietnam. Boosterism was in fashion. Mordecai Richler, an expatriate Montrealer who had deplored Canada's feeble cultural nationalism, now confessed that he no longer yearned for the day when the border would vanish. "Vietnam and Ronald Reagan," he wrote in 1967, ". . . have tempered my enthusiasm. Looked at another way, yes, we are nicer. And suddenly that's important."

Obviously, not everyone agreed. Still angry at Canadian criticism of his Vietnam policies, President Johnson paid a cold, perfunctory centennial visit. Quebec separatists fashioned licence plate tags proclaiming *100 ans d'injustice.* The violent student riots which had greeted a 1964 royal visit to Quebec were not repeated when the Queen opened Expo, but massive police precautions were unsettling reminders. The visit of Charles de Gaulle was a carefully orchestrated contrast. Ottawa was virtually excluded from the arrangements by Daniel Johnson and by Paris. The French president landed at Quebec and rode in a triumphal motorcade up the valley of the St. Lawrence. It was the glittering welcome Johnson had promised. At Montreal on July 14, the old general strode to the city hall balcony to deliver his regal greeting and concluded, arms outstretched, *"Vive Montréal! Vive le Québec! Vive le Québec libre!"*

Had vanity, mischief, or calculation led de Gaulle to shout the slogan of Quebec independence? It hardly mattered. He had had his vengeance on the Anglo Saxons. The euphoria of 1967 dissolved. "Canadians do not need to be liberated," sputtered a furious Pearson, and de Gaulle promptly returned to France. English Canada echoed the prime minister. As ever, Quebec responded defensively and angrily. *Le Devoir*'s Claude Ryan scolded Pearson for hysteria and fear; sixty per cent of Quebeckers condemned the prime minister's counterblast. The Saint-Jean Baptiste Society summoned its ranks of local worthies to a grandly named *Estates Général* and solemnly demanded associate statehood for Quebec, on a basis of full equality with the rest of Canada. René Lévesque, whom years of television commentary had made the best-known of Lesage's ministers, issued *Option Québec* in September, a clear demand for Quebec independence. When fellow Liberals hesitantly rejected the Lévesque program, he left the party. On November 18, 1967, Lévesque launched his *Mouvement souveraineté-association*.

In Canada's hundredth year, the forces of disintegration had finally found a compelling leader and a program. The logic and the example of a world of liberation movements had come to Quebec. The long tiresome arguments about language and powers and money could end if it was Québécois who were the majority and it was the English who could suffer the humiliations of a minority. It was the logic of Papineau, Mercier, and Duplessis, carried to its modern conclusion. For young, ambitious *Québécois*, frustrated by the persistent dominance of Montreal's English-speaking commercial elite, resentful of the burden of mastering a second language, independence was irresistibly seductive. For a decade, English Canadians had bored Quebeckers with the question "What does Quebec want?" René Lévesque had furnished a clear, disturbing answer.

The next question was what Canada would do about it. For a start, she would change, testing whether centennial euphoria really meant a new willingness to live on as a transcontinental nation. The armed forces, usually scorned or ignored in peacetime, became a controversial symbol of change. A stubborn, ambitious Paul Hellyer had been entirely in earnest about unification. A unified force in a single green uniform would not only win him renown for its originality and efficiency, it would break the last British links of uniform and tradition. The protests of admirals, generals, and air marshals were dismissed as mutinous threats to civil supremacy. On Canada's hundredth birthday, her three armed forces reluctantly became one. Other changes came even harder. At the end of 1967, the Royal Commission on Bilingualism and Biculturalism delivered its first report. The recommendations were predictable, sweeping, and now inescapable: the federal government must not only provide services in both official languages, it must provide a working environment where French as well as English Canadians could work in equal comfort.

More than language, uniforms, and symbols needed changing. The revolution in the status of women began hesitantly in the wake of Enovid, the first apparently safe oral contraceptive. Now it gathered momentum. The political response sought by Pearson's sole woman minister, Judy LaMarsh, was a Royal Commission on the Status of Women. Other problems, smaller or more urgent, were subjected to mere task forces. Embarrassment at the "Pearson Formula" led, in 1966, to a study of labour relations. To ease his political demotion, Walter Gordon sponsored a task force on foreign ownership, headed by a sympathetic but hitherto anti-nationalist economist, Melville Watkins.

If Canadians had given any message in 1965, it was that most of them wanted new political leaders. By 1967, New Democrats ranked with their rivals in the polls, but John Diefenbaker rejected the hint. The outcome was a harsh, year-long battle between his loyalists and the party's youth, financiers, and urban supporters. Dalton Camp, the Toronto advertising executive who engineered Diefenbaker's overthrow, was also sponsor of Robert Stanfield, his successor, an accident that preserved disunity in the party. Robert Stanfield, the premier of Nova Scotia, was a man of wit, integrity, and painfully cautious speech, and he deserved better. Diefenbaker fought to the end. His final bid for leadership, he insisted, was inspired by a convention resolution endorsing a Canada of two nations.

Lester Pearson, on the other hand, went quietly, content with his achievements and painfully aware that even the untried Stanfield had soared in the opinion polls as Canadians welcomed any new face. The Liberal inheritance drew half a dozen cabinet ministers, from the nakedly ambitious Paul Hellyer to aging veterans of the St. Laurent era such as Robert Winters and Paul Martin. All aspirants went against two Liberal traditions: the alternation of leaders from Ontario and Quebec and the preference for inexperience. Laurier, King, and even St. Laurent had served far briefer apprenticeships than had the more obvious claimants.

In November 1967, Ontario's Premier John Robarts summoned premiers to Toronto for a "Confederation of Tomorrow" conference, fulfilling an election promise, and expressing his own profound desire to save the country. Canadians watched Daniel Johnson dominate proceedings with a vision of a divisive future few of them welcomed. A few months later, in February 1968, the premiers came to Ottawa. This time, television watchers saw the new minister of justice answer Johnson with a blunt severity few of them could remember ever hearing from a federal spokesman. Pierre Elliott Trudeau's campaign for the leadership of the Liberal party was launched. By April 4, when Liberals met in Ottawa, he was the clear favourite. He won on the fourth ballot.

Pearson had expected the chance to say farewell to Parliament, but Trudeau dissolved it at once. Like Diefenbaker, he ran against his own party as much as against the opposition, but his style was utterly different from "the Chief's." Trudeau teased and challenged audiences and invested them with his own sophistication and style. The pride and self-satisfaction of 1967 revived and found fulfilment in a leader who seemed literate, eloquent, and adventurous. In a contest of images judged by the media, neither Stanfield nor the NDP's Tommy Douglas stood a chance. In the sole television debate they gave as good as they got, but journalists eagerly covered for their new hero. In Quebec, separatists and conservatives grumbled about Trudeau, but Stanfield's complex remedies, tendered in painful French, were no substitute for local pride. Even the rural, small-town base of conservatism was shaken by Diefenbaker's departure. Diefenbaker loyalists now voted NDP as once they had voted CCF. On June 25, Trudeau won the majority that Canadians had denied Pearson, with 155 seats to Stanfield's 72, and 22 for the NDP. Even the West had relented: the four western provinces had given 27 of its seats to Trudeau, 25 to the Conservatives, and 16 to the NDP.

It was a new era and Canadians had given a national mandate to a new leader.

PART V

A COUNTRY SHARED

I

Liberation

Ever since Confederation, Canadians had usually been more eager than Americans to use the power of governments to finance and administer great national undertakings, from the CPR of the 1880s to the nationwide health insurance program that finally took shape in 1968. On the other hand, Canadians believed that they were socially more conservative, law-abiding, and moral than their neighbours. Sir Wilfrid Laurier, for one, proudly pointed to comparative crime and divorce statistics to prove the happier state of Canadian society.

By 1968 the contrasts were blurred and, for some Canadians, even a source of embarrassment. Personal liberation had become a watchword, cherished as fiercely by separatist terrorists as by drop-outs in the drug culture. Liberation ranged from long hair and blue jeans to unblushing acceptance of premarital sex and unmarried cohabitation. Members of religious orders demanded freedom from their vows. Censorship became intolerable. So did the burdens of marriage, child-rearing, and family. Homosexuals emerged to defy the "straight" majority for the sake of "gay rights." A dependable and seemingly safe birth-control pill had ended the baby boom early in the sixties. Maternity, once defended by feminists as the highest role of womanhood, became an interlude that could be avoided at will. The consequences were unexpected. Quebec's birthrate fell from the highest to the lowest in Canada, raising alarm over French-Canadian survival. Traditional barriers to the employment of women, even in mines and construction sites, crumbled. The composition of the Canadian labour force changed from being one-quarter female to being almost one-half female within one generation.

In itself, liberation was not new; the young had regularly challenged their elders. But never had the defenders of authority and tradition collapsed so abjectly. Clergy, educators, editors, and politicians hastened to meet demands for change. Claude Bissell, president of the University of Toronto, hurried home from a traumatic year at Harvard to impose drastic changes on his elderly institution. Radicals abused him soundly for his pains. Electronic media disseminated a world-wide youth culture. Criminals, innovators, and rioters could share the psychic thrill of seeing themselves on television. Post-secondary education now embraced almost as large a share of the young as had the armed forces in two world wars. Colleges and universities became centres for the new culture of drugs, popular music, and protest. Superficial exposure to the social sciences bred faith in Marx, in pop gurus like Charles Reich of Consciousness III or Timothy Leary, prophet of LSD, and in the pseudo-science offered by groups like the Club of Rome. A Canadian, Marshall MacLuhan, was among the new Delphic oracles. Most ideas, from feminism to "participatory democracy," were imported from the United States and, more rarely, from Europe.

Fashions are never universal. Most Canadians avoided drugs, stayed married, and, for that matter, never voted for Pierre Elliott Trudeau. As a fashion, liberation was more conspicuous in British Columbia, big cities, and among the middle class than in Newfoundland, small towns, or among the poor. The unfashionable majority might wonder why priests urged secularism in education, or why governments financed the counter-culture through Opportunities for Youth and the Company of Young Canadians. Others took comfort in more enlightened fads. Roland Michener, the third Canadian-born governor general, made himself a model of physical fitness for a sedentary nation by promoting jogging.

Environmental concerns could also unite young and old, radical and conservative. Rage at polluting industries and the alleged hazards of nuclear power generation went hand-in-hand with an elitist disdain for the vulgarity and waste of mass affluence. The limits of growth would be reached more slowly if only the wealthy enjoyed nature's non-renewable resources of gasoline or silver. What united environmentalists with other crusaders of the age was a humourless intensity, often incapable of recognizing its own paradoxes. Legalization of marijuana could be urged by people who wanted to ban smoking. A passionate concern for baby seals coincided with a desire to preserve the folkways of Newfoundland outports. Native people must be protected from white meddling, but not if they continued their traditional discrimination against women.

In Pierre Elliott Trudeau, the Liberals offered Canadians a symbol of the liberation generation. As minister of justice, he had liberalized laws on divorce, abortion, birth control, and homosexuality. In his debates with Daniel Johnson, he had stressed individual rights over the group rights urged by the Quebec premier. By promising "no more free stuff," Trudeau condemned social programs which shared burdens collectively. Since liberation was largely a matter of style, its disciples adored a prime minister who wore sandals in the House of Commons, slid down a banister at a Commonwealth conference, and told a political opponent (in Trudeau's own sanitized version), to "fuddle duddle."

At forty-nine, Trudeau was not the youngest prime minister Canada had had, but he was the most inexperienced. Like most of the comfortable young Canadians who made him their hero in 1968, his wealth and success had been more the result of inheritance than of struggle. Whether as a world traveller, an outdoorsman, or as a critic of Duplessis in the 1950s, Trudeau had enjoyed the privilege of choosing his own challenges. So far, he had been spared the setbacks, frustrations, and personal financial insecurity that had taught caution and compromise to King, Laurier, or Macdonald.

As prime minister, Trudeau handled power with a firm and sometimes naive confidence. Pearson, the ex-bureaucrat, knew the power of deputy ministers and circumvented them. Trudeau simply switched them so frequently to new departments that they soon knew as little as their ministers. Cabinet meetings became seminars in which ministers were compelled to defend their own policies and programs without officials to protect them. Verbal agility mattered more than dull common sense. The prime minister's own office expanded dramatically. Youthful aides took over the regional responsibilities of cabinet ministers. Trudeau and his confidants insisted that the change guaranteed a rationalization of the political process.

Eager for a capsule phrase to sum up their leader's goals, Liberals had promised the "Just Society." But "justice" was not easily defined, and the phrase raised more hopes than it could satisfy. A 1969 white paper on Indian policy promised to abolish the Indian Act, a perennial focus for native grievances, replacing it with "full, free and nondiscriminatory participation of the Indian people in Canadian society." An embarrassed minister, Jean Chrétien, had to flee before cries of "cultural genocide." Indians wanted special status, not equality with whites. By 1974, native people had become a vocal, federally financed pressure group. White Canadians, who had imagined that land claims were ancient history, discovered that Indians and Inuit were claiming the North and much else besides.

The new prime minister had more success in imposing his views in external affairs and defence, if only because his opinions were closer to a familiar Canadian political tradition. Trudeau had publicly wondered whether defence dollars would be better spent on foreign aid. Canadian armed forces had endured the trauma of unification as the price for modern equipment. With Trudeau, that commitment died. Military manpower was slashed by a fifth, and Canada's NATO contingent was cut to half-strength – five thousand men. Obsolete ships, tanks, and aircraft remained. True to the new spirit of self-interest, allies were not consulted. Trudeau had had no respect for the pompous, English-speaking diplomats who had lived in Pearson's shadow. The new priority for Canada's missions abroad would be trade, not diplomacy. A collection of little booklets on Canada's new foreign policy insisted that self-interest, not self-importance, would be the guide. Even some of Trudeau's admirers were dismayed when he bluntly refused to engage himself in moderating the miseries of Nigeria's civil war. Aides reminded them that the prime minister was a man of contradictions.

Canada's relations with the United States were now more important and more complicated than ever. The rhetoric of special relations and undefended borders had worn thin. By criticizing American actions in Vietnam, even Lester Pearson had ignored the prudent doctrine that neighbourly differences were best discussed quietly. In Canada, anti-Americanism was a noisy feature of the youth culture, fed by draft dodgers and emigré academics. The simple-minded envy of the Kennedy years had become an equally simple-minded antagonism. Often the issues, the arguments, and the tactics echoed those in the strife-torn United States. Without the *Wall Street Journal* and the American Freedom of Information Act, it would, for example, have been difficult to document the alleged misdeeds of multinational corporations.

The most vociferous young nationalists (with Melville Watkins, formerly of Walter Gordon's task force on foreign ownership, at their head) migrated from Trudeaumania to the NDP in a bid to capture it for the newly fashionable academic Marxism. Enough nationalism remained in the older parties and in an elite-studded Committee for an Independent Canada to exercise a powerful influence on government. While Canada's external policies and foreign takeovers of Canadian companies were prime targets for the Committee, it was performers, publishers, and film producers who were the main beneficiaries of its lobbying. Canada was made safe for *Maclean's* magazine by the belated elimination of *Time's* Canadian edition. A new regulatory agency for broadcasting, the Canadian Radio and Telecommunications Commission, imposed Canadian quotas for television programs and broadcast music. Anne Murray and Gordon Lightfoot led a flood of suddenly popularized entertainers.

The issues raised by economic nationalists like Walter Gordon, Mel Watkins, and later by an outspoken Liberal minister, Herb Gray, went to the heart of Canada's industrial weaknesses. Inefficient branch plants would be vulnerable to the first serious economic down-turn. Head offices kept research and development at home, charged artificial prices for their services, and discouraged export efforts that might compete with the parent company. Yet millions of Canadians depended on foreign companies for their jobs, most Canadian business leaders fervently defended foreign investment (it guaranteed a market if they ever sold out), and economists had no trouble proving that Canada's prosperity depended on a regular "fix" of foreign capital.

Canada's vulnerability was driven home in 1971. European prosperity and the policy of borrowing to finance its Vietnam war effort drove the United States into intolerable financial difficulties. The 1944 world of Bretton Woods, with an almighty dollar and gold at $35 an ounce, suddenly ended. President Richard Nixon abandoned convertibility, sent gold prices soaring, and clamped down on exports of capital and imports of goods. With two-thirds of her exports bound for the United States, Canada was in a desperate plight: Nixon had forgotten to exempt her. By dint of much humble pleading, Canada finally got Washington partially to relent, but the price was Canadian acquiescence in American programs to repatriate capital and increase industrial exports.

For all their prosperity, the sixties had changed the balance of power among western nations. As an American economic dependent, Canada was on the losing side. Europe offered no alternative market. Neither did China. Trudeau had fulfilled an election commitment to recognize the Peking government, but the mainland Chinese took that as their due, and any brief economic advantage was promptly capped by President Nixon's unexpected overtures to China in 1971. Canadians, like Americans, began to lose interest in a world that seemed ungrateful and increasingly hostile. Affluence and cheap airfares allowed them to travel farther and more often, but they did so as tourists, not as world citizens. A few Canadians, secular missionaries from development agencies like CIDA and CUSO, returned to lobby for the needs of less-developed countries, but Canadians kept most of their sympathy and charity at home.

There was enough there to occupy them. Trudeau's single most substantive claim to power in 1968 was his strategy for keeping Canada united. In the euphoria of the election campaign his policies might be forgotten but they had been repeated – even in the interior of British Columbia – in both French and English. Recognition of a "two nations" version of Canada and of special status for Quebec, long buried in the NDP's program and later endorsed by Robert Stanfield of the Conservatives, Trudeau angrily dismissed. Canada must become a truly federal state with equality for all of its ten provinces. Canada must be a homeland for both French and English, without sacrifice of language or culture. The keystone of Trudeau's policy was the Official Languages Act of 1969, with its provision for bilingual districts and for the transformation of the federal government and its agencies into institutions where Canadians of either official language could find service and employment. It was a law solemnly endorsed by all parties and most MPS with the exception of John Diefenbaker and a small rump of his Tory supporters.

It was part of the faith of the liberation generation that history could be ignored or overturned. The Official Languages Act defined a vision of Canada which Cartier, Laurier, and the younger Henri Bourassa had sought but consistently failed to achieve. It was an attempt to annul novelist Hugh MacLennan's description of Canada as "two solitudes." To a prime minister with a superb cosmopolitan education and easy fluency in both languages, it seemed simple enough. It was not. In French Canada, nationalists now saw English as a deadly threat to French and demanded its repression in Quebec. In the West, Clifford Sifton's "national schools" had done their work. Generations of newcomers had sacrificed their linguistic heritage for English; nothing in their perception of Canada established special significance for French. In schools across Canada, the new fashion of student-selected courses drove second languages from the curriculum. It was "oppressive" to compel students to learn what they found difficult or unrewarding.

Yet the alternative to Trudeau's vision was far more threatening to national unity. If French Canadians were to be at home only in Quebec, there would be no logical destiny for them but national independence, with instalments of "special status" easing the process. The compromise of "associate statehood," now urged by the *Union Nationale*, was a reversion to the double majorities of the

1860s, this time with thirty per cent dictating to the other seventy per cent of the population. For all the grumbling about French on cereal boxes and the extravagance of making senior civil servants feebly bilingual, Trudeau was determined that his official languages program would persist.

The urgency was underlined by events in Quebec. In Montreal, nationalist riots became endemic. Trudeau's election victory had been enhanced by his coolness in the face of a bottle-throwing mob at the Saint-Jean Baptiste day parade in 1968; in the following year, rioters simply demolished the procession. In March 1969, massed demonstrators marched on Montreal's venerable McGill University, demanding its conversion to French. In October, police and firemen struck, leaving Montreal to looters and rioting taxi drivers. The underlying grievances in post-Expo Montreal were economic, but the inspiration came from revolutionary nationalists armed with a cause that drew grudging sympathy even from conservative Québécois.

Quebec Liberals had been leaderless since the retirement of Jean Lesage. They might have chosen a tough ex-judge, Claude Wagner, if Trudeau had not intervened. His choice was Robert Bourassa, a youthful economist who had married into wealth and who possessed a computer-age image of competence. Bourassa's opposition would not be the crumbling *Union Nationale* but the new *Parti Québécois*, René Lévesque's masterful welding of the disparate, quarrelsome independence movements. To meet their fiery appeals for an independent Quebec, Bourassa offered a vision of a "profitable Confederation" and firm promises of a hundred thousand new jobs. The outcome, in April 1970, was an easy Liberal victory, but the PQ, with a fifth of the votes, was in second place, with followers bitterly chagrined by failure and by Lévesque's personal defeat in a partly English-speaking constituency.

The victory was no prize. Quebec needed an economic wizard. The province was deep in debt. Too many of Quebec's industries – footwear, textiles, clothing – were obsolete and survived only because of mountainous federal tariffs. These were threatened by each step toward world trade liberalization. Quebec's hurriedly built, costly education system seemed to be staffed by teachers who were as orthodox in Marxism as they had once been in Catholicism. Their graduates were well indoctrinated but unemployable. Foreign investment, needed to keep Bourassa's promise, would be frightened off by social turbulence and whispers of revolution.

The challenge came quickly and unexpectedly. On October 5, 1970, James Cross, the British Trade Commissioner in Montreal, was kidnapped. It was a police matter, though a manifesto from the kidnappers, a pretentiously titled *"Front de Liberation du Québec,"* was solemnly broadcast. It was the FLQ's kidnapping, five days later, of Pierre Laporte, Bourassa's labour minister, that unleashed panic and confusion. Radicals, labour leaders, and French-speaking students sympathized deliriously and publicly with the kidnappers. A mass rally chanted "FLQ, FLQ" in a downtown arena, and a purported lawyer for the kidnappers held court before the admiring media. Claude Ryan of *Le Devoir* and René Lévesque of the PQ mustered prominent nationalists to provide Bourassa with their wisdom. Ottawa, they insisted, must not get involved. It was too late, a nervous Bourassa confessed, he had already asked for the army.

Troops were needed to relieve the strain on the competing and inexpert municipal, provincial, and federal police organizations. In Ottawa, the prime minister went much farther than "aid to the civil power." Before dawn on October 16, the government declared that an apprehended insurrection existed in Quebec and proclaimed the War Measures Act. As ten thousand soldiers in battle order swept into Montreal, Quebec, and Ottawa, police spread out to seize a total of 468 people. Some were cases of mistaken identity; most of them had merely enjoyed the heady thrill of preaching and promoting revolution.

A few days later, Laporte's strangled body was found, and terrorists were no longer heroes.

The man who had been elected as the embodiment of liberation in 1968 was the same man who dissolved that dream in 1970. The fun went out of revolution and, overwhelmingly,

Canadians approved – eighty-eight per cent across Canada, eighty-six per cent in Quebec. Trudeau's victims would not forget their humiliation; neither would erstwhile liberal admirers, horrified by so naked a use of force. They mistook his purpose. Trudeau's target was never the obscure terrorists of the FLQ, but the "self-appointed dictators," "the emergence of a parallel power which sets itself against the elected power in this country." To Trudeau, it was the chanting crowds, the coffee-table conspirators, and even men like Ryan and Lévesque who constituted the "apprehended insurrection." Bourassa's government might be feeble and frightened, but it had been elected democratically. By December the troops were gone. The police rescued Cross and found Laporte's murderers. Dismayed by its lack of information, the Trudeau government ordered the RCMP to spy on subversives and discreetly averted its eyes from the amateurish consequences. Terrorism passed from fashion.

Trudeau's critics also had a point. The War Measures Act created martyrs. It furnished ugly precedents. It casually shattered safeguards Canadians had taken for granted. Nor could Trudeau or his colleagues, Jean Marchand and Gérard Pelletier, publicly justify their role in the October crisis without explaining the intuitions gained in a lifetime of Montreal intellectual politics or without further damaging the frail credibility of Robert Bourassa's government.

Within a year, Trudeau's new Quebec enemies had their first revenge. While confessing that he was opening Pandora's box, Trudeau had returned to the old chore of constitutional reform. Perhaps to his surprise, he found that the provincial premiers agreed on a long list of issues, from shared-cost programs to a provincial role in choosing Supreme Court judges. At Victoria in June 1971, he and the premiers wrapped up trade-offs and compromises and an amending formula that limited veto rights to Ontario and Quebec. Together, they proclaimed a Victoria Charter. Even Bourassa agreed. But by the time Bourassa's plane had landed at Montreal, he had changed his mind. A storm of protest, much of it inspired by Ryan and *Le Devoir*, greeted him. Bourassa had won none of the constitutional panaceas that Ryan touted. There was no special status, equal status, or associate status for Quebec. On June 23, Bourassa declared that the deal was off.

Constitutional reform had a low priority for most Canadians; economic management held no great interest for the prime minister. The mismatch was unfortunate. For Canada, as for the United States, the easy post-war years were over. Confidence that Keynes had unlocked the secret of macroeconomic management was undermined by the co-existence of unacceptable levels of both inflation and unemployment. Keynesians like the Canadian-born economist John Kenneth Galbraith blamed the phenomenon on the price-setting power of great corporations and the wage-fixing influence of strong unions. The remedy, as in wartime, lay with selective wage and price controls. In Canada, both the problem and any solution was complicated by the split of federal and provincial powers and by the conviction that economic trends inevitably were determined by the American economy.

If economics mattered to the Trudeau government, it was because national unity or regional problems took on an economic dimension. Trudeau's version of federalism would have pushed Ottawa out of provincial fields like health, education, and welfare: provinces protested that Ottawa pressure and money had propelled them into costly programs in post-secondary education and medicare. Retreat was not easy. Meanwhile, in the Trudeau view, Ottawa had a clear responsibility for economic equalization among regions and even among individuals. In 1969, the government's array of development agencies and programs had been clustered in a new Department of Regional Economic Expansion (DREE) under Jean Marchand. By 1979, DREE was pumping half a billion dollars a year into Atlantic Canada and eastern Quebec with no conspicuous growth in local prosperity or contentment.

Unemployment insurance, devised as a benefit for jobless factory workers, had been transformed through the seasonal benefits invented in the Diefenbaker and Pearson years into an income subsidy for fishermen and loggers. In 1971, unemployment insurance was changed again into a vast income maintenance program for a wide range of Canadians, from artists to expectant mothers.

Higher-income employees were brought into the scheme. Benefits were improved to guarantee "individual development" as well as survival. Suspicious citizens complained that government was subsidizing the idle. Reporters duly uncovered "welfare bums."

The 1968 slogan of a "Just Society" implied progress on a long list of overdue reforms. Kenneth Carter, appointed by Diefenbaker in 1962 to study Canada's tax laws, delivered 2600 pages of expert opinion and a simple proposition: a dollar of income should be taxed as a dollar, however earned. Wage earners cheerfully agreed, but they carried no weight. By the time tax reform became law in 1971, lobbyists had done their work. A dollar earned by sweat was still taxed at full value; a dollar added from a windfall was taxed as fifty cents; gambling winnings were still tax-free. The moral lesson was clear. By 1975, lotteries in Canada had become a billion-dollar government enterprise.

Business had gutted tax reform. It buried legislation threatening time-honoured price-fixing and monopoly practices. It stalled the schemes of economic nationalists and channelled the government's anti-inflation efforts into a verbal assault on wages. Even having to struggle with Ottawa was tiresome. The Conservatives, bereft of business support since Diefenbaker, began to look more attractive.

In the West, Trudeau proved to have a gift for making enemies. He could not be blamed for sagging world sales of grain in 1969 and 1970, but his bad-tempered response to unhappy farmers – "Why should I sell your wheat?" – ignored the fact that the Wheat Board was a federal agency. Ottawa's response to surplus, a program designed to take wheat fields out of production, coincided with crop failures in China and the Soviet Union. Incomes soared with grain prices but not for those farmers who had taken Ottawa's advice. Western Canada might have tolerated Trudeau's concerns for bilingualism and constitutional reform if he had shown genuine concern for their preoccupations. He did not.

Liberals in 1968 had secured the foundation for a western revival. It vanished like a May snowstorm. In June 1969, New Democrats under Ed Schreyer accomplished the apparently impossible by winning a narrow victory in Manitoba. The extra votes came from provincial Liberals. In Saskatchewan, Ross Thatcher's Liberals had beaten a weary CCF in 1964, and won again in 1967. Not even the well-publicized coldness between Thatcher and Trudeau could save Saskatchewan Liberals in 1971, and Allan Blakeney became the province's second NDP premier. Within three years Saskatchewan Liberalism, the oldest and solidest branch of the party in western Canada, had virtually ceased to exist. In Alberta, the conservatism of Social Credit was replaced in 1971 by the younger but more authentic Conservatism of Peter Lougheed. In British Columbia, removed from the peculiar fervour of prairie grievances, Liberalism survived longest, helping to attract enough affluent votes in 1972 to aid Dave Barrett's NDP to win power. That trauma was sufficient to send British Columbia Liberals into Social Credit ranks by 1975, when the NDP fell before a right-wing phalanx.

The responsibility was more than Trudeau's. Polarization may have been inevitable in the western provinces with the growth of NDP support; resource-based economies were as unstable in their politics as they were in their markets. The crucial fact remained that the prime minister had inherited a national following and a commitment to national unity. By 1972, both Liberalism and Trudeau's party were in disarray.

Of this, Trudeau seems to have been blandly unaware. His advisers, appropriately influenced by Marshall MacLuhan, proposed that Trudeau's re-election would be a "dialogue with Canadians," under the slogan, "the land is strong." His squabbling rivals could be dismissed. Diefenbaker loyalists, dominant in the Tory caucus, had never ceased making what misery they could for Robert Stanfield. The NDP had replaced Tommy Douglas with David Lewis, a brilliant labour lawyer who had been chief architect of the CCF-labour marriage. It seemed a sad inheritance: the NDP had become the residual heir of the stormy, internecine politics of the liberation generation. Western victories were small compensation for civil war in the Ontario NDP and a Marxist-separatist takeover in Quebec. With broken enemies, the Trudeau magic, and so much expertise, the Liberals could not lose.

They got a surprise. For the NDP, Lewis turned the unpromising topic of tax reform into sensation by showing how huge firms – "corporate welfare bums" – deferred their taxes for years while ordinary citizens paid up. The facts won few converts, but the issue came as an overdue stimulus to troubled New Democrats. Tories translated Lewis's theme into an assault on more conventional "welfare bums," allegedly prospering under the costly new unemployment insurance scheme. On election night, a lacklustre election campaign became a cliffhanger. On October 30, Liberals emerged with only 109 seats, Conservatives with 107, and Lewis's NDP with 31. Réal Caouette's *Créditistes* kept 15 and independents, 2.

In 1972, the media had portrayed Trudeau as a spoiled brat, telling unemployed mail drivers to *"mange de la merde"* and dismissing journalists with icy aloofness. Perhaps he would now leave. Certainly there was a petulant edge to his explanation for the outcome: "Nine-tenths of politics appeals to emotions rather than to reason. I am a bit sorry about that, but this is the world we're living in, and therefore I've had to change."

Change he would. Quebeckers were informed that it was Trudeau's devotion to their interests that had cost the Liberals votes elsewhere in Canada. Inspectors were hired to hunt (in vain) for welfare bums. Since the Conservatives offered him no terms, David Lewis was compelled to take what Trudeau offered or force an early and possibly fatal election. Armed with budget surpluses, the government spent its way back to modest popularity, with bread and milk subsidies to offset inflation, and a Food Prices Review Board which, unexpectedly, denounced the government's marketing boards, not the supermarkets. That, of course, was a cue for the new agriculture minister, Eugene Whalen, to champion farmers and their right to a good price.

By 1973, European and American economies had recovered from mild recession. The long ordeal in Vietnam was approaching its painful conclusion, and optimists boasted that the world would benefit from a "peace dividend." In Canada, unemployment fell to under six per cent by 1973 and Liberal popularity climbed perceptibly, even in the West. In the summer of 1973, David Lewis tried to persuade his party to force an election, but the New Democrats were not interested.

Few Canadians even noticed that the major oil-exporting countries had met to consider their pricing policies. Even fewer recognized that petroleum had become virtually the only significant commodity whose price was immune to inflation. Ontarians grumbled that Alberta crude cost three dollars a barrel while Iranian oil sold for fifty cents. Suddenly, those days were memories. OPEC (Organization of Petroleum Exporting Countries) became a household acronym. By August, world prices of oil had risen fifty per cent in three months. In October 1973, when Egypt launched a massive and initially triumphant assault on Israel, Arab countries backed the war with an oil boycott of Israel's allies. By the end of the year, oil prices had quadrupled. A world economy based on cheap energy struggled desperately to readjust.

Canada was both a supplier and an importer. The Borden Line had given Alberta oil a protected market in Ontario. The American West imported about as much Canadian oil as the eastern provinces took from the world market. Oil company forecasts, devised to justify exports, had claimed in 1971 that Canada had enough reserves for hundreds of years. By odd coincidence, in 1973 the estimates suddenly shrank. Far from a happy immunity to the world crisis, Canadians were told that their energy reserves might vanish in a decade. It was also true that few sectors of the Canadian economy were more thoroughly dominated by multinational corporations and even more sadly true that the large oil companies had not enjoyed high public regard.

An economic crisis brought a political response. Alberta and Saskatchewan felt strongly that they had a right to the best available price for a non-renewable resource which, since 1930, they had undoubtedly controlled. Depression memories of poverty and dependence haunted people in both provinces. Without oil wealth, those days could return. The western provinces would be accommodating, but, as Allan Blakeney reminded Canadians, no one had ever suggested that Ontario sell its resources to western provinces at less than the world price. In Ottawa, the Trudeau government was unmoved. So was the NDP. Its pressure for economic nationalism had already won the promise of a Foreign Investment Review Agency. The oil crisis was a new opportunity to show what the New Democrats could do. Liberals swallowed hard and largely accepted the NDP's terms: a freeze on domestic prices; an export tax to subsidize eastern oil imports; a pipeline to carry Alberta oil to Montreal; and, at long last, a crown corporation, Petro Canada, to give Canada a stake in the oil industry. It was also time to begin, in earnest, development of the Alberta tar sands and a Mackenzie Valley pipeline to connect with expected Arctic oil deposits.

The program made political sense. Alberta would grumble but it now had no Liberal seats. Canadian consumers would see Ottawa protecting them from an artificial crisis contrived by foreigners and the oil companies. Americans would pay the export tax, and eastern Canadians, particularly Quebeckers, would see the benefits of Confederation. Even the West could hardly grumble, for it was now getting far more than it had ever expected for its oil, and salting away the proceeds in bulging "Heritage" funds. Economists took a different view. The "hidden hand" must rule. World prices would be painful but nothing less would shock Canadians into genuine conservation. It was too bad that the National Energy Board had never checked the exaggerated estimates of reserves, but the gloomy truth had to be faced. New oil finds would be remote, heavy, and very costly. Synthetic crude from the tar sands depended on expensive, environmentally questionable processes.

Politics prevailed. Alberta got more money, but not a world price. Most Canadians seemed pleased.

Liberal fortunes revived. In Newfoundland in 1972, Joey Smallwood had finally fallen to the Conservatives but Nova Scotia Liberals were back in power. In Quebec, Robert Bourassa tested his popularity with an electorate sick of public sector strikes, labour violence, and militant speeches. The result, in October 1973, was a Liberal landslide of 102 seats out of 110. The margin concealed a more disturbing statistic: *Parti Québécois* electoral support had climbed to thirty per cent.

As Liberal popularity revived, it seemed a good time for a federal election. It was not hard to arrange. An April budget distributed a gentle rain of tax cuts and a dollop of corporate welfare which Lewis and the NDP felt compelled to oppose. On May 8, 1974, to its complete satisfaction, the Liberal government fell, and the blame lay squarely with the NDP. For his campaign, the Conservative leader, Robert Stanfield, had consulted the experts and the newspapers, concluded that inflation was approaching a crisis, and promised a sixty-day wage and price freeze. Whatever its validity, neither the policy nor Stanfield made much impact. Good times and warm weather made Trudeau's audiences almost as forgiving as in 1968. He had changed, he admitted to whistle-stop audiences across Canada: "I have a train, and I have Margaret." A beautiful young wife, gushing with adoration, was the definitive answer to those who had depicted the prime minister as cold and unfeeling.

On July 8, 1974, urban Ontario and the working-class ridings of British Columbia deserted the Conservatives and the NDP to give Trudeau back his majority: 141 seats to only 95 for the Conservatives and a humiliating 16 for the NDP. The West gave Trudeau only 5 seats. In York South, a seat the CCF had first won in 1942, David Lewis was defeated. The Italian Canadians who now dominated his district voted Liberal. So, for the first time, did their wives. A growing "Right to Life" movement had persuaded them that Lewis favoured abortion.

The age of liberation was over. The counter-offensive had begun.

2

Affirmation

More than in 1968, Pierre Elliott Trudeau believed that his new majority gave him a mandate for his own approach to government. Ministers would now focus on long-term planning. A trusted friend, Michael Pitfield, took charge of the federal bureaucracy. A new jargon of policies and priorities permeated Ottawa. Rationality would surely follow.

Instead, Trudeau and his colleagues rediscovered that life in politics is lived in short gasps. Two old enemies, inflation and unemployment, would not wait for the bureaucratic seminar to end. In the minority interlude, the Liberals had echoed the theory that Canadian inflation was largely imported and beyond Ottawa's control. Quadrupled oil prices affected more than gasoline at the pump; tomatoes cost more because greenhouses were heated by oil, so did plastic gadgets since they came from an oil-based feedstock. Almost everything in Canada was transported by road or rail. In Atlantic Canada, oil-fired generators produced most of the electricity. Costs were passed on to the consumers at each stage.

The minority Liberal government's answer to inflation had been to tie wages, pensions, and many of its other payments to the consumer price index. At the same time, stealing a 1972 election promise from Robert Stanfield, John Turner, the finance minister, linked income tax deductions to the price index. This was even more popular, though it slashed Ottawa's revenue at a time when its expenses were certain to rise with inflation. Massive spending on housing programs delighted the construction and real estate industries and pleased young families eager for their own homes.

Once again, spending set house prices soaring. OPEC may have started an inflationary cycle but Ottawa's policies did nothing to hinder it.

Next to OPEC, oil companies, and Alberta's Premier Peter Lougheed, the most obvious scapegoat for inflation was labour. Unionized workers usually get their chance to raise their wages near the end of the inflation cycle. Fixed contract periods had been a proud feature of the Canadian industrial relations system, locking workers and employers into two- and three-year agreements, while prices rose resolutely but discreetly. Angry union members, bent on catching up and protecting themselves from future inflation, demanded settlements ranging from thirty to eighty per cent. Once editors and politicians admitted that inflation was a problem, unions presented themselves as a convenient and familiar villain. Since the public was the employer for some of the most militant unionists, notably in the post office, resentment was more easily mobilized than ever.

In his first term of inflation fighting, Trudeau had preferred lecturing business and labour: Canada had not imitated the short-lived American experience with controls. In the 1974 election campaign, Trudeau had delighted audiences by sneering at the folly of Robert Stanfield's proposed wage and price freeze. After the Liberal victory John Turner applied his undoubted charm to urging restraint on business and labour. Union leaders were tempted. The failure of the NDP in the 1974 campaign had been disillusioning, and never had Liberal politicians been more charming. What the Liberals could not seem to understand, however, was that it was union members, not leaders, who set bargaining demands. Officials of the Canadian Labour Congress might yearn to be statesmen but their jobs depended on votes from union militants and from younger members who expected fast results.

The pressures for controls grew. Elderly government officials remembered the triumph of the Wartime Prices and Trade Board. In the United States, John Kenneth Galbraith lent his credentials to the cause, and President Nixon's 1971 experiment with price controls looked better in retrospect than it had at the time. Turner's failure to win voluntary restraint deepened his personal antagonism to the prime minister; in 1974 he left the government and Parliament. On October 13, Canadians could rush out and buy copies of *Maclean's* citing the prime minister's firm opposition to controls. They could then rush home to their radios and hear him outlining a policy of mandatory wage and price guidelines of ten, eight, and six per cent in successive years, enforced by an Anti-Inflation Board (AIB). The further details were complex and they grew in complexity as their impact filtered through the economy.

Organized labour professed outrage. The brief flirtation with Liberalism ended. Unionists who had signed agreements before October 13 could pocket their gains; those who were too late were caught empty-handed. The AIB's officials showed no sensitivity to their plight. Serious collective bargaining had been suspended for the duration of controls; the Canadian Labour Congress devoted itself to demonstrations, a court challenge, and a "Day of Protest" involving a million workers on the anniversary of the Trudeau announcement. The experience was chastening. While business slowly came to share some of the union resentment at controls and their bureaucratic application, most Canadians (including union members) welcomed anything that promised to curb inflation.

Still faithful to the dream of long-range planning, the prime minister invited Canadians to contemplate a post-controls period when a kind of "social corporatism" might prevail. Labour leaders surpassed business in their initial horror at the notion. Then some of them were intrigued. For a few months, echoes of Mackenzie King's tripartism of government, business, and labour, and Henry Wise Wood's theory of "group government" wafted through the thinking of Canadian Labour Congress leaders and Liberal politicians, only to vanish. By 1978, a more aggressive CLC leadership had reaffirmed its commitment to the NDP, and notions of industrial democracy returned to the files.

Nowhere was labour protest louder or angrier than in Quebec. The era when Taschereau or Duplessis could promote the attractions of a cheap and docile labour force were gone. Industrial conflict took on political overtones, with *Parti Québécois* sympathizers in unions and the media eager to embarrass the Bourassa government. The centrepiece of Robert Bourassa's economic strategy was a vast hydro-electricity project on rivers leading into James Bay. Inflation and the price exacted by native bands for their land sent the costs of the project soaring. A scheme to win labour peace on the project by handing workers to one of Quebec's rival labour federations exploded in destructive riots in the winter of 1975. For all his huge majority, by 1976 Bourassa's government seemed to be in a state of siege with no relief in sight.

Beyond a faltering provincial economy, Bourassa's most serious problem was the language issue. Between them, the Laurendeau-Dunton commission and the 1971 census provided evidence that suggested that French was in deadly danger. Immigrants to Montreal learned English, not French. They also earned more than *Canadiens*. In 1951, French Canadians had formed eighty-three per cent of Quebec's population; by 1971 they had dropped to eighty per cent. Riots had exploded in the Montreal suburb of St-Leonard in 1969 because Italian immigrants had insisted on sending their children to English schools. Alarmists warned that Montreal would soon become an English-speaking city where the French would feel like foreigners. Nationalists blamed the 1970 defeat of the *Union Nationale* on its refusal to abolish the freedom of parents to choose the language in which their child would be educated. At a time when Trudeau urged bilingualism for Canada, nationalists demanded unilingualism for Quebec, and no one doubted that the demand was popular.

Bourassa had bought time with a commission of inquiry. The commission's report was moderate; its evidence should have been reassuring. It was not the French who were dwindling but the Anglo-Quebeckers. The huge investment in French education in the 1960s was already paying off in higher incomes and better jobs. Passions were not reduced. In 1974, Bourassa's Bill 22 proclaimed French the sole official language of Quebec and abolished the tradition of parental choice between French- and English-language schooling. To force immigrant children into French schools, toddlers would be subjected to a language test. No one, from the *Parti Québécois* to an English-speaking minority that had always voted solidly Liberal, seemed pleased. Foes of bilingualism elsewhere in Canada had new arguments to add to their case.

In 1970, Jean Drapeau followed his Expo triumph with a fresh announcement: in 1976 Montreal would be host to the Olympic Games. There was no echo of joy beyond the mayor's circle of admirers, nor did many believe Drapeau's boast that the Games could no more show a deficit than he could become pregnant. By the time the Games opened, the Expo miracle had not recurred. A grandiose eighty-thousand-seat stadium was unfinished, and not even a new Canadian appetite for buying lottery tickets could cover the sky-high costs for it and for other facilities. Federal sports subsidies and a vivacious sports minister, Iona Campagnolo, did not overcome Canada's mediocre record in most Olympic events, and the Montreal Games left debts, unemployment, and none of the euphoria of 1967. Instead, there was the sour awareness of corruption and incompetence.

Quebeckers yearned for a change of government; they did not want independence. On both points, the polls were unequivocal. René Lévesque was a realist; so were such key advisers as Claude Morin and Jacques Pariseau, both of them prominent veterans of the Quiet Revolution. The *Parti Québécois* would now proceed step by step, first winning power and then submitting the independence issue to a referendum. Voting PQ would get rid of the Liberals, not Confederation.

It was a shrewd idea and the PQ prospered in the opinion polls. It needed a little bit more, soon provided by a few hundred pilots and air traffic controllers. As federal minister of transport, Jean Marchand used his new authority to order that French as well as English could be used in the Quebec skies. Pilots and controllers, predominantly English-speaking, insisted that English was the international language of the air and, in June 1976, went on strike to support their opinion. A flood of support from English-Canadian editors, politicians, and ordinary citizens sent the government into retreat. The long, heaving flood of resentment at bilingualism suddenly burst, and just as suddenly was gone. English Canadians promptly forgot the issue and barely noticed a few years later when the arguments about safety had been demolished and bilingualism was in place. But French Canadians did not forget, and on November 15, 1976, they took their resentment to the polls. That night, René Lévesque stood triumphant amidst a huge, ecstatic crowd. From six seats, the PQ had soared to seventy-one. Bourassa was personally beaten; his Liberals kept only twenty-six seats, a mere twenty-three per cent of the popular vote, only half the *Parti Québécois* share.

Outside Quebec, Lévesque's victory was traumatic. The impossible had happened, and Canadians desperately wanted a leader.

Since 1974, the earlier hostility to Trudeau had revived. In 1975, a fifth of the delegates at a Liberal policy conference wanted a leadership review. In February 1976, after Robert Stanfield had gracefully resigned, the Tories had their chance to choose a new leader. Despite a strange, unpredicted bid by Diefenbaker to deliver the convention to an ex-Liberal from Quebec, Claude Wagner, delegates preferred an untried young Albertan named Joe Clark. The rest of Canada did not know him, but by that summer only twenty-nine per cent wanted Trudeau. The Lévesque victory changed that. "I say to you with all the certainty I can command," Trudeau reassured them, "that Canada's unity will not be fractured." By February 1977, half the electorate would have voted Liberal. In the spring, when Trudeau's wife left him for the role of flower child to the media, most Canadians sympathized with a lonely father left to raise three sons.

Almost as quickly as it had materialized, support dissipated. Separatism soon seemed to be no threat. In power, the *Parti Québécois* was more talented than the Liberals and no more radical than one of the prairie NDP governments. Government auto insurance and the takeover of the troubled asbestos industry were hardly revolutionary. Bill 101, the PQ's language legislation, might be absurd or oppressive in imposing French as the language of work, government, and even the signs of English bookshops, but Canadians outside Quebec were unaffected, and they never had shown much sympathy for Quebec's English-speaking minority.

The minority itself was confused, divided, and largely silent. Its younger members packed their bags. So did many of Montreal's head offices. Even Ottawa pleaded with businesses to stay. Separatists quietly rejoiced at the exodus.

In time, there would be a referendum. Meanwhile, both Trudeau and Lévesque competed vigorously for friends in New York and Washington – an uncomfortable reminder of where Canadian decisions were now appealed. A new federal task force, headed by Jean Luc Pepin of the Anti-Inflation Board and John Robarts, Ontario's retired premier, travelled the country, hunting for grievances in the name of national unity. Canadians returned, uncomforted, to their economic preoccupations.

In 1973, politicians had promised energy self-sufficiency. It was harder to attain than it looked. Private oil companies had been discredited by their role in the oil price crisis, but they were in full control of the industry. Most western Canadians preferred the wisdom of the Calgary "Oil Patch," the cluster of petroleum companies and their admirers to the policies of a Liberal Ottawa. Their provincial governments also controlled the resources. Only huge public investment helped the new Syncrude plant at Fort McMurray to turn tar sands into oil and two other vast projects stumbled through their planning stages as their private backers waited for the right price. Ottawa's promised participant in the oil business, Petrocan, had been too obviously a concession to the NDP. Its mere existence was an insult to the robust, American-style mood of the oil industry.

Beyond the provinces lay the fabled energy resources of the North West Territories, but the fable was unconfirmed and testing it would be enormously costly. Canadians had complacently viewed the Territories as a remote, uninhabited wilderness, to be exploited at future convenience. Belatedly, they were reminded that the Territories had a fragile ecology and a newly outspoken native population, as eager as any to profit from the energy crisis. An inquiry by Mr. Justice Tom Berger, a former NDP leader in British Columbia, publicized the problems of the proposed Mackenzie Valley pipeline, designed to carry Arctic gas to southern markets. His report neatly aligned native leaders, their white allies, and a largely sympathetic Canadian public. By 1977, the pipeline was dead.

It was all part of a leisurely, sometimes fatuous pursuit of energy self-sufficiency. Spared much economic urgency, Canadians could debate the merits of bio-mass and windmills, denounce the one substantive achievement of Canadian post-war technology, the CANDU reactor, and enjoy lower gasoline prices than Americans. In 1975, Ottawa and Edmonton had come to a reluctant agreement that Canadian oil prices would rise by 1979 almost to the rate set by the OPEC cartel, $14.75 a barrel. Thanks to the Iranian Revolution, OPEC chose that year to send prices zooming again. By the end of 1979, the world price had tripled and Canada's oil subsidy bill had climbed to $2.5 billion. With renewed fervour, the producing provinces demanded more money and the consuming provinces insisted on protection.

Oil prices were only one of many factors creating the combination of inflation and unemployment that infected most of the western industrialized nations. The analysis of the modern Keynesians was now discarded; their main policy – controls – offended labour and, in time, business. Older economic fashions fitted an increasingly conservative mood. Inflation, said the traditional textbooks, was due to too much money chasing too few goods. Monetarists promised that high interest rates would shrink a money supply inflated by excessive credit. "Supply-siders" insisted that lower taxes for the rich would give them an incentive to provide more investment capital. Money spent by governments was unproductive. Both doctrines delighted bankers and the wealthy; less influential folk went along with them since nothing else had worked.

In 1979, British voters gave Margaret Thatcher a mandate to test the old wisdom; American voters gave the same opportunity to Ronald Reagan and the Republicans in 1980. In Canada, Pierre Elliott Trudeau had not waited for an election to join the experiment. Sharing a summit with leaders of six other industrialized countries in 1978 provided the stimulus. On his return, he unceremoniously scrapped the Anti-Inflation Board, announced cuts in federal spending and programs, and promised tax reductions.

The impact on the economy and the government's fortunes was slight. A cluster of by-elections in the autumn of 1978 proved disastrous for the Liberals. Workers freed from wage controls discovered that their bargaining power had virtually vanished in an ensuing recession. Canadian industrial incomes, second highest in the world in 1970, had fallen to seventh by 1979 and would be fourteenth by 1982. Purchasing power had been outpaced by inflation since 1975, but economists unrepentantly insisted that wages had not been squeezed enough. Meanwhile, true to the tradition of James Coyne, the Bank of Canada returned to its old faith in tight money. Ottawa, to its own dismay, began to have to finance budgets that headed dramatically into the red.

Canadians had assumed since the war that the federal government could manage the economy effectively if it only chose to do so. The ingenious arrangement that allowed Ottawa to collect direct taxes for all but Quebec had been a guarantee of fiscal leverage. That leverage had dramatically dwindled. Instead of the ten per cent of federal income tax revenue they got in 1947, wealthier provinces like Ontario were taking forty-four per cent by 1977. Ottawa now insisted on limiting increases in its share of the costs of post-secondary education and medicare to no more than the growth of the gross national product. In return, provinces could spend the money as they chose. Fiscal decentralization would again result in local standards of health care and education.

Ottawa's fiscal plight was not understood. By 1978, earlier modest surpluses had turned into an annual deficit of almost $12 billion. Opposition critics complained of extravagance. Joe Clark, seizing a figure from the air, promised to eliminate sixty thousand government jobs. He also promised to let home-buyers deduct mortgage payments from their taxable income (a revenue giveaway of $3.5 billion), and to increase the size of Canada's admittedly under-strength armed forces. Ottawa could have eliminated the deficit by cutting its direct spending – if it could pay every federal expense, from the RCMP to lighthouse keepers, with $600 million. Thanks to a series of statutory programs no politician dared touch, Ottawa in 1978 paid out $14.6 billion to individuals, $10.5 billion to provinces, and $4 billion to businesses. Real federal spending was only a third of the budget.

The problem was not insoluble. In contrast to the hopeless dilemmas facing other nations in a decade of harsh economic shocks, Canadians were as fortunate as they ever had been. Problems might have been aggressively tackled. Instead, a sour, resentful mood developed. The underlying philosophy of the new economic dogmas was a conservative selfishness imported, like so much of Canada's intellectual climate, from the United States. The new mood was also a response to the disappointments of liberation. Freedom had brought pain and death. Between 1971 and 1978, the abortion rate in Canada doubled. So did murder convictions. Urban parents, once terrified by the drug culture, now worried that their offspring would be swept into exotic religious cults. Older churches, eager for "relevance" in liturgy and theology, saw the faithful depart for fundamentalist or charismatic sects. More than a third of all marriages now ended in divorce and the advance of feminism coincided with the spread of pornography and sexual assault.

Most Canadians remained in an amoral wasteland, cool to ideals or ideas. The old puritanism survived, but only when it stayed out of the line of fire. Lotteries, once illegal, had became a billion-dollar business for governments seeking funds for political favours. Liquor consumption tripled in the decade. Montreal and Toronto completed the cycle of spectator sports by acquiring major league baseball teams. Ontario politicians, guided by opinion surveys, banned beer from the ball parks. When opinion switched, in 1982, so did the regulations.

Social commentators spoke of the "me generation," or worried about a selfish narcissism. Pierre Elliott Trudeau might have claimed the credit for such developments. He had written and spoken eloquently of individualism as an ideal far higher than tribal or national loyalties. Canadians had not bothered to study

his philosophy nor to absorb the stoic demands of individual freedom. Young people, as in any age, wanted dreams greater than
themselves, but they could not create them and none were provided. They wanted leadership, too. How badly, they would soon
discover.

Outside Quebec, which now marched to a different political
rhythm, Canadians were disillusioned by Trudeau and unimpressed by Clark. A pitiless media had picked on Clark's appearance, his apparent clumsiness, and his lack of small talk. A world
tour, designed to expose Clark to international leaders, was
transformed by journalists into a saga of lost baggage, minor accidents, and the Tory leader's ignorance. Party strategists, sensing
victory and aware that Clark was the only leader they had, cautiously programmed him to avoid "uncontrolled situations."

Leadership had decided the 1974 election. Liberals believed it
would work again. When Trudeau finally called an election for
May 22, 1979, he offered another new image – the statesman
backed by a huge maple leaf flag, addressing high-school students
stagestruck with a celebrity. Clark, in contrast, spoke only to the
faithful, behind an entourage of aides. If leadership had mattered,
Ed Broadbent might have won. Chosen in 1975, the new NDP
leader was an autoworker's son, a politics professor with the look
of a game prize-fighter. Voters said they liked him but they did not
want a socialist. What they wanted was change and, narrowly,
they got it. The Liberals got more individual votes than the Tories,
and they won all but 8 seats in Quebec. Otherwise, they were
trounced. Only the NDP stopped a western Tory sweep and a Clark
majority. The new Parliament would have 136 Conservatives, 114
Liberals, 26 New Democrats, and 6 *Créditistes*.

Clark had thought hard about being prime minister – perhaps
too hard. Despite his painful efforts to become bilingual, Quebec
had ignored him, but he could appoint Quebec ministers from the
Senate. The Diefenbaker loyalists were bypassed and the new cabinet was at least as good as its Liberal predecessor. Trudeau had
filled the civil service with his appointees. Some must go. Michael
Pitfield, in tears, departed for Harvard; when the deputy minister

of finance followed, the sound of bureaucratic rumbling brought the decapitation process to a halt. Though a promise to move Canada's embassy in Israel from Tel Aviv to Jerusalem had not swayed Jewish voters, it had upset Arabs and their Canadian business partners. Once again, Clark's apparent toughness crumbled. Robert Stanfield was despatched to the Middle East to save the government's face.

A favourite election slogan, "community of communities," had depicted a Canada free of Liberal-induced regional strife. That seemed easier to accomplish. The Yukon would become a province. Newfoundland's Tory government would control its offshore oil. Arthur Tremblay, Duplessis's old constitutional adviser, would provide similar wisdom to Clark. In the forthcoming Quebec referendum, explained Clark, the prime minister would not intervene.

For a western-leaning government, energy issues were crucial. Clark had promised the abolition of Petrocan and effective bargaining with Alberta. In power, both promises looked more awkward. To eastern Canada, Petrocan looked like a lonely saviour against Arabs and Alberta. During a long, leisurely summer, Clark and his ministers met interminably, planned strategy, studied their departments, and negotiated, with no more evident success than Trudeau, with the Alberta government. The government, Clark explained, would act as though it had a majority. The figures showed that it did not; far from a honeymoon with gratified Canadians, the polls began to show a growing Liberal lead. Worried Tory MPs relaxed only on November 21 when, as expected, the former prime minister announced his departure from politics. At sixty, with three young children, Pierre Elliott Trudeau's political career was over. Relieved Tories could surpass Liberals in the warmth of their testimonials. A joyful finance minister, John Crosbie, could deliver a far tougher budget than he had originally planned. Indeed, he would revel in toughness to the delight of bankers, monetarists, and his own party's noisy right wing.

The outcome was utterly unexpected. Liberal members adjourned to a Christmas party, absorbed substantial courage, and accepted the advice of their house leader, Allan MacEachen, that they should vote with the NDP, beat the government, and win the next election. Conservatives, equally confident, scorned to win over *Créditiste* votes, sailed blithely into defeat, and promised themselves that they would repeat Diefenbaker's landslide of 1958. There were two modest differences. Their leader was Joe Clark, and the polls placed the leaderless Liberals twenty points ahead.

After a few days' wait had revealed which Liberals preferred his detested rival, John Turner, Trudeau modestly resumed the leadership. Liberals could almost have campaigned without him. In Ontario, where the real campaign was fought, Premier William Davis had already denounced the Clark government's budget. In time, Canadians would find out how modest that budget's eighteen-cent-per-gallon excise tax on gas at the pump (or about eighty-five per cent of world level oil prices) was. In the winter of 1980, Liberals portrayed such costs as intolerable. Caught unawares, the parties recycled speeches, candidates, and old election signs and privately rejoiced that since 1974 the taxpayer had met much of the cost of campaigning. The opinion polls remained rock-like from beginning to end. On February 18, Ontario, Quebec, and Maritime voters restored the Trudeau majority. By the time the polls closed in Manitoba, the election was over and so were Liberal victories. It did not matter. Trudeau would have 147 seats, Clark 103, Broadbent 32. In Quebec, the *Créditistes* had vanished with the death of Réal Caouette; the Conservatives had a single member. In the West, so had the Liberals. It was no national mandate.

"Welcome to the eighties," Trudeau greeted his triumphant followers. This time, there would be no leisurely reflections on priorities. He had gained his third majority government and he had promised it would be his last.

At gatherings of world leaders, Trudeau was now a survivor, longer in power than almost anyone. The leader of 1968, contemptuous of pompous diplomats and militarism, had learned painful lessons. Not security but European trade had forced re-equipment of Canada's NATO contingent. If Canada kept refusing to buy adequate aircraft to patrol her shores or guard her skies,

Americans would do it for her. The aircraft orders were placed, even if the prime criterion was job-creation, not suitability for service. Canadians in 1969 had been told to forget the idealism of the Pearson years and they had done so. Now, an older Trudeau had different ambitions. In a globe divided between a developed north and a hungry south, Trudeau claimed intermediary nations and leaders were needed. He would volunteer. If Canadians had remembered their world responsibilities, the prime minister suggested, would they have fallen into the mean-minded regionalism of the seventies?

In Quebec, there would be none of Clark's professed indifference to the referendum. It was all the more urgent that Jean Chrétien, now the minister of justice, take charge, because, to Trudeau's dismay, Claude Ryan was now provincial Liberal leader. The man who had done as much as anyone to bring down Robert Bourassa was now his successor. Ryan's nationalism and his independence from Ottawa would be an asset against Lévesque but his alternative to Quebec sovereignty dismayed Trudeau. A feeble federal government would be the creature of all-powerful provinces, with a provincially appointed "federal council" as trustee.

Lévesque's referendum strategy was clear: he would give Quebeckers a question to which they could not possibly say no. Market testing perfected the wording. It was deliberately complicated and innocuous. Would voters give their government a mandate to negotiate sovereignty-association with Ottawa? Any outcome would be put to a new referendum. *Oui* supporters could be mustered by the superb political machine of the *Parti Québécois*. The *non* campaign would have to be managed by a similar committee in which Liberals would quarrel with lesser allies and the stubborn, uncharismatic Ryan would argue with just about everyone.

History is full of surprises. The *non* campaign was smoother and more persuasive than Lévesque had expected, and the *oui* campaign was more fervid than planned. Lise Payette, a PQ minister, inadvertently prodded female *non* supporters into action by christening them "Yvettes," the French-Canadian "goody two-shoes" image of female submission. All the ingenious working of the question could not conceal the significance of the vote and no poll had ever found a separatist majority. On referendum day, May 20, 1980, 88 per cent of Quebeckers voted. The *oui* side won 40.5 per cent; 59.5 per cent voted *non*, a victory for federalism even if all the Anglophones' votes were deducted.

During the campaign, Trudeau and Jean Chrétien had promised that a *non* vote would launch immediate constitutional reform. Quebeckers might be excused for believing that such reform would reflect Claude Ryan's proposals for a divided, regionalized Canada as echoed by the 1979 report of the Robarts-Pepin task force. Trudeau had no such intention. He would resume where the Victoria Charter had stopped in 1971.

With Quebec secure, most provincial premiers now believed that they could dictate whatever their province or ego demanded. Since unanimity seemed to be the rule, each premier believed he had a veto. By 1980, few of them had much sympathy for Pierre Elliott Trudeau. Ed Schreyer, the New Democrat from Manitoba, had been closest in philosophy but he was defeated in 1977. A year later, Trudeau made him governor general. Only Richard Hatfield of New Brunswick and William Davis of Ontario, Conservatives both, backed the prime minister. Allan Blakeney, Saskatchewan's scholarly NDP premier, was a possible bridge to the region Trudeau had ignored for too long. Saskatchewan's attorney-general, Roy Romanow, joined Chrétien as negotiator, devising, promoting, and revising a shrinking list of constitutional proposals, from equalization to Senate reform. By September, the momentum was gone. A week-long conference, televised across Canada, showed that federal-provincial unanimity on a constitutional amending formula and reforms, so narrowly missed in 1971, was now out of the question.

The constitutional issue seemed dead but Trudeau would not bury it. It had become a personal crusade, the achievement that he wished to mark his long and seemingly futile period of national leadership. In October 1980, Trudeau astounded the experts. On three issues, "patriation" of Canada's constitution, an amending formula, and a charter of rights and freedoms, Parliament would act on its own. A Liberal majority would guarantee approval and the British could reject the package at their peril when it came to them for confirmation. Ontario and New Brunswick approved; the other eight provinces vociferously did not. While Broadbent and most New Democrats backed the government, Joe Clark prodded his uncertain Tory caucus into opposition. Manitoba and Quebec challenged Trudeau's procedure in their courts and lost; Newfoundland's judges ruled differently, forcing the issue to the Supreme Court of Canada.

On September 18, 1981, a majority of the Supreme Court's justices declared that the government's procedure might be strictly legal but it defied the "conventions" or customs of the past. Provincial unanimity, they added, was not necessary. (What the "correct" convention might be was left unsaid since, as Chief Justice Bora Laskin shrewdly noted in his dissent, it could not be found. The majority had simply rewritten history!)

In the spring of 1981, dissenting premiers (including René Lévesque) had finally offered their own meagre constitutional package, including an amending formula that allowed no province a veto. The proposal soon haunted its authors. In the wake of the Supreme Court decision, the NDP insisted on a final federal-provincial meeting. Before dawn on November 5, 1981, the logjam broke. Chrétien, Romanow, and all the premiers but Lévesque (asleep in his hotel room in Hull, across the river) found a compromise. Trudeau would have his Charter, the premiers would have their preferred amending formula and the right to opt out of the Charter's less basic provisions. Surely René Lévesque could have no complaints.

But he did. To the weary and triumphant premiers, Lévesque's denunciations of the compromise and his outrage at betrayal by his fellow premiers sounded forced. What the other politicians had forgotten was the situation that had revived the constitutional debate: Quebec's referendum. Now, revised and perhaps to be repented, the drafting was over. Canada would have a complicated amending process and a vast, rambling Charter of Rights which the judiciary would have enormous powers to define. Last-minute pressure from women and native organizations brought a few changes, but not many Canadians cared. Nor did most of the British politicians who wrestled briefly with the residue of colonialism as Indian demonstrators took their grievances to London. The British North America Act was dead; on April 17, 1982, the queen proclaimed the Constitution Act. At the cold, rainy Ottawa ceremony, Quebec was not represented.

3

Changes

The swift restoration of the Liberals to power in 1980 left the West profoundly dissatisfied. Electronics aggravated the sense of injury, proclaiming the Trudeau triumph before prairie votes had even been counted. At the same time, westerners had done less for their friends than they might have. Peter Lougheed's open disdain for his former assistance and public uncertainty over whether an oil-pricing agreement had even been reached with Alberta undermined Clark's frail image as a leader. The best Lougheed could now do was to disprove the Liberals' boast that they could get a better deal from the West than Clark could. For their part, Liberals still believed that the accidents of Middle East politics gave Alberta no right to an absurdly inflated world oil price. In 1980, Trudeau had promised sweeping tax reforms, economic nationalism, and a comprehensive plan to Canadianize the oil industry. Ten months later, his energy minister, Marc Lalonde, unveiled a National Energy Program (NEP) designed to cut foreign ownership of Canadian oil and achieve Canadian self-sufficiency by 1990. Instead of the old array of tax incentives, a new program would let Ottawa decide who got money for exploration and how much. A year later, in November 1981, the promised package of tax reforms formed the centrepiece of Allan MacEachen's first budget as minister of finance.

The timing was not ideal. A decade before, Lalonde's NEP would have found a stagnant, underpriced industry. It might have spared Canada some of the economic mishaps of the seventies. If tax loopholes had been plugged in 1971, not 1981, business groups would have moaned just as loudly, but the Carter royal commission report had provided the arguments. The seventies had changed both Canada and North America. In Washington, Ronald Reagan's new administration slashed taxes, not tax breaks, for the wealthy. In the halls of Congress, environmentalists scattered before oil company lobbyists. If exploration companies felt unwelcome in Canada, they could move their rigs south. Canadian companies, intended as beneficiaries of Lalonde's policies, sank in the undertow of a collapsing Canadian oil industry.

Good times make reform easier; times in the early 1980s were not good. The monetarist cure for inflation, applied by President Jimmy Carter and intensified under Reagan, drove the United States into deep recession. Canada followed, slowly at first, then plunging deeper than its neighbour. Interest rates had soared to record heights in 1979, hurting the Clark government when mortgaged homeowners turned their resentment into votes. By the end of 1980, prime rates reached 19 per cent. Canadians had always bought cars, refrigerators, and washing machines, as well as their homes, on credit. Now they stopped buying. Farmers made old machinery last another year. As in the 1930s, the economy slowly ground to a halt. Mass layoffs, bankruptcies, and reduced working hours were ugly reminders from the past. By the end of 1982, one and a half million Canadians were hunting for work; many more had abandoned the search.

The Canadian economy might have been stronger, more diversified, and more integrated if Canadians had used their post-war prosperity to achieve more than a comfortable standard of living. That was not their choice. Successive generations had agreed that Canada should remain a branch-plant economy with a stake in a continental automotive industry and an export role as resource-producer to the world. Prairie wheat farmers could profit from the failures of Soviet and Chinese grain harvests. British Columbia would be strip-mined to fuel Japanese industry. Mineral wealth would finance Canadian imports from the United States. Canadians who wanted more creative challenges could take their talent elsewhere.

In the 1980s, the cost of such post-war policies became more apparent, harder to pay, and even harder to avoid. Though few Canadians recognized the problem and even fewer sympathized, the economy of central Canada was in grave difficulties. The industries of the St. Lawrence-Great Lakes corridor had thrived on cheap energy, a steady flow of skilled immigrants, and proximity to the industrial heartland of the United States. By the seventies, energy was no longer cheap, highly trained workers earned more by staying in Europe, and American industry had fled south and west, leaving behind a "rust belt" of sullen slums and ravaged landscapes. Even northern lakes lost their attraction when sulphur dioxide, transformed into "acid rain," threatened vegetation and freshwater fish. For a time it was the Canadian West that grew. In the 1970s, only Alberta and British Columbia gained significant population. Though Toronto had already surpassed Montreal as Canada's largest city, Calgary and Edmonton were the boom towns of the decade. Head offices, fleeing Montreal for linguistic and political reasons, sometimes bypassed Toronto for the more entrepreneurial climate of Calgary. Edmonton, the metropolis of the newly rich Alberta, acquired the customary attributes of a subway, theatres, major-league sports teams, and a super-sized shopping centre, the West Edmonton Mall.

Western prosperity did not make tax reform or the National Energy Policy popular. Though Lalonde insisted that they had a better deal in Canada than in Mexico, Australia, or the North Sea countries, the oil giants packed their rigs and complained to Washington. By cutting oil shipments to eastern Canada, Lougheed extracted a new pricing agreement, but by then the OPEC cartel had cracked and world oil prices tumbled. By 1983, the western oil boom was a bust. Free to spend NEP money on remote drilling sites on the Beaufort Sea or off Newfoundland, Canadian firms spent billions, only to lose it when the cost of the oil they found far exceeded the falling world price. Other "mega-projects" encouraged by the NEP, including vast tar-sand conversion schemes, collapsed. The *Ocean Ranger*, an off-shore drill-rig, sank with all hands in 1982.

In the eighties, Canadians were older, on average, than in any decade since the thirties. They also grew more diverse. In the seventies, immigration laws finally discarded the last restrictions against non-white races. East Indians, Chinese, and West Indians joined the population mosaic. In some urban areas such as Toronto and Vancouver, "visible minorities" edged close to becoming a collective majority in the twenty-first century. In 1978, for the first time since the war, the average person lost purchasing power; the pattern persisted for most of the ensuing years. In many families, a second income cushioned the impact, but in 1990 double-income families also began losing purchasing power. Most Canadians were getting poorer; a few were getting richer. In the thirty years since 1950, income distribution between rich and poor had scarcely changed; now it began to shift slightly in favour of the affluent.

Of course, most Canadians were richer than their parents, and they enjoyed freedoms their parents had never imagined. More Canadians than ever before attended schools, colleges, and universities. Cynics might complain that the growth of learning had not kept pace with the years of schooling, though without educational growth would Canadian music, writing, and theatre have flourished as they did in the seventies and eighties – or would the legal and accounting professions? With education came greater freedom and individualism. Gays and lesbians began to challenge prejudice in the 1980s and, tragically, to seek greater action against the AIDS epidemic. In 1988, Svend Robinson became the first MP to proclaim his homosexuality. He was re-elected in his Vancouver constituency that year and again in 1993.

The application of knowledge to government was more controversial. The social-scientific rationality of Trudeau and his followers permeated every aspect of public policy, from defence to postal administration. It had not, however, added noticeably to the sum of national happiness. The main beneficiaries were senior officials, consultants, and experts in the newer techniques of information management. To non-admirers, they resembled the legendary people who sold the emperor his invisible new clothes, speaking a meaningless plastic language. The explosion of knowledge opened endless vistas of hope and fear. Canadians, in common with all humanity, found themselves vulnerable to nuclear annihilation. Technologies of mass destruction, spreading slowly from the great powers to mere power-seekers, ranged from chemical agents to biological toxins. Intellectual weakness in managing Canada's political and economic concerns was a troubling counterpoint to the utter dependence of Canadians on the intellect of strategists and military technologists. Understandably, some Canadians fled from such horrors into the escapist fantasy of pacifism. As Reagan expanded the American war machine and assured his people that a Strategic Defence Initiative could protect them from missile attack, some Canadians revived the old campaign for unilateral disarmament, and the prime minister himself set out on a 1983 world tour as the agent of peace and conciliation. Among allies, he was politely but not respectfully received.

Canadians were again out of love with Trudeau. They had their reasons. A federal deficit, born in 1974 but barely noticed until 1979, surpassed $30 billion a year by 1982 while doing little to curb a recession that devastated manufacturing and resource industries and left 1.3 million Canadians looking for work. As energy prices tumbled, Alberta and other producing provinces blamed Ottawa for killing their boom with the National Energy Program. Most other Canadians nursed grievances against a prime minister who seemed more preoccupied with constitutional change and his world image than the economic well-being of Canadians and their regions. Quebeckers had a further complaint: Trudeau had broken his apparent 1980 pledge to give them an acceptable constitution. It did not help that he denied even making the promise.

In April 1981, René Lévesque's *Parti Québécois* government won easy re-election on a record of honest reform and more subdued nationalism. In Newfoundland, Brian Peckford won a landslide by running against Ottawa. Other provincial premiers followed suit. In Saskatchewan, Allan Blakeney was flattened by the Conservatives, perhaps because he had been too close to

Trudeau in the 1980-82 constitutional negotiations. Whatever the government, conservatism flavoured the response to the new recession. Faced with a budget crisis, Quebec's re-elected *Péquiste* government cut public salaries in 1982, straining the allegiance of teachers, civil servants, and other former PQ militants. Quebec Liberals turned back to a newly conservative Robert Bourassa. In 1985 they won a landslide. Neo-conservatism, the philosophy of Ronald Reagan, crossed the Canadian border to inspire Saskatchewan's new premier, Grant Devine. Faced with deficits, governments borrowed, cut spending, and worried, but they refused to raise revenues to match needs. In British Columbia, Bill Bennett celebrated his re-election in 1983 by wiping out such agencies as the Human Rights Commission and by instituting changes in labour law that defied the province's powerful union movement. Protesters banded together in a "Solidarity" movement. Pollsters found that most people favoured Bennett. Union leaders counted heads and compromised. They had read the public mood. In 1986, Bennett's successor, Bill Vander Zalm, had no trouble winning an increased majority.

Faced with an unexpected chance to reverse their 1980 humiliation, the Tories chose to offer voters a fresh face. When the decent, luckless Joe Clark sought confirmation of his leadership, right-wingers spearheaded such a challenge that he felt obliged to invite a formal leadership convention. Brian Mulroney, a Montreal lawyer, had been a contender when Clark was chosen in 1976; he had bided his time, professed loyalty, and secretly promoted the anti-Clark cause. On June 11, 1983, Conservative delegates made him their leader. Born and bred in the little company town of Baie Comeau, Mulroney was handsome, smooth-tongued, and easily colloquial in French and English. Untested at the polls, he was a veteran of backroom politics and a telegenic veteran of a Quebec royal commission into labour racketeering. Mulroney had also managed the political feat of closing down much of the Iron Ore Company of Canada for its American owners without enraging unions or investors. Beyond promises to restore harmony to the Canadian federation, better relations with Reagan's White House, and "jobs, jobs, jobs," Mulroney was enigmatic about his political priorities. He distanced himself from the francophobia of Manitoba Tories and the public-sector bashing of British Columbia's Bill Bennett and assured anyone who asked him that Canada's social programs were "a sacred trust." Tory fortunes rose.

Then, with the departure of their chief target, they plummeted. On February 29, 1984, Pierre Elliott Trudeau went for a walk in an Ottawa snow-storm and returned to announce his imminent departure from public life. By then Liberals had convinced themselves that there could only be one successor, the handsome former finance minister and covert Trudeau critic, John Turner. Though a crowd of lesser contenders emerged, only the brash populist Jean Chrétien posed a real alternative. On June 16, 1984, Liberal delegates chose Turner. On June 30, he became prime minister.

With his party in power, a big lead in the polls, and first a royal visit and then Canada's first papal visit to add to his stature, Turner could be confident of victory. Some advisers urged him to take some time before calling an election so that voters could see the effects of his pro-business policies and forget the lavish patronage Trudeau had provided for his cronies. Others warned that his majority might drain away. Turner decided to act. Only then did he discover that his party was penniless and disorganized. The media found that years in a Toronto law firm, shooting sly barbs at Trudeau, had eroded his political skills. In a televised debate, Mulroney pinned him with the responsibility for approving many of Trudeau's patronage appointees. "I had no choice," mumbled Turner. His campaign never recovered.

The Tories had inherited a lead in English-speaking Canada, but they expected little from Quebec. Without Trudeau or Chrétien in the race, however, only Mulroney had any claim to be "un des nôtres." The rotting Liberal machine, discredited by the 1982 constitutional debacle, never knew what hit it. Armed with Mulroney's pledge to "bring Quebec into the Constitution with honour and enthusiasm," Conservative candidates found themselves riding a wave. In the West, suspicion that Mulroney and

Turner were "Bobbsey twins" for eastern business and Ed Broadbent's identification with "ordinary Canadians" hauled the NDP
back from oblivion. On September 4, Mulroney swept Canada
from coast to coast, almost matching Diefenbaker's 1958 landslide: 211 Tories to a mere 40 Liberals and 30 New Democrats.
More in pity than conviction, an affluent Vancouver riding gave
John Turner the only Liberal seat west of Ontario.

Some Tories claimed a mandate for massive "privatization,"
downsizing government, deregulation, slashing social programs,
even a return to hanging and an end to the metric system. The new
finance minister, Michael Wilson, burned with zeal to cut the $30
billion federal deficit. The energy minister, Vancouver's Pat Car-
ney, would kill the National Energy Program. A flotilla of "task
forces" promised business-pleasing recommendations on every
problem from Indian affairs to unemployment insurance. As civil
servants prepared for the new government, Mulroney warned that
all they could expect was "a pink slip and running shoes."

In fact, Mulroney was not a right-wing ideologue. His personal
goal was met by being prime minister. A voluble man with an urge
to please, Mulroney hoped that Tories might supplant the Liberals
as the natural governing party in Canada. That was why he had
cultivated Quebec. Wilson's plan to cap old-age pension payments
was dropped when French-Canadian seniors protested. Business
sense would have awarded a billion-dollar aircraft repair contract
to a Winnipeg firm; political instinct gave it to Montreal. Like
Maurice Duplessis, the political idol of his youth, Mulroney
believed in gratitude and loyalty. Unlike Duplessis, he cultivated
media affection and soon forfeited media respect. Ottawa's frugal
traditions, abandoned in the Trudeau years, soon became a distant
memory. The city swarmed with lobbyists, often Mulroney
cronies. Their task was easier because the Tories surrounded their
ministers with political staff. Tax changes gave the wealthy more
to spend. Trudeau's deficit faded as an issue when affluent and
influential voters showed no taste for tax increases and little for
spending cuts. In 1985, most of Wilson's early budget savings
were sacrificed to compensate depositors in two ill-managed,

worse-regulated Alberta banks. By the summer of 1986, six members of an admittedly oversized cabinet had departed under some shadow of failure or disgrace.

"Good relations, super relations with the United States, will be the cornerstone of our foreign policy," Mulroney promised the *Wall Street Journal* when he took power. When Ronald Reagan came to Quebec City in 1985, the two leaders charmed their friends with a joint rendition of "When Irish Eyes Are Smiling." Mulroney gave an early signal to Washington that Canada would meet Reagan's elaborate defence expectations. The obsolete DEW line was modernized as the North Warning System, the Liberal order for six new patrol frigates was doubled, and Canada's brigade in Germany was strengthened. A 1987 defence white paper proposed that nuclear-powered submarines patrol Canada's Arctic frontier. Anti-nuclear protests were predictable; Pentagon opposition was only a little more discreet. By 1988, the proposal was dead and the offending minister had been switched to a less sensitive post.

The Tory honeymoon was soon over. Provincial elections, familiar weather gauge of Canadian politics, showed the trend. In 1984, eight of ten provincial governments had been Conservative or sympathetic to Tory policies. Ontario's forty-two-year Tory dynasty had survived Diefenbaker but not Mulroney. A belated conversion to funding Catholic schools and a rightward tilt by Bill Davis's successor helped topple the Ontario Tories. David Peterson's Liberals formed a minority government. Peterson managed the province for two years, with the NDP providing most of his policies. In 1987, he won his own majority. In ultra-Tory Alberta, voters made the NDP the official opposition. The Lebanese roots of Joe Ghiz were no obstacle to a 1986 Liberal comeback in Prince Edward Island. Liberals won every seat in the New Brunswick legislature, ending the seventeen-year rule of Richard Hatfield. Nowhere was Mulroney a central issue but nowhere was he an asset. By 1987, he rivalled the unpopularity of Trudeau at his lowest. The only good news for Conservatives was their 1986 triumph over a Manitoba NDP government whose defence of French minority rights and high car-insurance premiums combined to annoy voters.

Good times had returned to southern Ontario and Quebec by 1985, though the recession persisted grimly in much of Atlantic Canada and remained as a cruel affront in the recently buoyant West. Ottawa badly needed some new ideas, and a Liberal-appointed royal commission provided them. During his 1983 leadership campaign, Mulroney had insisted that one item was not on his agenda: free trade. That issue, he maintained, had been settled in 1911. As prime minister, Mulroney changed his mind. He had help. At the depth of his recession, Trudeau had appointed a royal commission on the economic problems of the Canadian federation headed by Donald S. Macdonald. Academic economists urged an aged nostrum on the commission: free trade with the United States. Only within a guaranteed, protected North American market could Canadian exports compete with the goods and services of European and Asian trading blocs. Since Americans would protect their own shrinking industrial base, Canadians must get inside the U.S. wall or be cut off from the buyer of 80 per cent of their exports. When Macdonald presented his commission's report to Mulroney in 1985, he provided the Tories with a policy agenda. Mulroney was an instant convert. Business elites and the Reagan White House could both rejoice.

Once launched, there was no turning back. Ottawa negotiators might have won better terms if Mulroney's desperation for a deal had been less obvious. On September 23, 1987, chief negotiator Simon Reisman walked out of the talks. Mulroney promptly used his direct line to the White House. For a few cosmetic concessions, the deal was settled on October 4, 1987. Within ten years, all tariffs were to disappear. Americans would have full access to Canada's natural resources and to acquire financial and other service industries. Breweries and so-called "cultural industries" were protected, but Ottawa buried a proposed law to protect Canadian filmmakers. Free trade gave Mulroney an election issue.

It might seem an unlikely vote-getter. Most Canadians were opposed or at least suspicious. Formidable pressure groups, from feminists to nationalists, lined up against the deal. So did Liberals and the NDP. However, Mulroney had friends too. Big business, once solemnly protectionist, welcomed bigger markets and a Canada whose labour unions and social legislation would soon be "harmonized" with Ronald Reagan's America. Once a stronghold of protectionism, Quebec wanted to sell its electricity to the United States, and its opinion-leaders imagined that its new passion for business would make America Quebec's oyster. So did all other provinces, with the exception of Liberal Ontario and P.E.I. Special clauses persuaded farmers that their marketing boards were safe, and the sick and elderly that their social programs were still "a sacred trust." Even the hesitant wondered what alternatives anti-free traders could offer.

By the time Mulroney announced an election for November 8, 1988, his party's coffers were bulging and his popularity was reviving. In Quebec, Robert Bourassa was his ally, as were most moderate nationalists. An old friend, Lucien Bouchard, had won a by-election for the Conservatives. Elsewhere, $12 billion in pre-election promises, from $4 billion for day-care to a heavy oil upgrader for Saskatchewan, made more friends. So did an apology to Japanese-Canadians for their wartime internment and a $21,000 payment to each survivor. Just before Mulroney called the election, his scandal-plagued Nova Scotia allies narrowly won re-election. Being a Conservative was no longer a liability.

John Turner, in contrast, spent much of the pre-election period avoiding his own party's critics. Canadians who opposed the free-trade deal had to choose between the discredited Liberal leader or the NDP's Ed Broadbent, who had too many other issues on display. For a moment in the televised leaders' debate, Turner seized the lead, charging Mulroney with destroying Canada's national identity. Liberal fortunes rose, but the moment passed. By staging the debate early in the campaign, the Tories and business had time to offset the loss and win the contest. Turner became the target. Simon Reisman called him a traitor. Mr. Justice Emmett Hall, an architect of medicare, was brought from retirement to insist that health insurance was safe.

On November 21, 1988, with only 43 per cent of the vote, the Tories won 170 seats, virtually sweeping Quebec. Their two main opponents had 53 per cent of the vote, but the split gave the Liberals 82 seats and the NDP 43, not enough to stop the free-trade deal even if either party had dared to do so in coalition. Brian Mulroney had become the first Conservative prime minister since Sir John A. Macdonald to win back-to-back majorities. He was free to create "the level playing field" of free trade. Only the most attentive had noted the promise of a new Goods and Service Tax, a Canadian version of a European-style value-added tax. Set at 7 per cent and covering everything but food, rent, and the cost of financial services, the GST was awkwardly in place by January 1, 1990. It was not welcome, least of all in Alberta, where oil wealth had so far spared residents from any sales tax at all.

Alberta anger had a lasting political legacy. In May 1987, a clutch of disgruntled right-wing westerners had met in Winnipeg to create the latest in a long string of regional protest parties. To lead the new Reform Party, they chose Preston Manning, son of a former Alberta Social Credit premier, a man of evangelical faith and business orthodoxy. Manning had lost to Joe Clark in 1988, but the GST was a gift. Fury at the new tax, linked to old anger at bilingualism, bureaucracy, the NEP, the Senate, and a score of regional grievances brought Reform a hundred thousand members by 1992. A further bonus was Mulroney's second attempt to find a constitutional compromise acceptable to Quebec.

4

Futures

Since Trudeau presented them with their new Constitution and Charter in 1982, some Canadians had been preoccupied with testing its limits. Far from their traditional caution, judges all the way to the Supreme Court proved quite eager to use their new powers, striking down criminal sanctions against abortion, upholding francophone rights in Alberta and Saskatchewan and anglophone rights in Quebec, slowly giving hard meaning to the vague 1982 commitment to "aboriginal rights." The return to power of Robert Bourassa gave Mulroney a chance to complete what he and most Quebeckers saw as unfinished constitutional business. By dint of marathon sessions at the government's Meech Lake conference centre on April 30, 1987, and in Ottawa on June 3, Mulroney kept his 1984 promises. What Trudeau had refused, Mulroney and all ten premiers accepted: Quebec would be recognized as a "distinct society"; senators and Supreme Court justices would be chosen from provincial nominees; "major" constitutional amendments would need provincial unanimity; and provinces that opted out of federal programs in heath, education, welfare, and other provincial domains could claim full compensation.

To its supporters, the Meech Lake Accord was a milestone; to a growing number of critics, it was a stumbling block for their view of Canada. Satisfied that first ministers' conferences settled such matters, supporters assumed that the three-year wait imposed by the 1982 amending formula was a formality and settled down to wait. Critics moved. Trudeau denounced the Accord as a sell-out to the premiers and Quebec nationalists. Natives were angry that governments could agree on Quebec's demands but not on their rights. Special interest groups, from feminists to ethnic organizations, complained that there was nothing for them. The second meeting, in Ottawa, was an attempt to placate them.

Opponents of the Accord profited from a renewed hostility to Mulroney. The 1988 election had left lasting scars and the new Goods and Services Tax left others, particularly after Mulroney used a little-known constitutional procedure to create enough senators to push it through. If the detestable Mulroney was for the Meech Lake Accord, many reasoned, it must be bad. Those who did read it predicted a weaker central government, stronger provinces, and a vague special status for Quebec. Early in 1990, pressed by Quebec nationalists, Bourassa used the 1982 "notwithstanding" clause to ban English-language outdoor signs. A country that had almost ignored the impact of Bill 101 on Quebec's English-speaking minority suddenly felt affronted. In 1989, Newfoundland returned to the Liberals and a new premier, Clyde Wells, a former Trudeau aide. Other premiers elected since 1987, notably New Brunswick's Frank McKenna and Manitoba's Gary Filmon, had been uncertain about Meech; Wells simply told his new legislature to reject it. As the ratification deadline of June 28 approached, Meech Lake was no longer an Accord.

Mulroney responded with a desperate national search for compromise. Bourassa, who had greatly modified his own demands to get a deal in 1987, would not budge. When a young minister, Jean Charest, came back with proposals, Quebec members in both the Tory and Liberal caucuses rebelled. Lucien Bouchard quit as minister of the environment, denouncing Mulroney as a traitor. A handful of dissidents joined him in a *Bloc Québécois*. If Canada could not accept Meech, then Quebec sovereignty was inevitable and even overdue. Mulroney tried a renewed bargaining session. Billed as a dinner for the premiers on June 3, the few hours turned into an almost unbroken week of meetings. At one point Alberta's premier, Don Getty, a former football player, rose to stop Clyde Wells from leaving. At another moment, Bourassa withdrew in despair. Somehow Mulroney kept the sessions going until, near midnight on June 9, a complex parallel agreement could be announced to a national television audience.

Was the Accord saved? It seemed so. But who would have reckoned on the *Globe and Mail* printing an interview in which Mulroney described himself as "rolling the dice." Insulted by Mulroney's arrogance and vulgarity, Wells announced that his grudging consent was gone. Newfoundland's House of Assembly would vote, but his opposition would be clear. Manitoba's political leaders had come to Ottawa, accepted the compromise, and returned home to find provincial opinion solidly opposed to them. They were saved by Elijah Harper, a Cree member of the Legislative Assembly, who made use of procedural delays on the grounds that aboriginal rights had been slighted. When Manitoba's legislature adjourned on June 22, a day before the deadline, Harper could claim that he had killed the Meech Lake Accord.

While some suggested that he might have killed Canada, too, and its tradition of compromise, native leaders showed no regret. Nor did others who denounced constitution-making by "eleven middle-class men in suits." In September, Ontario premier David Peterson was defeated by the NDP. His conspicuous role in trying to bridge the obstacles to the Meech Lake Accord was cited against him. In the West, fury at Meech added supporters to the Reform Party. If the Accord caused fury in English-speaking Canada, its rejection was presented to Quebeckers as a new humiliation. Henceforth, Bourassa announced, he would not meet with other premiers. Instead, a commission, jointly chaired by prominent businessmen Michel Bélanger, a federalist, and Jean Campeau, a sovereigntist, would advise Quebeckers on their future. Nationalists congratulated themselves on the "serene certainty" that independence was now inevitable.

Quebeckers were less serene about another crisis that summer. If Elijah Harper forced Canadians to consider native concerns, so did Mohawk communities near Montreal. In the spring, a violent dispute over gambling shattered the peace of the Akwasasne reserve that straddled the Quebec, Ontario, and New York State borders. Across the Ottawa River, near Oka, Mohawks with heavy weapons established a roadblock as part of their campaign to regain lands granted them as refugees from the American Revolution. On July 11, after months of legal wrangling, Quebec police advanced on the barricade. In a fusillade of shots, a police officer died and his comrades fled, leaving their cars to be piled on the barricade. At Kahnewake, outside Montreal, other armed Mohawks blockaded a bridge and closed a major commuter route to the south shore of the St. Lawrence. Across Canada, natives briefly blocked roads and rail lines and toppled an occasional hydro pylon, but Montreal provided television with a summer-long focus. The dispute fed on the issues of a turbulent year. Indian affairs were a federal matter; law and order was a provincial responsibility. The Mohawks spoke English and attracted sympathy from journalists and civil libertarians outside Quebec; their angry victims were French-speaking. On August 17, Bourassa asked for troops. For more than a month, soldiers camped at Oka and Kahnewake and, with a patience bred of peacekeeping training, pushed the natives back from the blockades until September 25 when, after some final tense moments, resistance folded.

To many Canadians, Meech Lake and Oka were distractions. So was the Gulf War, the American-led UN response to Iraq's sudden conquest of Kuwait. With a speedy deference to the White House that some of his critics condemned, Mulroney despatched two elderly destroyers and a supply ship to the Gulf. Later, a squadron of CF-18s moved to Qatar. Canada's fifth war of the century was also the least bloody: no Canadian died.

By mid-1991, when the ships and aircraft came home, Canada was in the grip of a new, more pervasive and damaging recession than any since the 1930s. Within two years, three hundred thousand manufacturing jobs had vanished in Ontario alone. The 1990s recession had more parallels with the 1930s than its size. Like the earlier disaster, it grew out of an era of wild speculation and political conservatism as well as being part of the predictable boom-bust cycle. A speculative buying fever had allowed solid companies to be bought up, plundered of capital, and left vulnerable to an increasingly global competition. In the 1990s recession, long-established companies collapsed, merged, or endured a drastic "downsizing" that reached into the executive offices and emptied whole floors of the computer-literate information handlers who had had the future in their hands.

Though interest rates fell and inflation almost vanished, the fear of unemployment killed consumer spending. Shops began their Boxing Day sales before Christmas in a desperate bid to move inventory. Warehouse stores offering lower prices emptied malls and drove established retail chains into liquidation. In Toronto, Vancouver, and other cities, property values had soared in the 1980s, leaving banks and trust companies dangerously exposed. Now values tumbled, taking the development and construction industries with them. In the 1980s it had been considered dangerously rude to question the real value of Paul and Albert Reichmann's world-wide assets. Their collapse was only the biggest. Quebec's confidence in its new business acumen survived the collapse of Robert Campeau – he was from Sudbury and Ottawa, after all – but such erstwhile powerhouses as Provigo and the engineering firm Lavalin had to be rescued by the province's investment fund.

Not only the corporate world was in trouble. Years of overfishing off the Atlantic coast by domestic and foreign fleets, compounded by changes in water temperature, had their inevitable outcome. After years of reports, warnings, and denial, Canadian-based fishing had to be banned, beginning with Newfoundland's northern cod and gradually extending along almost the entire Atlantic coast. Not only the economic staple but also the way of life for hundreds of communities was finished for at least a decade, perhaps forever. Meanwhile, farming faced a comparable challenge as prairie wheat growers watched prices fall below the cost of production. The United States and the European Community could afford the subsidies of a grain price-war; like other smaller producing countries, Canada could not. Wheat farmers could hope for a settlement as part of a major agreement under the General Agreement on Tariffs and Trade (GATT). If that happened, dairy, egg, and poultry producers, chiefly in Quebec and Ontario, would lose their system of supply-management and only huge corporate production units could hope to survive.

During the 1930s, John Maynard Keynes had offered a persuasive remedy for curing depressions: governments could spend to spur the economy because they had taxed and saved in periods of prosperity. But when was Canada so completely prosperous that it could accept Keynesian saving? And neo-conservatism argued that individuals, not governments, should do the spending. In the prosperous years, government deficits had deepened as Canadians protested their tax burdens while defending their benefits and services. When companies and jobs vanished, so did tax revenues. The new GST replaced a much higher but hidden manufacturers' sales tax, but it hit a vastly greater range of products and services, depressing the economy at a time when it desperately needed stimulus. John Crow, governor of the Bank of Canada, insisted that inflation and excessive public debt were bigger problems for Canada than a short-lived recession.

Most governments agreed. A year of Keynesian stimulation took Ontario past its borrowing limit. Ontario's NDP premier, Bob Rae, imposed drastic public-sector cutbacks. In 1993, Rae enraged his erstwhile union allies by imposing wage cuts and unpaid holidays as an alternative to layoffs. A labour movement now dominated by public-sector unions promptly turned its back on the NDP. It was hardly different in Saskatchewan, where the NDP defeated the Conservatives in 1991 only to inherit the heaviest per-capita debt load of any province. In British Columbia, Bill Vander Zalm's mingling of personal and public business cost him his job. Social Credit picked Rita Johnson as Canada's first woman provincial premier, but she could not save her party from defeat by the NDP. Less scathed than others by the recession, Mike Harcourt's new government preferred to sacrifice some of Clayoquot Sound's old-growth forests rather than shut down much of the province's most profitable industry. Tough times meant tough, unpopular choices. It was not a good time to be in government.

That was certainly Brian Mulroney's conclusion in 1992 as he entered what should have been an election year. Never had pollsters found a more unpopular leader. It was small comfort that a government task force, headed by Keith Spicer, found that voters despised all politicians. The third year of recession and dropping real incomes, the GST, and the elimination or privatization of public enterprises from Canada Post to Air Canada had made him few friends. Family allowances, born in 1945, died in 1992 in favour of a tax credit supposedly targeted at the needy. The 1988 promise of a national day-care system was formally scrapped.

Though it felt helpless to do anything about the recession or other regional economic miseries, Ottawa could go back to the Constitution. Perhaps it had no choice. Quebec's Bélanger-Campeau commission agreed on very little, but Robert Bourassa accepted its advice to set October 26, 1992, as the deadline for a referendum on Canada's constitutional offer. Since the rest of Canada had rejected the Meech Lake Accord, it was its turn to make an offer. But even formulating an offer would be almost impossibly difficult. The Canadians who talked to a government task force sent to take the national pulse were united mainly in their distaste for their political leaders and for "kowtowing" to Quebec. Elijah Harper and the Mohawks had helped ensure that the First Nations would be consulted, but in four separate groups: "status" and "non-status" Indians (those who lived on and off reserves), the Métis and the Innu. The Territories would have to be included too. Quebec, however, refused to be part of any negotiations. Like it or not, the rest of Canada would have to recognize that Quebec was not a province like the others. Two other provinces, British Columbia and Alberta, had been content to let the premier and the legislature approve amendments: now they required a province-wide referendum.

The two western provinces also insisted on a "triple-E" Senate – elected, equal, and effective. Instead of a quarter of the Senate seats, Quebec or Ontario would have no more than P.E.I., and the new senators would matter a lot more. Native leaders insisted that any new constitution must recognize their "inherent" – and hence nondebatable – right of self-government. Provinces, though not necessarily their citizens, demanded transfer of federal powers. From the fall of 1991 to the spring of 1992, a succession of committees wrestled with the task of producing an acceptable constitutional package. Switched from External Affairs, Joe Clark shuttled his new diplomatic experience to provincial capitals, seeking consensus.

With nine premiers, two territorial leaders, four First Nations groups, and Ottawa directly involved, and a host of pressure groups demanding a place or at least influence, and Quebec even more eloquent in its absence, agreement seemed impossible. To give himself leverage, Mulroney adopted referendum legislation. His advisers even hoped that the provinces would come to a deadlock. Then Mulroney could devise a package Quebec would accept, fight a referendum campaign with or without the premiers' backing, and then offer himself in his third federal election as a national saviour. Instead, on July 8, Clark proudly announced a consensus. In return for an equal, elected, but less effective Senate and more seats in the House of Commons for bigger provinces, Ontario's Bob Rae had persuaded western provinces to accept aboriginal demands. All had accepted an entrenched commitment to medicare and other social programs. Even Newfoundland's Clyde Wells now agreed that Quebec was a distinct society. To his dismay, Clark got a scolding for allowing the agreement to jell, though it was enough to bring Bourassa back to negotiate. More days of intense negotiation in Ottawa and a largely symbolic visit to the "Cradle of Confederation" on August 28 produced the Charlottetown Accord.

For those enmeshed in the process, it seemed a miraculous manifestation of that spirit of compromise Canadians preached to a conflict-strewn world. A "Canada clause" would remind judges that Quebec's distinctiveness, the Charter, linguistic duality, social justice, and regional redistribution were all part of the national fabric. The triple-E Senate, with power over key federal appointments, resource taxes, language and culture, would be balanced by a larger House of Commons in which Quebec, thanks to deft wording by Saskatchewan's Roy Romanow, would always have a quarter of the seats (about its normal share). Aboriginals could thank themselves and Bob Rae for inclusion of their "inherent right to self-government." Scores of other issues were settled in a document which, in its final version, was as thick as a small telephone book.

If this was Canada's proposal, Quebeckers would decide its fate on October 26. As would the rest of Canada. Using his new referendum law, Mulroney could satisfy the widespread demand for individual participation. Or could he? Those who had created the

Charlottetown Accord, who rejoiced at a seeming nation-saving compromise, or who liked one or more of the provisions could range with the Yes side. They included three of the national parties, every premier, business and labour leaders, and most editorial boards. Ranged on the other side in Quebec were Lucien Bouchard and Jacques Parizeau, insisting that the Accord offered too little; outside Quebec, after a brief hesitation, Preston Manning insisted that the Accord gave Quebec too much. Almost his echo was the still-powerful voice of Pierre Elliott Trudeau. Aboriginal groups, promised much in the Accord, split when dissidents insisted that they could have even more. Most important as the No campaign surged in the polls was a phalanx of Canadians who resented everything that had happened to them under the rule of Brian Mulroney, from the GST to the recession. In September, polls had shown that the Yes side might even take Quebec; by October 26, the Charlottetown Accord was doomed outside Newfoundland, P.E.I, New Brunswick, and, by the narrowest of margins, Ontario. In all, six provinces, both territories, and 54 per cent of Canadians had voted No.

Canadians had defied their chosen leaders. Inside Quebec, support for independence rose. Outside Quebec, political leaders agreed that it would be suicidal to raise constitutional issues again for a long time to come. Rejection of the Charlottetown Accord was both a repudiation of Brian Mulroney and a reflection of how Canada had changed in his years of power. Canadians were told that the UN regarded them as second in the world for well-being, but most of them were disconcerted by the deterioration of their schools and hospitals. There was a sense of panic as secure jobs evaporated and familiar companies vanished into receivership or forced mergers. Inevitably Canadians blamed their government for the recession, but what was the cure? Was Canada's economy sick because of me-first individualism and short-run profit-seeking? Where, in the Mulroney vision, was the long-term thinking that might have saved the Atlantic fishery or British Columbia's old-growth forests? Or was a recession merely a feature of healthy capitalism, as economists had urged in the 1930s?

Despite record unpopularity, Mulroney was convinced that he could win another election. A surprisingly staunch caucus was reminded, regularly, that Mulroney had come back after the depths of 1987. The recession could not last forever; government officials announced its end early in 1993. The next stage of Reagan's vision, a North American Free Trade Agreement that included Mexico, promised the Tories a winning argument with its business backers: new markets, cheap labour, and minimal environmental standards. A divided opposition would do the rest. By choosing Yukon MP Audrey McLaughlin in 1990, the NDP had done little more than give itself the first woman federal party leader. When the Liberals, later that year, picked Jean Chrétien as John Turner's successor, he was promptly dubbed "yesterday's man." Quebec would not forget a man who had echoed Trudeau on the Meech Lake Accord. In opinion polls, Chrétien was far ahead; in many Liberal minds, he was a terrible mistake.

Months of persuasion by friends and the media finally convinced Mulroney that he, personally, could not win. After a feast of patronage for his friends, a mawkish farewell tour of world capitals, and a delay to make sure his detested rival, Joe Clark, quit first, Mulroney announced his resignation on February 24, 1993. "This is a beautiful view," he told reporters at his residence on Sussex Drive, "but it ain't free." With 3,082 days in office, he had outlasted all but four Canadian prime ministers. He had forced through free trade with the United States, slashed spending, made the rich richer, doubled the national debt, and still faced the same $35 billion deficit he had encountered in 1984. When more prominent lieutenants announced their departure, the succession seemed to fall almost inevitably to a forty-five-year-old Vancouver woman he had promoted to defence minister only weeks before. Kim Campbell was attractive because she was much that Mulroney was not: a westerner, witty but abrasive, a newcomer elected only in 1988, unconnected with Tory old-boy networks. Twice divorced, she did not seem to have many friends, but suddenly she had a bandwagon, with hundreds of ambitious Tories clambering aboard. The media and some Tories had second thoughts. Jean

Charest, an impeccably bilingual minister from Sherbrooke, was the beneficiary. He was too late. On June 13, 1993, Campbell took the leadership convention on the second ballot, and on June 25 she became Canada's nineteenth prime minister.

Like Trudeau in 1984, Mulroney had given his successor little time to get known. Unlike Turner, Campbell took all the time she could, with a summer of friendly cross-country travel. She handed out promises as she went. The deficit would vanish in five years, with no cuts to social programs. As defence minister, she had defended the purchase of costly helicopters; as prime minister, she would cut them back. If Quebec wanted to control manpower training, it could have the money too. By the time she called the election, Campbell's support had almost crawled ahead of the Liberals. Tory hopes rose. With twenty-four parties in the race and five of them serious contenders, a good campaign could make all the difference. Hadn't a new Tory leader, Ralph Klein, recently wiped out the NDP opposition in Alberta?

But Canada was not Alberta and the Tory campaign was not good. Campbell's opening admission that she could not overcome serious unemployment much before the year 2000 was probably true, but her manner suggested that it did not matter very much. A Tory attempt to capitalize on Chrétien's reputation by focusing on his partial facial paralysis, the legacy of a childhood disease, backfired. Instead, the Liberal leader profited from low expectations and concentrated on a simple message of hope and a red book full of promises few people even read. McLaughlin and her NDP had sunk to a miserable seven per cent in the polls long before the campaign and they never revived. The real running was made by Preston Manning, whose Reform Party had spread from the West to rural and small-town Ontario, and by Lucien Bouchard's *Bloc*, which simply swallowed Mulroney's former Quebec support. A week before election day, the outcome was obvious, but it seemed so impossible that no one really believed it.

On October 25, the Conservatives elected only two members (one of them was Jean Charest), and the NDP saved a mere nine of the forty-three seats they had held at dissolution. By sweeping the Maritimes, taking ninety-eight of Ontario's ninety-nine seats and

winning a scattering of western ridings, Jean Chrétien had 177
seats, making him prime minister. A mere sixteen per cent of the
national vote, all of it in Quebec, gave the *Bloc* fifty-four seats and
made Bouchard leader of Her Majesty's Official Opposition. Close
behind, with fifty-one seats from the West and one from Ontario,
was Preston Manning. It was, a commentator noted, the kind of
parliament Canadians could expect after the referendum a year
before. As if he needed a bigger challenge, the new prime minister
learned that he had inherited a $40 billion deficit as well as a reces-
sion and 1.4 million unemployed from his presumably cost-
conscious and businesslike predecessors.

History is another word for experience; it is not a form of
prophecy. History tells Canadians only that they live in a tough
old country, that they have a tradition of compromise, an aversion
to violence, and a gift for survival. Only Switzerland and the
United States have older federal systems, and both of them have
survived cruel civil wars. Twenty-six million Canadians live in a
country that has stayed together for almost a hundred and thirty
years, and, whatever the temptation, geography makes it very difficult for them to live apart. In those years, Canadians mastered
the self-restraint of democracy, learned to live in peace, if without
much affection for each other, and adapted to an environment others would consider harsh and unforgiving.

Certainly it is the only homeland most Canadians will ever
know. Beneath their shell of cynicism and self-deprecation, Canadians are as proud of their land as any people on earth. Make no
mistake about it.

Index

DATE DUE

GAYLORD   PRINTED IN U.S.A.